WILL NOT RETURN VOID

WILL NOT RETURN VOID

The Use of Scripture in Evangelistic Writings
in the Greek Patristic Tradition

JOHN ALLEN DEARING III

WIPF & STOCK · Eugene, Oregon

WILL NOT RETURN VOID
The Use of Scripture in Evangelistic Writings in the Greek Patristic Tradition

Copyright © 2021 John Allen Dearing III. All rights reserved. Except for brief quotations in critical publications or reviews, no part of this book may be reproduced in any manner without prior written permission from the publisher. Write: Permissions, Wipf and Stock Publishers, 199 W. 8th Ave., Suite 3, Eugene, OR 97401.

Wipf & Stock
An Imprint of Wipf and Stock Publishers
199 W. 8th Ave., Suite 3
Eugene, OR 97401

www.wipfandstock.com

PAPERBACK ISBN: 978-1-6667-1303-9
HARDCOVER ISBN: 978-1-6667-1304-6
EBOOK ISBN: 978-1-6667-1305-3

10/15/21

"Scripture quotations taken from the (NASB®) New American Standard Bible®, Copyright © 1960, 1971, 1977, 1995, 2020 by The Lockman Foundation. Used by permission. All rights reserved. www.lockman.org"

Scriptures taken from the Holy Bible, New International Version®, NIV®. Copyright © 1973, 1978, 1984, 2011 by Biblica, Inc.™ Used by permission of Zondervan. All rights reserved worldwide. www.zondervan.com The "NIV" and "New International Version" are trademarks registered in the United States Patent and Trademark Office by Biblica, Inc.™

Scripture quotations from The Authorized (King James) Version. Rights in the Authorized Version in the United Kingdom are vested in the Crown. Reproduced by permission of the Crown's patentee, Cambridge University Press.

To my loving, supportive wife, Andrea,
and our children, Jack, Charis, and Lizzy.

Contents

1 | Introduction   1
2 | The Use of Scripture in the Evangelistic Writings of Justin Martyr   17
3 | The Use of Scripture in the Evangelistic Writings of Origen   39
4 | The Use of Scripture in the Evangelistic Writings of Athanasius   54
5 | The Use of Scripture in the Evangelistic Writings of John Chrysostom   86
6 | The Use of Scripture in the Evangelistic Writings of John of Damascus   120
7 | Conclusion   137

Bibliography   149

1

Introduction

When one considers the early Christian church, one is immediately struck by the exponential growth that the church experienced. When recounting the events surrounding the resurrection of Christ, Paul writes,

> He [Christ] appeared to Cephas, then to the twelve. After that he appeared to more than five hundred brethren at one time, most of whom remain until now, but some have fallen asleep; then he appeared to James, then to all the apostles; and last of all, as to one untimely born, he appeared to me also (1 Cor 15:5–8).[1]

From this passage, one is given a starting number of at least five hundred Christians at the time of Christ's resurrection. From this point, the church of Jesus Christ grew rapidly. According to Acts 2, three thousand more converts were added to the church soon after the ascension of Christ. These converts "from every nation under heaven" were likely instrumental in the spread of Christianity to every corner of the Roman Empire, which saw the establishment of at least forty-five Christian churches in the empire by AD 100.[2] Because Roman census data did not record the religious affiliations of its citizenry, it is difficult to determine exactly how many people converted to Christianity in the patristic period, though some suggest that the church's pace of growth increased throughout the period.[3] Rodney Stark holds to

---

1. All Scripture NASB unless otherwise indicated.
2. Van der Meer and Mohrmann, *Atlas of the Early Christian World*, 2.
3. Wilken, *First Thousand Years*, 65–66.

Erwin Goodenough's[4] suggestion that at the time of the Edict of Milan in AD 313, there were over six million Christians in the Roman Empire, constituting 10 percent of the general population and suggesting that the early church grew at the incredible rate of 40 percent per decade.[5] Perhaps the greatest estimation of the number of Christians in the Roman Empire by the fourth century is L. von Hertling's figure of fifteen million,[6] though this figure is considered high by most historians.[7]

The inevitable question one must ask when considering the early church's rapid rate of growth is "How did it happen?" Traditionally, church historians have attributed the rapid rise of Christianity to the outworking of the Holy Spirit, as manifested through the mass conversions of various people groups. This position was first voiced by Eusebius of Caesarea in his *Ecclesiastical History* and has continued to be advocated by scholars such as Ramsay MacMullen in his *Christianizing the Roman Empire*.[8] Modern historians frequently look to other possible causes for the rapid spread of Christianity. Some, such as W. H. C. Frend, attribute the spread of Christianity to the existence of the widespread Hellenistic Jewish Diaspora, which preceded the spread of Christianity.[9] Others argue that Christianity spread because of its ideological superiority. N. T. Wright asks, "Why then did early Christianity spread? Because early Christians believed that what they had found to be true was true for the whole world. The impetus to mission sprang from the very heart of early Christian conviction."[10]

Rodney Stark, a sociologist by trade and training, has become an influential voice in understanding the early church due in large part to his methodology of "contribut[ing] to studies of the early church [through] better

---

4. Goodenough, *Church in the Roman Empire*, 87.

5. Stark, *Rise of Christianity*, 7. Stark comes to this number through statistical inference as opposed to an existing historical record. He dismisses the number of Christians recorded in the biblical record and instead supposes that there were one thousand Christians in AD 40. Stark gives no reasoning for this number, but it gives him a starting point to begin his calculations. As noted, he then cites Goodenough's figure of six million Christians as his ending point. From this, he calculates that the early church grew at a rate of 40 percent. Stark notes that this figure is plausible to him due to the fact that many "new religions," such as Mormonism, tend to have a similar rate of growth early in their history.

6. Von Hertling, "Die Zahl der Christen," 245–64.

7. Grant, *History of Rome*, 241.

8. See Eusebius, *The Ecclesiastical History of Eusebius Pamphilus*, 37; and MacMullen, *Christianizing the Roman Empire*, 29.

9. Frend, *Rise of Christianity*, 89.

10. Wright, *New Testament and the People of God*, 360.

social science—better theories and more formal methods of analysis."[11] Drawing from this methodology, Stark contends that a number of sociological factors contributed to the rise of Christianity.[12] The first major sociological factor Stark considers in the establishment of the church is the class basis of early Christianity.[13] Citing Engels, Deissman, Troeltsch, and Goodenough, Stark notes that many historians have focused upon Christianity's acceptance among the lower classes of Roman society. Drawing from new research from scholars such as E. A. Judge, Stark argues that Christianity's acceptance by the middle and upper classes of Roman society cemented its position as a legitimate religion as these converts provided the financial, intellectual, and social standing needed to merge into the mainstream of Roman society.

A second sociological factor that Stark examines is the apostolic church's mission to the Jews.[14] Stark argues that the mission was a short-term failure, leading the church to adopt a wider horizon and begin establishing churches among gentile populations and allowing Christianity to be viewed as a distinct religion by the Romans. At the same time this was a long-term success, offering a sense of continuity to Hellenistic Jews that had been marginalized by their Roman neighbors. Stark also argues that the various epidemics that swept through the late Roman Empire were a major contribution to the growth and acceptance of Christianity.[15] These epidemics had the effect of destabilizing Roman society, allowing new ideas and movements to take root while also giving Christians a very public platform to minister to their communities.

A fourth factor considered by Stark is Christianity's appeal to women in the Roman Empire.[16] Stark notes that the ratio of women to men in the ancient church was rather high, which contributed the natural growth of Christianity through the birth of children raised as Christians and through the secondary conversion of husbands. Another sociological factor Stark examines in depth is the church's focus on evangelizing cities in the Roman Empire.[17] In *Cities of God*, Stark argues that Roman cities were fertile

11. Stark, *Rise of Christianity*, xii.
12. Stark, *Triumph of Christianity*, 89.
13. Stark, *Rise of Christianity*, 29.
14. Stark, *Rise of Christianity*, 49.
15. Stark, *Rise of Christianity*, 73.
16. Stark, *Rise of Christianity*, 95.
17. Stark, *Rise of Christianity*, 129.

grounds for Christian evangelism as they provided the social networks required for the spread of new ideas.[18]

The sixth factor Stark examines is the role that the martyrs and the Christian view of martyrdom played in the growth of the ancient church.[19] Stark notes that the number of martyrdoms experienced by the church was relatively low, but the steadfastness of these martyrs helped to strengthen other believers and gain the admiration of pagans outside of the church. A final factor to the growth of the ancient church Stark investigates is the culture of the church and the culture of Roman society.[20] Due to the pluralistic nature of Roman society, it was relatively easy for converts to leave a pagan religion and adopt Christianity. However, due to the exclusivistic nature of the Christian church, it was difficult for Christians to leave the church and adopt a pagan religion.

While social forces, plagues, politics, and ideological competitions were certainly factors in the growth of Christianity, one would be remiss to not consider the methodology behind the considerable evangelistic effort made by the patristic church. During the apostolic era, church writers were most concerned about establishing a proper faith and practice among Christian churches. By the dawn of the patristic period, however, church thinkers began focusing their efforts toward writing Scripture-oriented apologetic works meant to defend the faith and encourage conversions.[21] Central to the apologetic writings of the ancient Christian leaders were the Scriptures. Michael Haykin describes the importance the fathers placed upon the Scriptures in *Rediscovering the Church Fathers: Who They Were and How They Shaped the Church*. Haykin considers the reasons behind Origen's use of Scripture:

> Central to Origen's engagement with Greco-Roman culture was the Bible. Although the Scriptures were often regarded as "barbaric" writings by educated Greeks and Romans, they played a vital role in the evangelization of the Roman Empire. Both Tatian (fl. 170s) and Theophilus of Antioch, for instance, directly attributed their conversions to reading the Scriptures. Origen was firmly convinced that the Bible could effect such conversions because these "sacred books are not the works of men, but . . . they were composed and have come down to us

---

18. Stark, *Cities of God*, 14.
19. Stark, *Rise of Christianity*, 163.
20. Stark, *Rise of Christianity*, 191.
21. Haykin, *Rediscovering the Church Fathers*, 50.

as a result of the inspiration of the Holy Spirit by the will of the Father of the universe through Jesus Christ.[22]

The early church fathers valued the written word of God highly, as demonstrated by their consistent use of the Scriptures in their sermons, letters, personal writings, and commentaries. Bruce Metzger notes, "So extensive are these citations [of Scripture] that if all other sources for our knowledge of the text of the New Testament were destroyed, they would be sufficient alone for the reconstruction of practically the entire New Testament."[23] The fathers sought to conform every area of their life with Scripture, whether it was ecclesiastical faith and practice, family relationships, work, or, as I propose, evangelistic methodology.

DEVELOPMENT OF EVANGELISTIC WRITING IN THE ANCIENT CHURCH

The first recorded work bearing the title of an "apology" (*apologia*) is a formal speech delivered by Socrates[24] in which he defended himself against the capital charge of "corrupting the young, and by not believing in the gods in whom the city believes, but in other daimonia that are novel," as recorded by Plato.[25] Deriving its meaning from Socrates's defense, the term *apology* and its genre of writings are known for providing a defense for a person, institution, or worldview. Within the Christian worldview, Christians are allowed to make a defense for themselves before the world but are commanded to "be prepared to give an answer [*apologia*] to everyone who asks you to give the reason for the hope that you have" (1 Pet 3:15). Accordingly, throughout the history of the church, Christians have produced apologetic works designed to defend the person of Christ, the church, and the Christian worldview against criticisms and attacks from the outside world.

H. B. Swete notes that as one migrates from the writings of the apostles found in the New Testament to the earliest writings produced by the apostolic fathers that "there is no immediate change in the form of the writings; the earliest remains of the sub-apostolic age consist of letters addressed to churches or individuals after the model of the Apostolic Epistles."[26] Initially, works by the apostolic fathers focused upon church order, discipline, and

22. Haykin, *Rediscovering the Church Fathers*, 80–81.
23. Metzger and Ehrman, *Text of the New Testament*, 87.
24. Harvey, "Martyr Passions and Hagiography," 549.
25. West, *Plato's Apology of Socrates*, 8.
26. Swete, *Holy Spirit in the Ancient Church*, 3.

moral and theological instruction. This emphasis can be clearly seen in works such as Clement of Rome's *Epistle to the Corinthians*, which encouraged the church to practice personal humility and forgiveness. However, as the Christian faith expanded and came under both social and political attacks, the church began to respond with apologetic works designed to answer their society's questions about Christianity as well as demonstrating its superiority over other worldviews.[27]

While Tertullian was the first Christian writer to title one of his own works as an apology,[28] he was not the first to offer a defense of the faith. In the *Epistle of Barnabas*, one finds an argument against the Jewish interpretation of the Scriptures in favor of a Christian interpretation, and in the *Epistle to Diognetus* the writer attempts to show the superiority of the Christian life, but these writings are somewhat fleeting and insubstantial.[29] The earliest and most influential Christian apologist is Irenaeus who, in many ways, defined the genre of Christian apologetics. J. K. S. Reid notes,

> For the first time an attempt is made to go beyond unsystematic apologetic practice and to define the principles of apologetics. Irenaeus is not content simply to select form the riches of the classical world what suits or is congruous with Christianity and to reject what contradicts or conflicts with it. He passes beyond such eclecticism to study not only what is heretically said, but also what heresy in itself is; and proceeds not only to approve particular elements in the non-Christian world, but to construct a strategy of Christian defense. Scientific apologetics begins to take shape and to replace amateurish apologetic activity.[30]

Pre-Nicene apologetical writers such as Irenaeus, Origen, and Tertullian tended to focus upon proving seven primary tenets: Christians were innocent of the crimes they were commonly accused of; paganism was ignorant of Christianity; pagan morals were corrupt, while Christian morals were pure; Christian beliefs aligned with the best philosophies; Christianity was an ancient religion; and Christianity was verified by the fulfillment of scriptural prohecies.[31]

In the post-Nicene era of the ancient church, Christian thinkers continued to contend for the faith against their pagan culture, but also began to

---

27. Haykin, *Rediscovering the Church Fathers*, 78.
28. Harvey, *Oxford Handbook of Early Christian Studies*, 550.
29. Reid, *Christian Apologetics*, 54.
30. Reid, *Christian Apologetics*, 54.
31. House and Jowers, *Reasons for Our Hope*, 146.

contend with others in the church over proper theological beliefs.[32] This is perhaps best seen in the example of Athanasius who sought to both convert pagans to Christianity as well as convince wayward Christians to embrace orthodox theologies.

As Christianity began to be tolerated and even accepted in the late Roman Empire, the need of apologetic writings began to decline. Perhaps the last great Christian apologetic from the early church was Augustine's *City of God*.[33] This work was written following the sack of Rome by the Goths in 410. Pagan critics of Christianity used the fall of Rome to argue that Christianity was detrimental to the empire and that the rejection of the old gods had caused its downfall.

One constant found in the apologetical literature produced by the ancient church was the writer's trust in the power of the Scriptures to produce salvation in their readers. This is evident in Justin Martyr's *First Apology* where, after reviewing Old Testament prophecies, he concludes, "Since, then, we prove that all things which have already happened had been predicted by the prophets before they came to pass, we must necessarily believe also that those things which are in like manner predicted, but are yet to come to pass, shall certainly happen."[34] This is also evident in Origen's assertion to Celus: "The prophecies . . . are sufficient to produce faith in any one who reads them."[35]

STATEMENT OF THE PROBLEM

The goal of this dissertation is to demonstrate that arguments from Scripture were extensively used in the apologetic and evangelistic writings produced by Christian leaders within the Greek patristic tradition due to their belief that Scripture was the primary tool given by God for the conversion of souls. I wished to explore this issue for a number of reasons. Foremost, as previously noted, the patristic church experienced a growth rate of approximately 40 percent per decade,[36] a growth rate considerably greater than the current growth rate of the Christian faith. As modern Christians consider how they might better reach the lost in their context, it is wise to consider how the earliest Christians successfully reached the lost in their context.

---

32. Swete, *Holy Spirit in the Ancient Church*, 65.
33. Harvey, *Oxford Handbook of Early Christian Studies*, 560.
34. Justin Martyr, *Apologies* 1.180.
35. Origen, *Contra Celsum* 4:397b.
36. Stark, *Rise of Christianity*, 7.

In many ways, considering the evangelistic methodology of the patristic church may be very productive for modern Christians because people living in the "post-Christian age"[37] view Christianity in a very similar light as did people living in the "pre-Christian age." For example, in contemporary culture, many view the Bible as a collection of writings produced by a superstitious culture attempting to understand their world, though lacking the scientific knowledge needed to do so.[38] This view, of course, is similar to the first-century Roman view of the Bible, which was that it was a writing consisting of "foreign superstition" produced by unenlightened authors.[39]

Following contemporary culture's diminished view of the Scriptures, some evangelists have found themselves using the Scriptures less in evangelistic appeals. In *The Church on the Other Side*, Brian McLaren argues that using Scripture in an apologetic for the Christian faith in the contemporary culture constitutes circular reasoning:

> When everyone de facto believes the Bible, we can afford to prove our points with proof-texts. But as the world changes and more and more people show themselves ignorant or skeptical of the Bible, saying "The Bible says" doesn't prove anything. The old

---

37. Jenkins, *Next Christendom*. Post-Christianity, or the post-Christian age, is the loss of a Christian "monopoly" in political, cultural, and social affairs in areas where the Christian worldview had previously flourished.

38. Sam Harris states:

> There is not a single line in the Bible or the Koran that could not have been authored by a first-century person. There is not one reference to anything— there are pages and pages about how to sacrifice animals, and keep slaves, and who to kill and why. There's nothing about electricity, there's nothing about DNA, there's nothing about infectious disease, the principles of infectious disease. There's nothing particularly useful, and there's a lot of iron age barbarism in there, and superstitions. (Sam Harris, "Sam Harris: On Interpreting Scripture.")

Christopher Hitchens writes:

> Religion comes from the period of human prehistory where nobody—not even the mighty Democritus who concluded that all matter was made from atoms—had the smallest idea what was going on. It comes from the bawling and fearful infancy of our species, and is a babyish attempt to meet our inescapable demand for knowledge (as well as for comfort, reassurance, and other infantile needs). Today the least educated of my children knows much more about the natural order than any of the founders of religion. (Hitchens, *God Is Not Great*, 64.)

39. Tacitus, *The Annals, The Reigns*, 286. Tacitus records that Pomponia Graecina, the wife of Senator Plautius, "was accused of foreign superstition" and handed over to her husband for judgment. Marta Sordi makes a compelling case that the "foreign superstition" in question was Christianity. Sordi, *Christians and the Roman Empire*, 28.

apologetic was effective when it was helping nominal Christians, who assumed biblical authority, discover a vital faith. It has been losing effectiveness as nominalism (i.e., being Christian in name only) gives way to secularism (i.e., dropping the Christian label as well) and as biblical authority is either questioned or unheard of rather than assumed. On the other side, the Bible serves less as the authoritative foundation for apologetics as a part of the fabric of the message itself.[40]

Using the same line of reasoning, Dan Kimball states that evangelism "is more dialogue and listening than preaching and telling,"[41] arguing that personal experiences and the building of relationships should be the primary tools of evangelism. The evangelistic methodology of the patristic church can speak to this mindset. The fathers lived in a world largely ignorant and antagonistic to both the Scriptures and to the Christian faith. While engaging the lost in their context, however, the fathers still used Scripture as a primary means of evangelization as they believed that the word of God carried with it the power of God and was the only way to break the power of sin in one's heart.

A secondary issue that this thesis addresses is the claim made by Michael Green in *Evangelism in the Early Church*, in which he focuses upon the idea and practice of evangelism in the apostolic church, frequently using examples from later periods of the church as illustrations. However, while frequently using patristic writings to illustrate his claims, Green is also somewhat dismissive of the evangelistic literature produced by the fathers, arguing that they are acrimonious and counterproductive to the evangelistic pursuit. Green writes,

> But unfortunately tendencies which were already beginning to make themselves felt in the New Testament documents became heightened in the Apologists. It has long been recognized that there is a strong anti-Jewish element in parts of St. Matthew's Gospel, and in St. John too, where "the Jews" are always mentioned in contradistinction, if not open opposition, to Christian believers . . . At all events, in most of the second-century pieces of apologetic that we possess there is a hardness of approach which could hardly have been calculated to win the friendship and goodwill of the non-Christian readers. There is acrimony about Justin's *Dialogue* with the Jew, Trypho, a biting scorn for the pagan gods among Apologists like Tatian and Tertullian, which almost certainly frustrated the genuine evangelistic concern

40. McLaren, *Church on the Other Side*, 74–75.
41. Kimball, *Emerging Church*, 286.

these men undoubtedly possessed. To launch a full-scale and at times bitter assault on someone's cherished beliefs is not the best way of inducing him to change them . . . The love must have been there, as is clear from the way in which these Apologists lived and died; but it is to a large extent masked in their writings, and to that extent one may well imagine that not many pagans or Jews were won to the faith through these documents, if in fact they read them were they written more perhaps in the interests of Christian readership than for external consumption? There is, to my knowledge, no example of an outsider being converted to Christianity by reading an apologetic writing.[42]

In many respects, Green is shortsighted in his view of second-century apologetic writings. This dissertation shows that the patristic writers were bold in their defense of the gospel and that this boldness was founded upon their intrinsic trust in the Scriptures to effect salvation in the heart of their readers.

DEFINITIONS

To better define the parameters of this dissertation, it is wise to clarify some of the nuances and details of the terms and phrases used. In the following paragraphs, I define the terms and phrases *fathers*, *Greek fathers/tradition*, *Scripture*, and *evangelistic writings* as they are used in this dissertation.

Fathers. The term "patrology" was coined by Lutheran scholar J. Gerhard in his posthumous work *Patrologia sive de primitivae Ecclesiae Christianae Doctorum vita ac Lucubrationibus* and is derived from the Latin and Greek terms for "father" (*pater*).[43] From this, it is held that the term "church fathers" refers to "persons to whom is owed spiritual generation and formation in teaching and style of life."[44] In *Rediscovering the Church Fathers: Who They Were and How They Shaped the Church*, Michael Haykin offers the following definition, which I use for this dissertation:

> In an entry on "patristics" in *The Oxford Dictionary of the Christian Church*, a standard reference work of Christianity, the church fathers are described as those authors who "wrote between the end of the 1st cent . . . and the close of the 8th

---

42. Green, *Evangelism in the Early Church*, 350–51.

43. Di Berardino, *Encyclopedia of Ancient Christianity*, 92. In *Patrologia, sive De Primitivae Ecclesiae Christianae Doctorum vita ac Lucubrationibus*, Gerhard included authors from Hermas to Bellarmine.

44. Ferguson, ed., *Encyclopedia of Early Christianity*, 345.

cent.," which comprises what is termed the "patristic age." These authors, this entry continues, defended the gospel against heresies and misunderstandings; they composed extensive commentaries on the Bible, explanatory, doctrinal, and practical, and published innumerable sermons, largely on the same subject; they exhibited the meaning and implications of the creeds; they recorded past and current events in church history; and they related the Christian faith to the best thought of their own age. In another major reference work dealing with Christianity's history and theology, *Christianity: The Complete Guide*, it is noted that while there is no official list of the fathers, there are at least four characteristics that denote those meriting the title of "church father": their orthodoxy of doctrine, their being accepted by the church as important links in the transmission of the Christian faith, their holiness of life, and their having lived between the end of the apostolic era (ca. 100) and the deaths of John of Damascus (ca. 655/675–ca. 749) in the East and Isidore of Seville (ca. 560–636) in the West. Recent study of the fathers, this article goes on to observe, has tended to broaden the category of church father to include some figures many in the ancient church viewed with suspicion—namely, figures like Tertullian and Origen (ca. 185–254). This article also notes that, owing to the rise of feminist historiography, scholarship of this era is now prepared also to talk about church mothers ("matristics"). There is no doubt that feminist concerns have highlighted the way in which much of church history has been taught from an exclusively male perspective. But the problem with this category of "matristics" is that there are very few women in the ancient church who can be studied in similar depth to the fathers since they left little textual remains.[45]

Greek fathers. The *Catholic Encyclopedia* notes,

> In order to get a good view of the patristic period, the fathers may be divided in various ways. One favorite method is by periods; the Ante-Nicene Fathers till 325; the Great Fathers of the fourth century and half the fifth (325–451); and the later fathers. A more obvious division is into Easterns and Westerns, and the Easterns will comprise writers in Greek, Syriac, Armenian, and Coptic. A convenient division into smaller groups will be by periods, nationalities, and character of writings; for in the East and West there were many races, and some of the ecclesiastical

---

45. Haykin, *Rediscovering the Church Fathers*, 16.

writers are apologists, some preachers, some historians, some commentators, and so forth.[46]

For this dissertation, I subdivide the fathers between the Greek fathers and Latin fathers. The Latin fathers are those church fathers who wrote in Latin, such as Augustine of Hippo, Cyprian of Carthage, and Tertullian. The Greek fathers consist of those fathers who wrote in Greek, such as Irenaeus of Lyons, Origen of Alexandria, and John Chrysostom. The "Greek Patristic Tradition" would consist of the writings, ideas, and theologies derived from the Greek fathers.

Scripture. When commenting upon the Lausanne Covenant, John R. W. Stott writes,

> It may seem strange that the Lausanne Covenant, which is primarily concerned with worldwide evangelization, should include a statement about biblical authority and indeed emphasize it by putting it in such a prominent place . . . [but] both evangelism and the nurture of converts involve teaching and therefore raise the question, "What shall we teach?" As Dr. Francis Schaeffer wrote in his later paper, "The Gospel we preach must be rich in content." And this content must be biblical content.[47]

Equally, it may seem strange to define the term *Scripture* in a dissertation written for an evangelical seminary; however, given the diverse number of opinions on what constituted Scripture in the patristic period, such a definition is wise. For this dissertation, I use the definition adopted by the Third Council of Carthage in AD 397:

> The canonical Scriptures are these: Genesis, Exodus, Leviticus, Numbers, Deuteronomy, Joshua the son of Nun, Judges, Ruth, four books of Kings, two books of Paraleipomena, Job, the Psalter, five books of Solomon, the books of the twelve prophets, Isaiah, Jeremiah, Ezechiel, Daniel, Tobit, Judith, Esther, two books of Esdras, two books of the Maccabees. Of the New Testament: four books of the Gospels, one book of the Acts of the Apostles, thirteen Epistles of the Apostle Paul, one epistle of the same [writer] to the Hebrews, two Epistles of the Apostle Peter, three of John, one of James, one of Jude, one book of the Apocalypse of John. Let this be made known also to our brother and fellow-priest Boniface, or to other bishops of those parts, for the

---

46. Herbermann, *Catholic Encyclopedia*, 5.
47. Stott, *Lausanne Covenant*, 8.

purpose of confirming that canon. because we have received from our fathers that those books must be read in the church.[48]

While exploring the fathers' use of Scripture in their evangelistic writing, I focus solely upon their use of Scripture as recorded in the Old Testament and New Testament while disregarding references to apocryphal or non-canonical works.

Evangelistic writings. One of the great strengths of the Church Growth Movement is that it has properly rejected the evangelism/discipleship divide arguing that the goal of evangelism is not to just create converts, but to create converts who become fully-functioning disciples of Jesus Christ.[49] The Church Growth Movement's influence upon the Lausanne Congress is obvious in its definition of evangelism. In the Lausanne Covenant, evangelism is defined as follows:

> To evangelize is to spread the good news that Jesus Christ died for our sins and was raised from the dead according to the Scriptures, and that as the reigning Lord he now offers the forgiveness of sins and the liberating gifts of the Spirit to all who repent and believe . . . But evangelism itself is the proclamation of the historical, biblical Christ as Savior and Lord, with a view to persuading people to come to him personally and so be reconciled to God. In issuing the gospel invitation we have no liberty to conceal the cost of discipleship. Jesus still calls all who would follow him to deny themselves, take up their cross, and identify themselves with his new community. The results of evangelism include obedience to Christ, incorporation into his church and responsible service in the world.[50]

Given the Lausanne Congress's definition of evangelism, for this dissertation an *evangelistic writing* consists of any writing written for the purpose of convincing a lost person to convert to Christianity and grow as a disciple of Christ. This definition includes the apologetic writings of the Greek fathers, meant to convince people of the legitimacy of the Christian faith, as evangelistic writings.

---

48. Westcott, *General Survey*, 440.
49. McGavran, *Bridges of God*, 13.
50. Stott, *Lausanne Covenant*, 20.

RESEARCH METHODOLOGY

This dissertation relies primarily upon the extant writings of the fathers in the Greek tradition to determine if the patristic church relied upon the Scriptures in their evangelistic writings and the fathers' reasoning behind such a reliance. Given that Jacques Paul Migne's 166-volume collection *Patrologia Graeca* documents over ten thousand works produced by more than eight hundred Greek patristic writers,[51] a sufficient number of primary sources are available to complete this dissertation.

The early church fathers studied, wrote on, preached to, and commented on a broad range of issues related to the founding, growth, theology, and praxis of the early church, as well as issues within their culture at large, thus producing a large volume of work. As previously noted, Migne's *Patrologia Graeca* records over ten thousand writings produced by more than eight hundred Greek patristic authors. When this collection is combined with Migne's 221-volume *Patrologia Latina* and the unfinished collection of Rene Graffin's *Patrologia Orientalis* (now at forty-one volumes), as well as the 240 volumes of the *Corpus Scriptorum Christianorum Orientalium* published by the Catholic University of Louvain, one finds a body of writings that would be nearly impossible for a solitary student to study and understand, and is certainly beyond the scope of this dissertation.

This dissertation was delimited to the apologetic literature produced by the Greek fathers. Thus, relevant writings outside of the Greek patristic tradition such as Tertullian's *Apologeticus pro Christianis*, though a wonderful and scripturally-driven apologetic for the Christian faith, must be passed over and left for future study.

Additionally, this dissertation was delimited to writers within the Greek patristic tradition who produced both apologetic writings as well as theological and hermeneutical writings. This is necessary as the goal of this dissertation was not only to demonstrate that Scripture drove the evangelistic writings of the Greek fathers, but also to investigate why Scripture was given such a central role in their apologetic writings. As such, writings such as Marcus Minucius Felix's *Octavius*, *The Apology of Aristides* and the *Letter to Diognetus* were not considered in this dissertation because these works are written by either anonymous or unknown writers or they represent the only surviving writing produced by their author. Therefore, while one may be able to demonstrate that these writings made extensive use of the Scriptures, it would be impossible to ascertain why they did so.

---

51. Migne, "Patrologia Graeca."

Chapter 2 examines the use of Scripture in the evangelistic writings of the Greek fathers by exploring the writings of Justin Martyr, perhaps best known for his role in arguing that Christ is the Logos of God.[52] After offering a brief biography, I conduct a general survey of his writings to better understand his theology of Scripture and to demonstrate how his high view of Scripture educated his evangelistic method. My primary goal of this chapter is to argue that Justin's theology of Scripture led him to use Scripture as a primary tool in his evangelistic endeavors. In this chapter I survey Justin's First and Second *Apology, Dialogue with Trypho, On the Sole Government of God, On the Resurrection,* as well as various fragments of his writings.

Chapter 3 explores the writings of the most prolific Bible commentator from the patristic period, Origen. Following a biography on Origen, I examine his theology of Scripture as found in his exegetical works, such as Origen's various homilies, commentaries, and the extant fragments of his *Hexapla*. In this chapter I demonstrate that Origen's theology of Scripture drove the content of his evangelistic works such as his *On First Principles* and his response to the Middle Platonist Celsus in *Against Celsus*.[53]

Chapter 4 considers the writings of Athanasius, perhaps best remembered for his opposition to Arianism and his defense of Trinitarianism. Following Athanasius's biography I explore his views upon the Scriptures as found in his theological and exegetical works, such as his *First Letter to Serapion* and the remaining fragments of his comments of Genesis and Psalms. Following this I examine Athanasius's evangelistic writings, such as *Against the Heathen* and *The Incarnation of the Word of God*. In this chapter I show that Athanasius's high view of Scripture led him to use Scripture as a primary means to prove the divinity of Christ and one's need to trust in him.

Chapter 5 begins to examine the writings of John Chrysostom, known today in large part due to his renowned preaching ability. After looking at John's biography I offer a general survey of the vast number of his extant works, including his liturgies, homilies, and commentaries, to establish his views pertaining to the Scriptures. The primary purpose of this chapter is to argue that John Chrysostom's theology of Scripture led him to use Scripture as a primary tool in his evangelistic endeavors. In this chapter I survey John's apologetic literature such as his *Demonstration against the Pagans That Christ Is God*.

Chapter 6 explores the writings of John of Damascus, perhaps best known for being the first major Christian thinker to address the Islamic

---

52. Rokéah, *Justin Martyr and the Jews*, 22.
53. Herzog and Schaff, *New Schaff-Herzog Encyclopedia*, 466.

religion in an apologetic fashion. After presenting a brief biography, I consider John's views on the Scriptures from works such as *The Fountain of Wisdom, On Right Thinking,* and *Elementary Introduction into Dogmas.* Following this I consider how his theology of Scripture educated the content of his evangelistic writings.

Chapter 7 concludes the dissertation with an overarching summary of the use of Scripture in the evangelistic writings of the Greek fathers, as well as considerations for contemporary evangelicals. Additionally, I suggest streams for future research and study.

2

The Use of Scripture in the Evangelistic Writings of Justin Martyr

By the dawn of the second century AD, the Christian faith had experienced a time of rapid transition. By AD 100, Christian churches had been established in major cities throughout the Roman Empire, such as in Alexandria, Ephesus, and even the capital city of Rome itself. While the spread of the faith gave Christians the opportunity to reach large numbers of lost people with the gospel, it also exposed the church to a number of criticisms as well. Internally, the church found itself in a struggle against the heresy of Gnosticism. Regarding the gnostics, Justo Gonzalez writes,

> The gnostic movement was not a well-defined organization in competition with the church, but a vast, amorphous movement that existed within, and beyond, the church . . . According to the gnostics, they possessed a special, mystical knowledge, reserved for those with true understanding. That knowledge was the secret key to salvation.[1]

Externally, the church found resistance from both Jewish and Roman sources. Springing from the roots of Judaism, Christians first faced opposition from the Jewish people. This resistance ranged from simple resistance to Christian teachings to the execution of Christian leaders, such as James

---

1. Gonzalez, *Early Church to the Dawn of the Reformation*, 58.

the Just under the leadership of the High Priest Annas.[2] This early Jewish resistance to Christianity may in part stem from the early Jewish view that Christianity was a heretical sect of Judaism. Claudia Setzer writes,

> Jews did not see Christians as clearly separate from their own community until at least the middle of the second century. Thus, acts of Jewish persecution of Christians fall within the boundaries of synagogue discipline and were so perceived by Jews acting and thinking as the established community. The Christians, on the other hand, saw themselves as persecuted rather than disciplined.[3]

As the Christian church expanded beyond Israel into gentile lands, the church also began to experience resistance from its Roman neighbors. Initially, Roman resistance to Christianity was largely social in nature. Frederic Farrar notes,

> They looked on the worship of One who had been crucified as the lowest abyss of religious infatuation. Further than this, they were maddened by the moral inflexibility which prevented the Christians from taking any part in public amusements or social gatherings . . . The heathen looked on them as morose and fanatical intruders, whose ostensible innocence was a rebuke to the commonest and most harmless practices of daily life. What made them still more indignant was that they believed the rigid exterior of Christians to be the cloak for deeds of nameless abomination. They could not shake off the effects of the persistent calumny that such crimes were carried on in secret gatherings.[4]

Once Christians had been established as social pariahs in first-century Roman society, it was easy for Roman leaders to use Christians as scapegoats to deflect from scandals within their own administrations. This is seen in the example of Emperor Nero blaming the great Roman fire on Christians to redirect the charges that he was responsible for it.

As the Christian church entered the second century, it found itself in need of a leader with sound philosophical training and a background with both the pagan and Jewish cultures. Fortunately, the ancient church found such a leader in Justin Martyr.

---

2. Wand, *History of the Early Church*, 13.
3. Stetzer, *Jewish Responses*, 89.
4. Farrar, *Lives of the Fathers*, 125.

BIOGRAPHY

The limited information about Justin's life comes from his own hand, recorded in his now-extant works. Scholars estimate that Justin was likely born at the end of the apostolic age around AD 100.[5] Justin notes that he was born in the town of Flavia Neapolis in Palestine,[6] founded in AD 72 on the same site of the Samaritan town of Mabartha. Today the town is known by its Arabicized name, Nablus. Given that the city of Flavia Neapolis lied just to the west of Shechem and just to the north of Mt. Gerizim, it is likely that Justin had some familiarity with Judaism as a child. Though he self-identified as a "Samaritan,"[7] Justin was a gentile, as evidenced by the Grecian names of his father (Priscus) and grandfather (Bacchius)[8] and the fact that he was never circumcised.[9]

In many respects, Justin could be referred to as a "seeker," as he found himself in a nearly constant quest for the knowledge and wisdom that led to God.[10] Justin began his quest for the wisdom of God by studying within the Stoic school of thought. Justin notes that he "surrendered" to the teachings of a Stoic instructor and spent a "considerable" amount of time with him learning the tenets of Stoicism.[11] While Justin gives no indication of how long this "considerable" amount of time lasted, he does note that it was long enough that his teacher eventually dismissed him, noting that he had nothing more he could teach Justin about God.[12]

Following his tenure with Stoicism, Justin began studying with an itinerant philosopher in the area.[13] After several days with this philosopher, however, Justin began to question the philosopher's motives and teaching after he began to negotiate payment. Soon after, Justin began following a Pythagorean philosopher whom he greatly respected.[14] However, Justin

---

5. *New Catholic Encyclopedia*, 93.
6. Justin Martyr, *1 Apology*, 1.
7. Justin Martyr, *Dialogue*, 120.
8. Justin Martyr, *1 Apology*, 1.
9. Justin Martyr, *Dialogue*, 128.
10. Justin Martyr and Athenagoras, *The Complete Works of Justin Martyr and Athenagoras*, 1. During his trial before the Prefect Rusticus, Justin is reported to have said, "I have endeavoured to learn all doctrines; but I have acquiesced at last in the true doctrines, those namely of the Christians, even though they do not please those who hold false opinions."
11. Justin Martyr, *Dialogue*, 2.
12. Justin Martyr, *Dialogue*, 2.
13. Justin Martyr, *Dialogue*, 2.
14. Justin Martyr, *Dialogue*, 2.

quickly became discouraged with his new teacher due to the numerous prerequisites to study that were expected of him. The Pythagorean philosopher told Justin that he would need a background in disciplines such as music, geometry, and astronomy. Unwilling to delay his quest for God, Justin moved on to a teacher versed in Platonism.

Regarding his Platonic studies, Justin writes,

> In my helpless condition it occurred to me to have a meeting with the Platonists, for their fame was great. I thereupon spent as much of my time as possible with one who had lately settled in our city, a sagacious man, holding a high position among the Platonists, and I progressed, and made the greatest improvements daily. And the perception of immaterial things quite overpowered me, and the contemplation of ideas furnished my mind with wings, so that in a little while I supposed that I had become wise; and such was my stupidity, I expected forthwith to look upon God, for this is the end of Plato's philosophy.[15]

As Justin grew in his understanding of Platonic thought, he began to seek out solitude to reason with himself. On one of these outings, he met a man looking for a member of his household.

Recognizing Justin as a philosopher, this anonymous man began to discuss how one might come to know God. After several lines of reasoning, the man had demonstrated to Justin's satisfaction that man cannot find God through human philosophy[16] and that if God is to be known, he must make himself known through his own revelation of himself.[17] Fortunately, according to this man, God has revealed himself through his Holy Spirit to various prophets throughout the ages, who have sought to teach the people around them of God. Furthermore, their writings are still extant in the Christian Scripture, which points people to find salvation through Jesus Christ.[18]

At the conclusion of his gospel presentation, the man encouraged Justin to think upon their conversation. And though Justin never saw him again, his impact upon Justin's life was unmistakable. Justin writes,

> Straightway a flame was kindled in my soul; and a love of the prophets, and of those men who are friends of Christ, possessed me; and whilst revolving his words in my mind, I found this philosophy alone to be safe and profitable. Thus, and for this reason, I am a philosopher. Moreover, I would wish that all, making

15. Justin Martyr, *Dialogue*, 2.
16. Justin Martyr, *Dialogue*, 6.
17. Justin Martyr, *Dialogue*, 7.
18. Justin Martyr, *Dialogue*, 7.

a resolution similar to my own, do not keep themselves away from the words of the Savior. For they possess a terrible power in themselves, and are sufficient to inspire those who turn aside from the path of rectitude with awe; while the sweetest rest is afforded those who make a diligent practice of them.[19]

Following his conversion to Christianity, Justin took on the robe of a philosopher and began to formulate arguments to defend both Christians and the Christian faith. Justin refers to a treatise written against "all heresies" in his *First Apology*[20] and Eusebius records that Justin also penned an apology against Marcion,[21] though these works have been lost to history. Three of Justin's works are extant today, known from one manuscript, the *parisinus graecus*, dated September 11, 1363.[22] Justin's first work is his *First Apology*, written to Emperor Titus, his sons Verissimus, Lucius, Pius, the Roman Senate, and the people of Rome.[23] The purpose of this apology was to demonstrate that Christians were innocent of the crimes with which they were typically charged and argued that they should be given fair trials. Additionally, Justin argues that Christianity is the source of truth, concluding with an explanation of the life and theology of the church. Justin's *Second Apology* was, in many ways, an addendum to his *First Apology*.[24] Justin's final extant work is his *Dialogue with Trypho the Jew*, in which Justin recalls a multi-day debate between Justin, Trypho, and several of Trypho's friends.[25]

Justin's apologetic ministry soon brought him into confrontation with several people, including a philosopher by the name of Crescens who held to philosophical Cynicism. According to Eusebius, Justin had debated Crescens a number of times, and following a public humiliation in AD 165 he sought to accuse Justin before the Roman authorities.[26] The *Martyrdom of Justin* records that Justin was arrested along with four other Christians.

---

19. Justin Martyr, *Dialogue*, 8.
20. Justin Martyr, *1 Apology*, 26.
21. Eusebius, *Ecclesiastical History* 18.9.
22. Sibinga, *Old Testament Text of Justin Martyr*, 13.
23. Parvis and Foster, *Justin Martyr and His Worlds*, 24. There is some debate concerning the order in which Justin's works were written. In *Justin Martyr and His Worlds*, Paul Parvis notes that people view Justin's first and second apology in three primary ways: (1) the two apologies are two separate apologies; (2) they constitute one apology; (3) they constitute an apology with an appendix. For the sake of this dissertation, I assume the first view and examine these works separately.
24. Litfin, *Getting to Know the Church Fathers*, 60.
25. Litfin, *Getting to Know the Church Fathers*, 59.
26. Eusebius, *Ecclesiastical History* 4.16.

After a brief questioning by the Prefect Rusticus, he pronounced judgment. The *Martyrdom* records,

> Rusticus gave the prefect pronounced sentence, saying, "Let those who have refused to sacrifice to the gods and to yield to the command of the emperor be scourged, and led away to suffer the punishment of decapitation, according to the laws." The holy martyrs having glorified God, and having gone forth to the accustomed place, were beheaded, and perfected their testimony in the confession of the Savior. And some of the faithful having secretly removed their bodies, laid them in a suitable place, the grace of our Lord Jesus Christ having wrought along with them, to whom be glory for ever and ever. Amen.[27]

JUSTIN'S THEOLOGY OF SCRIPTURE

Before considering Justin's theological understanding of Scripture, it may be prudent to examine his conception of what constituted Scripture in this lifetime. While the consideration of Justin's understanding of what writings should carry the designation of "Scripture" may seem superfluous, it is necessary due to the contention of some that the ancient church did not possess a set of writings widely seen as authoritative within their context.[28]

Justin's Old Testament Text

By the time of Justin's birth around AD 100, the text of the Old Testament (Jewish Tanakh) had largely been settled. Evidence suggests that, within Judaism, the Old Testament was canonized in phases beginning with the acceptance of the Torah around 400 BC and concluding with the acceptance of the Writings in the late first century AD.[29] A significant amount of evidence indicates that the ancient church followed Judaism in accepting their Tanakh as the Christian Old Testament. The earliest extant list of books contained in the Christian Old Testament comes from Bishop Melito of Sardis

---

27. Justin Martyr, *Martyrdom*, 5.

28. Ehrman, *Lost Christianities*, 250. Ehrman argues that within pre-Constantinian Christianity, there were a number of competing ideas of what constituted true Christianity. As such, there was a wide opinion on what constituted "scripture" in the early church. According to Ehrman, the push for a recognized canon of Scripture was necessary to establish an Orthodox faith, thus making the canonization of the New Testament in 419 as much of an ecclesiastical victory as it was a political victory.

29. McDonald and Sanders, *Canon Debate*, 4.

in AD 170.³⁰ Bishop Melito lists all the books found in modern Protestant Old Testaments, though he combines the book of Lamentations with the book of Jeremiah and the book of Nehemiah with the book of Ezra. In the third century, Origen echoed Melito's list, as recorded in Eusebius's *Ecclesiastical History*.³¹ Additionally, in the late fourth century in his *Prologus Galeatus* and other works, Jerome agreed with Melito and Origen while adding the apocryphal books in a secondary position.³²

While examining Justin's extant writings, it quickly becomes evident that the aforementioned views of the content of the Old Testament were also held by Justin, as evidenced by his practice of regularly quoting from the Old Testament. In *Justin Martyr: His Life, Writings, and Opinions*, Charles Semisch notes,

> Of the canonical books of the Old Testament, Justin makes use of about two-thirds, mostly in the way of direct quotation, but sometimes in more general references to their contents. The books of Moses, the Psalms, and the Prophets, but especially Isaiah, are most frequently employed. The books that are passed over in entire silence are, of the historical books, Judges, the second book of Chronicles, Ruth, Ezra, Nehemiah, and Esther; the Prophets, Haggai, Zephaniah, Habakkuk, Nahum and Obadia [sic]; of the didactic poetical books, Ecclesiastes and Solomon's Song. Those passages of the Old Testament of which Justin makes use are uniformly quoted in the translation of the LXX [Septuagint].³³

It is not surprising that, while quoting from the Old Testament, Justin primarily focused on prophetic literature as one of the primary proofs to demonstrate the truthfulness and antiquity of the Christian faith by examining the prophecies fulfilled by the coming of Jesus Christ.³⁴

Justin's New Testament Text

While the content of the Old Testament had been settled prior to Justin's birth, in many respects the content of the New Testament was in a state of

---

30. Archer, *Survey of Old Testament Introduction*, 80.
31. Eusebius, *Ecclesiastical History* 6.25.
32. Pfeiffer, *Introduction to the Old Testament*, 69.
33. Semisch, *Justin Martyr*, 254.
34. Bush, *Classical Readings in Christian Apologetics*, 3.

flux during Justin's lifetime. As such, determining what Justin would have considered to constitute the New Testament is somewhat difficult.

The works that would later be confirmed as part of the New Testament canon were all written and in circulation among Christian churches by the time of Justin's birth in AD 100. However, there existed no universal consensus on which apostolic writings should be equal in weight to the Old Testament Scriptures. Bruce Metzger summarizes the situation:

> During the course of the second century most churches came to possess and acknowledge a canon which included the present four Gospels, the Acts, thirteen letters of Paul, 1 Peter, and 1 John. Seven books still lacked general recognition: Hebrews, James, 2 Peter, 2 and 3 John, Jude, and Revelation . . . On the other hand, certain other Christian writings, such as the first letter of Clement, the letter of Barnabas, the Shepherd of Hermas, and the Didache, otherwise known as the Teaching of the Twelve Apostles, were accepted as scriptural by several ecclesiastical writers, though rejected by the majority.[35]

While a general consensus upon what constituted the New Testament remained in a state of slight flux at the beginning of the second century, by the dawn of the third century the ancient church began to settle upon which apostolic writings should be considered Scripture alongside the Old Testament. This is evident in Eusebius's list of accepted writings in his *Ecclesiastical History*, in which he listed every book of the modern New Testament as generally accepted Scripture by the ancient church,[36] with the same nature and authority of the Old Testament Scriptures.[37]

In many respects, the ancient church's first venture into the canonization of the New Testament began during the course of Justin's life and ministry. This is due in large part to heretical sects producing their own letters claiming apostolic authorship and Marcion's publication of his canon in the mid-second century. To answer the challenges presented by these various sects, men like Irenaeus began to investigate which texts should be

---

35. Metzger, *The New Testament*, 274.

36. Eusebius, *Ecclesiastical History* 3.25. Eusebius divides the writings in question into three classes. First, twenty-two books generally acknowledged to be canonical. These were the four Gospels, fourteen letters of Paul (in which Eusebius included the book of Hebrews), 1 John, 1 Peter, and Revelation. The second class of writings were those widely, though not universally, accepted. These were James, Jude, 2 Peter, and 2 and 3 John. The final class of writings were those universally rejected as scripture. These included the Acts of Paul, the Shepherd of Hermas, the letter of Barnabas, and the Didache.

37. Von Harnack, *Origin of the New Testament*, 43.

considered legitimate and authoritative Christian writings. As Christian leaders began discerning between legitimate apostolic writings and spurious writings, they began producing lists of accepted texts. One such list is the Muratorian fragment, which was written around AD 170 and lists nearly all the books found in the New Testament.³⁸ Based upon the aforementioned instances, scholars argue that the earliest attempts to codify the New Testament had begun in the mid-second century, with a definite form emerging between AD 180 and AD 200.³⁹

In the course of his writings, Justin only directly referenced a New Testament writing once, the Apocalypse,⁴⁰ when he noted, "A man among us named John, one of the apostles of Christ, prophesied in a revelation made to him."⁴¹ In addition to this one direct quote to John's Apocalypse, Justin also references the "memoirs of the apostles,"⁴² which corresponds to the four canonical gospels of Matthew, Mark, Luke, and John. When referencing the practice of Christian worship, Justin notes,

> And on the day called Sunday, all who live in cities or in the country gather together to one place, and the memoirs of the apostles or the writings of the prophets are read, as long as time permits; then, when the reader has ceased, the president verbally instructs, and exhorts to the imitation of these good things.⁴³

The fact that it was the practice of churches to publicly read these memoirs alongside the writings of the "prophets" during their worship services indicates that these writings held significance for the early Christians.⁴⁴

Though Justin did not make many direct references to New Testament writings, it should not lead one to believe that Justin was unfamiliar with these writings or held to a narrow view of what constituted Christian Scripture.⁴⁵ On the contrary, while rarely directly referencing New Testament works, Justin made the regular habit of quoting New Testament texts, though it should be noted that Justin frequently provided loose quotes from the New Testament, leading many to believe that these quotes were written from memory.⁴⁶ Regarding the manner in which Justin quoted the New

38. Metzger, *Canon of the New Testament*, 200.
39. Von Harnack *Origin of the New Testament*, 95.
40. Justin Martyr, *Works Now Extant*, vii.
41. Justin Martyr, *Dialogue*, 81.
42. Justin Martyr, *1 Apology*, 66; Justin Martyr, *Dialogue*, 103.
43. Justin Martyr, *1 Apology*, 67.
44. Justin Martyr, *Works Now Extant*, viii.
45. Justin Martyr, *Works Now Extant*, vii.
46. Justin Martyr, *Works Now Extant*, xi.

Testament and which New Testament writings Justin referred to, Willis A. Shotwell notes,

> As it has been pointed out, Justin made use of both Paul and the writer of Hebrews. However, he does not quote long sections verbatim from either writer. His references to the New Testament Epistles are made by way of allusion and not by direct quotation. Purves has found evidence for Justin's acquaintance with Acts, Romans, 1 Corinthians, 2 Thessalonians, Galatians, Philippians, Colossians, Hebrews, and 1 John. It must be noted that this conclusion is based on similarities of thought and vocabulary, and not on a direct quotation by Justin from any of these books.[47]

While Justin did not quote from every New Testament book, one should not infer that Justin was unaware of the writing or that he did not accept it as Christian Scripture. Instead, it is most likely that Justin simply did not have the need to quote from these books as proofs of the legitimacy of Christianity. Given Justin's penchant for orthodoxy, it is highly likely that he agreed with his contemporaries on the content of the New Testament[48] and viewed these writings as equal in nature and authority to the Old Testament writings.[49]

Perhaps the most troubling aspects of Justin's writings, when trying to determine the content of the New Testament according to Justin's understanding, is Justin's use of what Shotwell refers to as "Christian Haggada";[50] or, references to the life and work of Jesus that are extra-canonical. This "Christian Haggada" would include Justin's assertion that Jesus' birth took place in a cave[51] and that he was born with a deformity,[52] that Jesus began working miracles as a child,[53] and that the Magi came from Arabia,[54] among

---

47. Shotwell, *Biblical Exegesis of Justin Martyr*, 23. See also Williams, *Justin Martyr*, 173; and Purves, *Testimony of Justin Martyr*, 238–41.

48. One of Justin's own writings, now lost, that could shed substantial light on his understanding of what constituted Christian Scripture was his argument against the heretic Marcion. Because Marcion produced his own version of the Bible, those Christian leaders that argued against him typically included in their writings a brief synopsis of what they believed to be Christian Scripture. It is quite possible that Justin did the same in his writings against Marcion.

49. Justin Martyr, *1 Apology* 1.28.

50. Shotwell, *The Biblical Exegesis of Justin Martyr* 26.

51. Justin Martyr, *Dialogue*, 78.

52. Justin Martyr, *Dialogue*, 14, 49, 85, 100, 110, and 121.

53. Justin Martyr, *1 Apology*, 22.

54. Justin Martyr, *Dialogue*, 78.

others. Given that Justin's extra-canonical references to the life and work of Christ closely match Christian literature such as the Clementine Homilies, the Gospel of the Ebionites, and the *Protevangelium,* this strongly suggests that Justin did indeed use extra-canonical writings in his apologetic writings,[55] though that does not necessarily mean that he viewed them as possessing the same characteristics of the Scriptures publicly read during Christian worship.

Justin on the Proper Interpretation of Scripture

One of the cornerstones of Justin's theology of Scripture was his position that only Christians can rightly interpret Scripture whether it be contained in the Old Testament or New Testament. Justin believed that only Christians can properly interpret God's word because only Christians are indwelt and illuminated by the Holy Spirit. Both in his *First Apology* and *Dialogue with Trypho* Justin contends that, following the resurrection of Christ he empowered his followers with the Spirit to be able to accurately understand and interpret the scriptures. Justin writes,

> Accordingly, after he was crucified, even all his acquaintances forsook him, having denied him; and afterwards, when he had risen from the dead and appeared to them, and had taught them to read the prophecies in which all these things were foretold as coming to pass, and when they had seen him ascending into heaven, and had believed, and had received power sent thence by him upon them, and went to every race of men, they taught these things, and were called apostles.[56]

Similarly, during his debate with the Jew Trypho, Justin considered the nature of one's understanding of the Scriptures and concludes that no one— not even the apostles themselves—was able to understand the Scriptures prior to Christ's explanation of their meaning. Justin notes, "The prophets declared obscurely that Christ would suffer, and thereafter be Lord of all, yet that could not be understood by any man until he himself persuaded the apostles that such statements were expressly related in the Scriptures"[57]

One should not conclude, however, that Justin shared in the gnostic belief that Christ had given the apostles special knowledge. Instead, Justin believed that the ability to understand and interpret Scripture was available

---

55. Shotwell, *Biblical Exegesis of Justin Martyr,* 28.
56. Justin Martyr, *1 Apology,* 50.
57. Justin Martyr, *Dialogue,* 76.

to all Christians who had turned to Christ in faith. Justin demonstrated this contention with his description of the early ministries of the apostles:

> For the Jews having the prophecies, and being always in expectation of the Christ to come, did not recognize him; and not only so, but even treated him shamefully. But the gentiles, who had never heard anything about Christ, until the apostles set out from Jerusalem and preached concerning him, and gave them the prophecies, were filled with joy and faith, and cast away their idols, and dedicated themselves to the Unbegotten God through Christ.[58]

Justin repeats this description of how the apostles were instructed to understand the Scriptures by the resurrected Christ, and then took it upon themselves to teach others in his *Dialogue with Trypho*, when he notes,

> Moreover, the prophet Zechariah foretold that this same Christ would be smitten, and his disciples scattered: which also took place. For after his crucifixion, the disciples that accompanied him were dispersed, until he rose from the dead, and persuaded them that so it had been prophesied concerning him, that he would suffer; and being thus persuaded, they went into all the world, and taught these truths.[59]

Elsewhere, Justin suggests that those who are indwelt by Christ possess a special understanding of the Scriptures, as the same Christ who first inspired the prophets to write is the same Christ that now inspires the Christian to understand. Reminiscing upon his conversion, Justin records the words of the man who led him to Christ,

> There existed, long before this time, certain men more ancient than all those who are esteemed philosophers, both righteous and beloved by God, who spoke by the Divine Spirit, and foretold events which would take place, and which are now taking place. They are called prophets. These alone both saw and announced the truth to men, neither reverencing nor fearing any man, not influenced by a desire for glory, but speaking those things alone which they saw and which they heard, being filled with the Holy Spirit . . . pray that, above all things, the gates of light may be opened to you; *for these things cannot be perceived*

---

58. Justin Martyr, *1 Apology* 49.
59. Justin Martyr, *Dialogue* 53.

> or understood by all, but only by the man to whom God and his Christ have imparted wisdom.[60]

In his *First Apology*, Justin makes a similar argument to the Roman government. Justin notes that his message comes from the prophets and from Christ himself as he explains that the Scriptures will form the basis of his defense of the faith:

> And that this may now become evident to you—that whatever we assert in conformity with what has been taught us by Christ, and by the prophets who preceded him, are alone true, and are older than all the writers who have existed; that we claim to be acknowledged, not because we say the same things as these writers said, but because we say true things.[61]

Throughout the course of his writings, Justin repeatedly argues that Christians possess a privileged insight into the meaning of the Scriptures. Justin makes this claim by noting that, due to their possession of Christ, Christians also possess a divine grace that allows them to understand the Scriptures that people do not possess while in their natural, sinful state. In *Dialogue with Trypho*, Justin states that the grace required to properly understand the Scriptures requires a divine enablement that comes via the work of the Holy Spirit:

> For such institutions seemed to be unreasonable and unworthy of God to many men, who had not received grace to know that your nation were called to conversion and repentance of spirit, while they were in a sinful condition and laboring under spiritual disease; and that the prophecy which was announced subsequent to the death of Moses is everlasting . . . And that we, who have been made wise by them, confess that the statutes of the Lord are sweeter than honey and the honey-comb, is manifest from the fact that, though threatened with death, we do not deny his name.[62]

---

60. Justin Martyr, *Dialogue* 7, emphasis added.

61. Justin Martyr *1 Apology* 23. The Benedictine editor, Maranus, Otto notes that Justin has three primary arguments in his work: (1) that Christian doctrines alone are true, and are to be received, not on account of their resemblance to the sentiments of poets or philosophers, but on their own account; (2) that Jesus Christ is the incarnate Son of God, and our teacher; (3) that before his incarnation, the demons, having some knowledge of what he would accomplish, enabled the heathen poets and priests in some points to anticipate, though in a distorted form, the facts of the incarnation.

62. Justin Martyr *Dialogue* 30. During his debate with Trypho, Justin returned to this point a number of times, which is not surprising given that this debate was an argument concerning the proper interpretation of a number of Old Testament texts.

In *Dialogue with Trypho*, Justin recollects his conversion and considers the nature of Scripture:

> There existed, long before this time, certain men more ancient than all those who are esteemed philosophers, both righteous and beloved by God, who spoke by the Divine Spirit, and foretold events which would take place, and which are now taking place. They are called prophets. These alone both saw and announced the truth to men, neither reverencing nor fearing any man, not influenced by a desire for glory, but speaking those things alone which they saw and which they heard, being filled with the Holy Spirit. Their writings are still extant, and he who has read them is very much helped in his knowledge of the beginning and end of things, and of those matters which the philosopher ought to know, provided he has believed them.[63]

This selection strongly suggests that Justin believes the divine grace afforded to Christians to properly understand the Scriptures closely corresponds to the divinely inspired nature of the Scriptures themselves. According to Justin, the Scriptures can only be rightly understood by Christians indwelt by the Holy Spirit because the same Spirit that now illuminates Christians is the same Spirit that originally inspired the authors of Scripture.

Christ as the Logos of God

While Justin was deliberate in using an appeal from Scripture as his primary means of argument,[64] scriptural reasoning was not the only tool he employed. Justin also quoted several pagan philosophers and alluded to a number of philosophical ideas in his defense of the faith.[65] One philosophical

---

In *Dialogue* 58, Justin tells Trypho that "God's grace alone has been granted to me to the understanding of his Scriptures." In *Dialogue* 78, Justin encouraged Trypho and his fellow Jews, saying, "It would be becoming for you, sirs, to learn what you have not perceived, from those who have received grace from God, namely, from us Christians." In *Dialogue* 92, Justin states, "Unless, therefore, a man by God's great grace receives the power to understand what has been said and done by the prophets, the appearance of being able to repeat the words or the deeds will not profit him." Again in *Dialogue* 100, Justin contends, "He revealed to us all that we have perceived by his grace out of the Scriptures, so that we know him to be the first-begotten of God." And finally, in *Dialogue* 119, Justin poses the question, "Would you suppose, sirs, that we could ever have understood these matters in the Scriptures, if we had not received grace to discern by the will of him whose pleasure it was?"

63. Justin Martyr, *Dialogue* 7.
64. Justin Martyr, *1 Apology* 23.
65. Justin rejected a number of the Greek philosophies, such as the Cynics, whom

idea favored by Justin in his apologies was the concept of the logos, which Justin Christianized to refer to the illumination of Christ in men. According to Bryan Liftfin in his *Getting to Know the Church Fathers*, Justin's Christianization of the logos served two purposes. First, it demonstrated that Christian theology was compatible with generally accepted philosophical truths. This allowed Christians a formal way to conceptualize the relationship between Father, Son, and Holy Spirit that maintained a belief in a Supreme Being, which was seen as the highest form of religion within Greek philosophies. Second, Justin's use of the logos allowed him to appropriate the very best lessons from pagan philosophies and claim them to be Christian.[66] Justin was able to accomplish this marriage of Greek philosophy and Christian theology by arguing that the highest ideals of Greek philosophy were inspired by Christ, who also inspired the Christian scriptures.

Within the Greek philosophical system, the philosopher Heraclitus was the first to begin using "logos" as a technical term.[67] To Heraclitus, the logos represented a universal cosmic law that unified rational discourse and the structure of the rational world and were common in all things.[68] Stoic

---

he saw as enemies of Christ, and the Epicureans, whom Justin described as immoral. However, Justin also held a number of Greek philosophers in high regard, including the Stoics, whom Justin referred to as "admirable," though he rejected their teachings on fate and their pantheistic tendencies. Justin's reference to the Pythagorean school of philosophy is brief and only reveals that Justin held them in at least modest regard. Justin twice refers to Heraclitus, whom Justin refers to as a Christian, perhaps due to his understanding of the logos. Justin held Socrates and Plato in the highest regard, believing them to be a source of Godly truth. Justin saw in them a pattern of bold witness and patient suffering similar to that encouraged by Christ. While Justin referred to these men as sources of truth, he saw them not as Christians but as pre-Christian pagans. In his "L'Influence du Timee de Platon sur la Theology de Justin Martyr," 172, E. de Faye claims that Justin refers to the writings of Plato forty times, including Plato's *Apology, Crito, Phaedrus, Phaedo, Republic,* and *Timaeus*. Although, Erwin Goodenough would strike from that list the *Crito* and *Phaedrus*, Goodenough, *Theology of Justin Martyr,* 82.

66. Litfin, *Getting to Know the Church Fathers,* 66.

67. Peters, *Greek Philosophical Terms,* 110. Regarding logos's transition from a common term for knowledge to a technical philosophical term, Peters notes,

> A major difficulty in the interpretation of logos is determining when this common and amorphous Greed word is being used in a technical, specialized sense. Thus, Heraclitus, in whom it first plays a major role, frequently employs it in its common usage, but he also has a peculiar doctrine that centers around logos in a more technical sense: for him logos is an underlying organizational principle of the universe, related to the common meaning of logos as proportion, the rule of change so frequently associated with Heraclitus's thought . . . This logos principle, though it is hidden and perceptible only to the intelligence, is still material, as can be seen from the identification of the Heraclitan logos with cosmic fire, and his description of the process of thinking.

68. Guthrie, *Greek Philosophers,* 43.

philosophers continued to expand upon the Greek's understanding of the logos, arguing that the logos created, animated, and maintained the material universe. As such, the Stoics frequently referred to the *seminal logos*[69] representing a divine principle at work in the universe and living within all people and all things.[70] The Hellenized Jewish philosopher Philo, whose work attempted to syncretize Greek philosophy with Judaism, continued to expand the concept of the logos in philosophical circles. Following the Platonic distinction between imperfect matter and perfect form, which required an intermediary being to bridge the gap between God and people, Philo argued that the divine logos was this intermediary figure that Philo described as the firstborn of God and represented in the Old Testament as the "Angel of the Lord."[71]

It is interesting to note that when Justin refers to the logos in his writings, his description of the logos fluctuates depending upon who is in his audience. When writing to the Roman court in his *Apologies*, Justin uses the term in a way they would understand, using the Stoic understanding of the seminal logos to describe the work of Jesus Christ. However, in his *Dialogue with Trypho*, Justin refers to the Philonic understanding of the logos, arguing that Jesus Christ alone is the intermediary between God and man.

In his defense of the Scripture to the Roman court, Justin borrows from the Stoic understanding of the logos:

> For each man spoke well in proportion to the share he had of the spermatic word, seeing what was related to it. But they who contradict themselves on the more important points appear not to have possessed the heavenly wisdom, and the knowledge which cannot be spoken against. Whatever things were rightly said among all men are the property of us Christians. For next to God, we worship and love the word who is from

---

69. In Stoic philosophy, *logos spermatikos* represented the generative principle of the universe, which creates all things.

70. Tripolitis, *Religions of the Hellenistic-Roman Age*, 38. Describing the Stoic's view of the logos, Tripolitis writes,

> The Stoics claimed that the universe is a single ordered whole, a perfect organism that unites within itself all that exists in the world. It is ruled by a supreme cosmic power, a firey substance the Stoics called Logos, Divine Reason, or God. The logos is the organizing, integrating, and energizing principle of the whole universe. As a perfect entity, the universe combines within itself the Logos or Divine Reason, which is its soul, and matter, which serves as its body. Since everything is derived from God, everything is a part of God, but not separated or cut from the whole. Each individual soul is a fragment of the universal Logos or God.

71. Copleston, *History of Philosophy*, 459.

the Unbegotten and Ineffable God, since also he became man for our sakes, that, becoming a partaker of our sufferings, he might also bring us healing. For all the writers were able to see realities darkly through the sowing of the implanted word that was in them. For the seed and imitation imparted according to capacity is one thing, and quite another is the thing itself, of which there is the participation and imitation according to the grace which is from him.[72]

Here, Justin demonstrates his belief that the Stoic's understanding of the seminal logos was, in fact, a vague understanding of the inspirational work of Christ at work in all of mankind. Thus, by using the concept of the seminal logos, Justin was able to contend that Christianity was not completely at odds with pagan philosophy. Instead, Christianity was the greatest expression of philosophy, as what the Greek philosophers could discern from the logos at work in them was made perfect in the logos's inspiration of the Christian Scriptures.

While Justin relied upon a Stoic framework of the logos to describe Christ to a Roman audience in his *Apologies*, in *Dialogue with Trypho* Justin borrowed from the Philonic understanding of the logos to describe the work of Christ to a Jewish audience. Justin writes,

"I shall give you another testimony, my friends," said I, "from the Scriptures, that God begat before all creatures a Beginning, a certain rational power from himself, who is called by the Holy Spirit, now the Glory of the Lord, now the Son, again Wisdom, again an Angel, then God, and then Lord and Logos; and on another occasion he calls himself Captain, when he appeared in human form to Joshua the son of Nave. For he can be called by all those names, since he ministers to the Father's will, and since he was begotten of the Father by an act of will . . . The word of Wisdom, who is himself this God begotten of the Father of all things, and Word, and Wisdom, and Power, and the Glory of the Begetter."[73]

In *Dialogue with Trypho*, Justin uses the term *logos* to depict Christ as a mediator between God and men who relate messages from God.[74] During the period of the Old Testament, this was achieved via illumination and theophanies of the pre-existent Christ. Justin's understanding of the work of the logos allows him to forge a continuity between the Jewish and Christian

72. Justin Martyr, *2 Apology* 13.
73. Justin Martyr, *Dialogue* 61.
74. Goodenough, *Theology of Justin Martyr*, 163.

Scriptures. Justin argued that the same logos that inspired the Old Testament texts also inspired the New Testament Scriptures, which now, through the Holy Spirit, continue to divulge their true meaning to those who now follow Christ.

EXAMINATION OF JUSTIN'S USE OF SCRIPTURE IN EVANGELISM

Turning to the writings of Justin Martyr, one finds a set of works saturated with references to, and direct quotations of, the Scriptures. In many respects, Justin used the Scriptures to form the foundation of his arguments for the Christian faith, and when Justin needed some proof for his arguments he always turned to the Scriptures to provide that proof. In many respects, the exposition of the Scriptures took a central place in Justin's apologetic literature.

Justin's Use of Scripture in his Apologies

In *First Apology* Justin indicates that, as the foundation of truth, Scripture will rightly take a central place in his arguments. In chapter 23, which serves as the thesis of his *Apology*, Justin states that the core of his message comes from the prophets and Christ himself as recorded in the Scriptures:

> And that this may now become evident to you—that whatever we assert in conformity with what has been taught us by Christ, and by the prophets who preceded him, are alone true, and are older than all the writers who have existed; that we claim to be acknowledged, not because we say the same things as these writers said, but because we say true things.[75]

In *First Apology*, Justin begins his argument for the Christian faith by describing Jesus Christ as the pre-existent logos to demonstrate that the Christian faith is a philosophy that rivals that of the Greeks. Justin writes,

> And reckon ye that it is for your sakes we have been saying these things; for it is in our power, when we are examined, to deny that we are Christians; but we would not live by telling a lie. For, impelled by the desire of the eternal and pure life, we seek the abode that is with God, the Father and Creator of all, and hasten to confess our faith, persuaded and convinced as we are that

---

75. Justin Martyr, *1 Apology* 23.

> they who have proved to God by their works that they followed him, and loved to abide with him where there is no sin to cause disturbance, can obtain these things. This, then, to speak shortly, is what we expect and have learned from Christ, and teach. And Plato, in like manner, used to say that Rhadamanthus and Minos would punish the wicked who came before them; and we say that the same thing will be done, but at the hand of Christ, and upon the wicked in the same bodies united again to their spirits which are now to undergo everlasting punishment; and not only, as Plato said, for a period of a thousand years.[76]

In this section, Justin begins by demonstrating to his pagan audience that the teachings of Christ and the teachings of the Greek philosophers are not at odds with one another. Justin's comparison here achieves the twofold purpose of demonstrating the truthfulness of the Scriptures while also suggesting the unjust nature of Roman laws that punish those following the teachings of Christ, but not those following Plato's teachings.[77] In the opening sections of *First Apology*, Justin uses pagan philosophy as a bridge to the Scripture. However, as Justin's apology progresses, he makes the case that the Scriptures represent true knowledge[78] while the writings of the Greek philosophers should be rejected as a demonic misrepresentation of the scriptures.[79]

Chapters 31–53 are a central component of Justin's argument for belief in Christ. As Justin argues for the truth of Christianity, he does so by exegeting Old Testament Scriptures that pointed to the life and work of Jesus Christ. Beginning in chapter 31, Justin describes the nature of the inspiration of the Hebrew Scriptures, how the Septuagint was created for the Library of Alexandria, and concludes by saying,

> In these books, then, of the prophets we found Jesus our Christ foretold as coming, born of a virgin, growing up to man's estate, and healing every disease and every sickness, and raising the dead, and being hated, and unrecognized, and crucified, and dying, and rising again, and ascending into heaven, and being, and being called, the Son of God. We find it also predicted that certain persons should be sent by him into every nation to publish these things, and that rather among the gentiles [than

76. Justin Martyr, *1 Apology* 7.

77. See also chapters 20–22, in which Justin discusses a number of analogies to Christ, Christian doctrine and practice, as well as Christ's relationship with the Father, found in the writings of pagan philosophers.

78. Justin Martyr, *1 Apology* 23, 44, 54, 59.

79. Justin Martyr, *1 Apology* 54–58.

among the Jews] men should believe on him. And he was predicted before he appeared, first five thousand years before, and again three thousand, then two thousand, then one thousand, and yet again eight hundred; for in the succession of generations prophets after prophets arose.[80]

In chapter 32, Justin begins to consider the prophecies of Moses, taken from Genesis 49:10. Justin argues from this passage that the birth of Jesus coinciding with Roman assumption of power over Judea proved that Jesus was the long-expected Messiah. Additionally, Justin argues that this verse also foretold this immaculate conception and the means of his crucifixion. In chapters 33 and 34, Justin uses prophecies from Isaiah and from Micah to demonstrate that the birth of Jesus was predicted by the Jewish Scriptures. Justin continues to argue from the Old Testament for the coming of Jesus, his crucifixion, ascension, ministry, rejection by the Jews, and scourging.

Beyond this lengthy exposition, Justin also undergirds every point he made in his *First Apology* by quoting Scripture in support of his arguments. In chapter 55, while discussing symbols of the cross found in pagan philosophies, Justin refers to Lamentations 4:20 to prove that pagan symbolism was part of God's general revelation received, and misunderstood, by pagan peoples. In chapter 59, Justin considers Plato's understanding of the forms and quotes from Genesis 1 to demonstrate that this philosophy was borrowed from Moses.

In Justin's *First Apology* one finds that the author consistently used Scripture as the source of truth for his apologetical arguments. Though his Roman audience would have viewed the Jewish and Christian Scriptures as vulgar writings, Justin saw them as the foundation of truth and, as such, gave the Scriptures a central place in his *First Apology*.

Justin's Use of Scripture in His Dialogue with Trypho

While Scripture served as the foundation of Justin's argument in his *Apologies*, the Scriptures were both the foundation and the content of his *Dialogue*. Justin's *Dialogue with Trypho* records a debate between Justin and Trypho, a refugee who fled Judea during the Bar Kokhba war. Philip Bobichon argues that this *Dialogue* is actually an exegetical exposition of the Scriptures which takes a dialogical format.[81] This is most evident in Justin's contention that he bases his arguments in the *Dialogue with Trypho* "on scriptures and

---

80. Justin Martyr, *1 Apology* 31.
81. Bobichon, *Justin Martyr*, 126.

facts,"[82] and at the conclusion of the debate encourages Trypho to meet with him again to continue "studying the scriptures."[83]

Trypho begins this exegetical debate in chapter 10 by asking Justin how Christians can expect to be accepted by God when they do not observe the Mosaic law in matters such as the Sabbath or circumcision. In chapter 11, Justin answers Trypho by arguing that Christians are not bound by the law of Moses, but by the law of Christ, which was predicted by the Old Testament prophets. Justin quotes from Isaiah 51:4–5 and Jeremiah 31:31–32 to argue that the Mosaic law has been superseded by Christ. Justin continues his exposition of Isaiah to demonstrate that Christ was sent as the atonement for sin, that men are accepted by God through faith in Christ and can only be considered righteous when possessing the alien righteousness of Christ.

In chapter 32 Trypho challenges Justin, arguing that Christ should be rejected as the Messiah because he was "dishonorable and inglorious, so much so that the last curse contained in the law of God fell on him, for he was crucified."[84] Justin answers Trypho's charge by quoting from Isaiah and Psalm 110 to demonstrate that the prophets foresaw the humility of Christ during his earthly ministry.

In chapter 48, Trypho argues that the Christian doctrine of Christ existing as both God and man is both "paradoxical and also foolish."[85] To this charge Justin appealed to the life of Elijah and the belief that he will precede the Messiah. Justin then offers a lengthy commentary on Isaiah to demonstrate that Jesus was the Messiah anticipated by the Old Testament prophets. Finally, Justin and Trypho conclude their debate as Justin argues from Micah, Isaiah, and the Psalms to demonstrate that the true Israel are not those who are physical descendants of Abraham, but the spiritual descendants of Abraham through faith in Christ.

CONCLUSION

During his description of his conversion to Christianity, Justin noted that the Scriptures, the only source of truth, played a significant role in convincing him of the truth of Christianity. It is no wonder then that Justin would give the Scriptures such a central place in his evangelistic writings. According to Justin, the Scriptures themselves served as the foundation of

82. Justin Martyr, *Dialogue* 28.
83. Justin Martyr, *Dialogue*, 142.
84. Justin Martyr, *Dialogue*, 32.
85. Justin Martyr, *Dialogue*, 48.

his arguments for Christianity in both his *Apologies* and his *Dialogue with Trypho*. Justin used the Scriptures in his evangelistic writings because he believed that they possessed the power of God to turn people away from sin and toward Christ.

3

The Use of Scripture in the Evangelistic Writings of Origen

By the end of the second century AD, the Christian faith had taken root in every stratum of Roman society and for the first time began to produce second-generation Christians; that is, Christians who did not convert away from a pagan religion to Christianity, but were born into a Christian household and were taught, from birth, to know and follow Jesus Christ.[1] Perhaps the best known second-generation Christian born in this period is Origen Adamatious, born in approximately AD 184.

Though immersed in the church from birth, few figures from the early Christian church were as controversial as Origen. He was lauded by Eusebius for his exemplary piety,[2] while also condemned by Jerome for unorthodox theologies, such as his view on the pre-existence of souls and a universalism

---

1. Draper, "Second Generation Syndrome." Draper notes that the position of a "second-generation Christian" is a difficult one, as second-generation Christians tend to lose the zeal found in their parents' faith, who were converted "out of the world." As such, it is common for second-generation Christians to be nominal in their faith and follow the "status quo" as opposed to following God. Draper goes on to argue that being a second-generation Christian can also be a great blessing, they have the opportunity to spend their entire life knowing and following Christ. Knowing the dangers of the "second-generation Christian syndrome," Draper encourages parents to train their children in spiritual disciplines such as Bible study, involvement in the church, and faith and forgiveness. Origen's own zeal and faithfulness could perhaps be attributed to the fact that Origen's father, Leonides, instilled such disciplines into his son's life.

2. Eusebius notes "Origen seems to me worthy of mention, even, so to speak, from his swathing-bands." Eusebius, *Ecclesiastical History* 6.2.

that allowed for the possibility of all creatures, including Satan, to be finally reconciled to God. To modern historians, Origen is frequently praised as a pioneer in the fields of biblical exegesis, hermeneutics, textual criticism, and pastoral theology, though he is frequently criticized for his reliance upon an allegorical interpretation of the Scriptures.[3] George Scholarius, the first patriarch of Constantinople following its capture by the Turks, summarizes Origen well:

> The Western writers say, "Where Origen was good, no one is better, where he is bad, no one is worse." Our Asian divines say on the one hand that "Origen is the whetstone of us all," but on the other hand, that "he is the fount of foul doctrines" . . . Both are right: he splendidly defended Christianity, wonderfully expounded Scripture, and wrote a noble exhortation to martyrdom. But he was also the father of Arianism, and, worst of all, said that hellfire would not last forever.[4]

ALEXANDRIAN THOUGHT IN THE TIME OF ORIGEN

Founded by Alexander the Great in 331 BC, Alexandria quickly became an important Hellenistic center in Egypt.[5] In addition, Alexandria also became an important city for the Jewish Diaspora.[6] Alexander invited a number of Jewish officials to help found the city, and in the following centuries many more migrated to the area seeking work, education, and a welcoming community.[7]

As it drew much of its population from the Jewish Diaspora, Alexandria also became a major center for Jewish thought. Alexandrian scholars produced the Septuagint at the request of Philadelphus, the second Ptolemy king, to better accommodate Alexandria's large Jewish population who were fluent in Koine Greek but had lost their grasp upon the Hebrew language.[8] Alexandria was also the birthplace of the Middle Platonic philosophy of Philo, born in the first century BC to a wealthy Alexandrian family who

---

3. Chadwick, *Early Christian Thought*, 95.
4. Chadwick, *Early Christian Thought*, 95.
5. De Berardino, *Encyclopedia of Ancient Christianity*, 78.
6. Forster, *Alexandria*, 120.
7. Josephus, *Antiquities* 12.7–9.
8. Bridger and Wolk, *New Jewish Encyclopedia*, 186.

sought to syncretize Jewish thought with Platonic philosophy.[9] To achieve this synchronization, Philo developed an allegorical hermeneutic for the Jewish Scriptures that allowed him to be bound by the Scriptures while allowing for a degree of latitude in its interpretation.[10]

Philo did not invent the idea of an allegorical interpretation of texts. Instead, Stoic scholars first applied allegorical principles to Homer's works of *The Iliad* and *The Odyssey*.[11] Philo, however, was the first to use an allegorical framework to understand the Jewish Scriptures. As Philo sought to understand the Jewish Scriptures, he did so with a two-tiered view.[12] First, Philo considered the literal meaning of the text, which then drove his understanding of the deeper, spiritual meaning of the text. Philo's work in hermeneutics and understanding Greek philosophy through the lens of Scripture laid the groundwork for the early church's understanding of Christian Scripture and its place in the philosophical world, as evidenced by Clement of Alexandria's adoption of Philo's hermeneutic and by his successor, Origen.[13]

BIOGRAPHY

Any biographical accounts that Origen may have left behind have been lost to history. As such, almost the entirety of what is known of Origen's early life comes wholly from Eusebius's *Ecclesiastical History*. Eusebius notes that "Origen seems to me worthy of mention, even, so to speak, from his swathing-bands,"[14] and begins his history of Origen's life by recalling his father's martyrdom. Eusebius records that during the persecution under Severus, Origen desired martyrdom for himself—a desire that peaked when his father Leonides was arrested and sentenced to death. After his father's arrest, it is recorded that the only thing that prevented Origen from turning himself in to the authorities was his mother, who hid his clothes, thus preventing her son from leaving the house due to his modesty.[15]

Origen's devotion to both his father and his God is the result of his father's love for Origen and the discipleship Leonides cultivated in the boy.

---

9. Di Berardino, *Encyclopedia of Ancient Christianity*, 174.
10. Sandmel, *Philo of Alexandria*, 18.
11. Sandmel, *Philo of Alexandria*, 19.
12. Sowers, *Hermeneutics of Philo and Hebrews*, 28.
13. Fairweather, *Origen and Greek Patristic Theology*, 3.
14. Eusebius, *Ecclesiastical History* 6.2.
15. Eusebius, *Ecclesiastical History* 6.2.

Eusebius records that Origen's piety and desire for knowledge caused his father to have a great deal of love and respect for his son. Eusebius writes,

> But by himself he rejoiced greatly and thanked God, the author of all good, that he had deemed him worthy to be the father of such a child. And they say that often, standing by the boy when asleep, he uncovered his breast as if the Divine Spirit were enshrined within it, and kissed it reverently; considering himself blessed in his goodly offspring. These and other things like them are related of Origen when a boy.[16]

As a part of his duties as a father, Leonides gave his son a liberal arts education, which was typical for its time. But beyond this education, Leonides also taught Origen Greek science and literature. In addition to his secular studies, Leonides introduced his son to the studies of Scripture and Christian theology. Origen pursued all his studies with vigor, at times bringing the rebuke of his father for pursuing subjects beyond his age.[17]

After his father's arrest and martyrdom, Roman authorities seized Leonides's property and assets, leaving his family destitute. It was then, at the age of seventeen, that Origen began teaching in a local school and fell under the patronage of a wealthy Christian woman in Alexandria, which allowed him to support himself and his family.[18] While teaching in a secular school, Origen became concerned about the catechetical school in Alexandria whose teachers had all been driven away by the threat of persecution. Thus, at the age of eighteen, Origen began his work as a catechist, discipling new converts in preparation for baptism,[19] though without an ecclesiastical endorsement.[20] Origen was immediately successful in his role as a

---

16. Eusebius, *Ecclesiastical History* 6.2.

17. Eusebius, *Ecclesiastical History* 6.2. It should be noted that while Eusebius's writings are seen as the definitive biography of Origen's life, it is not the only account of his early life. Porphyry, for example, a critic of Christianity and its leaders—specifically Origen—writes that Origen was born into a pagan home and lived as a pagan until later in life. Porphyry's desire to discredit Christianity and its leaders, however, should give one pause before uncritically accepting his account of Origen's life. Granted that Eusebius himself was not an unbiased observer of Origen, but held him in high regard. Chadwick, *Early Christian Thought*, 67, writes, "For Eusebius Origen is a supreme saint and hero, the realization of his highest intellectual and spiritual ideals. The life of Origen is written in a hagiographical tone, and freely uses oral tradition and gossip." Given that both writers possessed certain biases, who should be believed? Eusebius's diligence in collecting and quoting letters between Leonides and Origen lends credence to his description of Origen's home life.

18. Eusebius, *Ecclesiastical History* 6.2.

19. Eusebius, *Ecclesiastical History* 6.3.

20. Eusebius, *Ecclesiastical History* 6.2. Chadwick surmises that Origen's decision to

catechist, drawing attention from secular authorities who wished to close his school,[21] as well as attracting large numbers of seekers and new converts into the student body. Origen's catechetical school drew so many students that Origen first stopped teaching in a secular setting to devote himself to discipling converts,[22] and eventually was forced to divide his school into separate classes. Origen appointed Heraclas, who would later become a bishop in Alexandria,[23] to train new converts in the elementary disciplines of the Christian faith, while Origen retained the duty of training advanced students.[24]

Origen's popularity and success began to draw out his own ascetical nature. After resigning from his position of instructor at his secular academy, Origen lived on the donations given to him by his catechetical students.[25] To help supplement his lifestyle, Origen also sold his personal library and chose to live a very rigid ascetic life. Origen fasted often, slept little, and when he did sleep, he did so on the bare ground. Wishing to follow Christ's exhortation in Matthew 5, Origen possessed only one cloak and went barefoot much of his life.[26] It was also during this time that Origen underwent what Eusebius refers to as "Origen's daring deed." Eusebius writes,

> At this time while Origen was conducting catechetical instruction at Alexandria, a deed was done by him which evidenced an immature and youthful mind, but at the same time gave the highest proof of faith and continence. For he took the words, "There are eunuchs who have made themselves eunuchs for the kingdom of heaven's sake" [Matthew 19:12], in too literal and extreme a sense. And in order to fulfill the Savior's word, and at the same time to take away from the unbelievers all opportunity for scandal,—for, although young, he met for the study of divine things with women as well as men,—he carried out in action the word of the Savior.[27]

---

assume the role as a catechist without the bishop's approval was the genesis of the eventual divide that occurred between Origen and the bishop of Alexandria, Demetrius. Chadwick, *Early Christian Thought*, 69.

21. Eusebius, *Ecclesiastical History* 6.3.
22. Eusebius, *Ecclesiastical History* 6.3.
23. Chadwick, *Early Christian Thought*, 70.
24. Eusebius, *Ecclesiastical History* 6.15.
25. Fairweather, *Origen and Greek Patristic Theology*, 47.
26. Eusebius, *Ecclesiastical History* 6.3.
27. Eusebius, *Ecclesiastical History* 6.8. Frederic Farrar dismisses a literal interpretation of this passage. He argues that the phrase "made themselves eunuchs for the kingdom of heaven's sake" was understood to be a Jewish idiom which implied

In some respects, Origen's financial situation improved when he influenced a wealthy Christian named Ambrose away from the Valentinian heresy and into Orthodoxy.[28] Out of appreciation for Origen's correction and a desire to learn more from him, Ambrose began to sponsor Origen's study and writing. Ambrose provided Origen with seven writers so that he only needed to dictate his thoughts. Additionally, Ambrose hired a number of copyists and girls skilled in calligraphy.[29] Under Ambrose's patronage and due to his high expectations,[30] Origen was able to produce more writings than any other early church leader besides John Chrysostom.[31] During this period, Origen continued his work on the *Hexapla*, wrote his *Treatise on Prayer*, the *Exhortation to Martyrdom*, *On the Resurrection*, *On First Principles*, and his *Miscellanies*, which is now lost to history.[32] Also during this time, Origen completed his voluminous works of scriptural commentaries that, according to Eusebius, were the primary cause of Ambrose's patronage.[33]

As Origen's writings began to spread, so too did his reputation. Soon, Christians throughout the Roman Empire and beyond began to look to Origen to speak on theological or hermeneutical debates. Origen's endeavors took him to teach in places such as Arabia,[34] Antioch,[35] Greece,[36] and into Palestinian lands such as Judea, Jerusalem, and Caesarea.[37] As Origen began his travels, his relationship with Demetrius, the bishop of Alexandria, began to deteriorate. Perhaps in fear of losing such an influential thinker,

---

unbroken chastity. As such, Farrar argues that Origen did not literally mutilate himself, but instead chose to remain celibate to avoid charges of impropriety. Farrar supports this supposition by noting that Origen took an allegorical approach to Matthew 12 in his writings, and that Origen's many critics never made this issue a point of contention. Despite his arguments, Farrar does concede that his opinion is a minority view and that for much of church history, historians have taken Eusebius's account literally. Farrar, *Lives of the Fathers*, 398.

28. Eusebius, *Ecclesiastical History* 6.18.
29. Eusebius, *Ecclesiastical History* 6.23.
30. Nautin, *Lettres et Ecrivains Chretiens des II et III Siecles*, 250. Origen notes that Ambrose's love for sacred scriptures and desire to know more about them left Origen working to the extent that he was unable to enjoy a meal, walk, or even a full night's sleep in an attempt to meet Ambrose's deadlines.
31. Kraft, *Early Christian Thinkers*, 51.
32. Farrar, *Lives of the Fathers*, 409.
33. Eusebius, *Ecclesiastical History* 6.23.
34. Eusebius, *Ecclesiastical History* 6.19.
35. Eusebius, *Ecclesiastical History* 6.21.
36. Eusebius, *Ecclesiastical History* 6.23.
37. Eusebius, *Ecclesiastical History* 6.27.

Demetrius recalled Origen on several occasions to resume his duties in Alexandria.[38] When Origen worked in Palestine, Alexander, bishop of Jerusalem, and Theoctistus, bishop of Caesarea, encouraged him to stay in the area as a teacher and eventually ordained Origen.[39] Demetrius saw the ordination of Origen, an Alexandrian, by the church in Caesarea to be extraordinarily out of order,[40] and convened a series of synods to condemn him, eventually leading to Origen's excommunication from the Alexandrian church.[41] Following his excommunication from the Alexandrian church, Origen resided in the city of Caesarea until his death.

In AD 249, Decius became the new emperor of Rome, and in the following year made an edict ordering every inhabitant within the empire to sacrifice to the emperor before a magistrate, who would then issue a certificate of sacrifice.[42] Unable to escape from this empire-wide persecution, Jerusalem's Bishop Alexander was placed in prison as well as Origen. Concerning Origen's imprisonment, Eusebius writes,

> But how many and how great things came upon Origen in the persecution, and what was their final result,—as the demon of evil marshaled all his forces, and fought against the man with his utmost craft and power, assaulting him beyond all others against whom he contended at that time,–and what and how many things he endured for the word of Christ, bonds and bodily tortures and torments under the iron collar and in the dungeon; and how for many days with his feet stretched four spaces in the stocks he bore patiently the threats of fire and whatever other things were inflicted by his enemies; and how his sufferings terminated, as his judge strove eagerly with all his might not to end his life; and what words he left after these things, full of

---

38. Eusebius, *Ecclesiastical History* 6.19.
39. Eusebius, *Ecclesiastical History* 6.27.
40. Kraft, *Early Christian Thinkers*, 51.
41. Farrar, *Lives of the Fathers*, 413.
42. Potter, *The Roman Empire at Bay*, 209, writes,

> All the inhabitants of the empire were required to sacrifice before the magistrates of their community "for the safety of the empire" by a certain day (the date would vary from place to place and the order may have been that the sacrifice had to be completed within a specified period after a community received the edict). When they sacrificed they would obtain a certificate (*libellus*) recording the fact that they had complied with the order. That is, the certificate would testify the sacrificant's loyalty to the ancestral gods and to the consumption of sacrificial food and drink as well as the names of the officials who were overseeing the sacrifice.

comfort to those needing aid, a great many of his epistles show with truth and accuracy.[43]

The sudden death of Decius in AD 251 ended the Decian persecution, allowing Origen to leave prison with his life, but at the age of sixty-seven, Origen would never recover from the hardships he experienced there. Origen died at the age of sixty-nine, two years after his release and was buried "in the wall behind the high altar of the church of Tyre."[44]

ORIGEN'S THEOLOGY OF SCRIPTURE

Like Justin Martyr before him, Origen lived in a time prior to the Council of Carthage's pronouncement of the canon in AD 397. As such, while works such as Athanasius's *Thirty-Ninth Festal Letter* presented a list of authoritative works similar to contemporary lists, there still was some debate surrounding the question of which writings should be viewed as authoritative for Christians.[45] Origen acknowledged the debate surrounding the canonicity of several books, though he made few attempts to argue for or against the authenticity of the disputed writings.[46] This is perhaps due to the fact that, though the early church had not made a definitive list of authoritative writings, the writings used by individual Christian churches had already assumed a discernable shape.[47] Whatever the case may be, it may be wise to ask "What did Origen consider to be Scripture?" before examining his overall theology of Scripture.

Origen's Old Testament Text

Regarding the Old Testament, Origen benefited greatly from the Jewish scholars that preceded him in Alexandria.[48] Origen accepted the books

---

43. Eusebius, *Ecclesiastical History* 6.39.
44. Farrar, *Lives of the Fathers*, 424.
45. Ehrman, *Lost Christianities*, 250.
46. Martens, *Origen and Scripture*, 201. Fairweather writes, "With Origen the New Testament was still less of a fixed quantity than the Old. In admitting books to canonical rank he was careful, however, to exclude such as could not lay claim to general ecclesiastical recognition, even although he himself believed them to be genuine apostolic records." Fairweather, *Origen and Greek Patristic Theology*, 66.
47. Martens, *Origen and Scripture*, 201.
48. It appears that Origen was either unaware of, or rejected, the canon as stated by Melito of Sardis. According to Eusebius, Melito, the first to coin the term "Old Testament," limited the books of the Old Testament to their current form while excluding the

published in the Greek Septuagint and their order as inspired Scripture, even when he believed there to be textual errors in the Septuagint. In his *Commentary on Hosea*, Origen argues that it was inappropriate to amend the text of the Septuagint, even when it appeared nonsensical.[49] Additionally, Origen began to consider the intertestamental books with a greater deal of seriousness than did previous scholars.[50] In *Ecclesiastical History*, Eusebius looks to Origen's commentary on the Psalms, which, in the course of Origen's examination of Psalms 1:2, provides a listing of what he considers authoritative Scripture in the Old Testament. Eusebius writes,

> When expounding the first Psalm, he gives a catalogue of the sacred Scriptures of the Old Testament as follows: "It should be stated that the canonical books, as the Hebrews have handed them down, are twenty-two; corresponding with the number of their letters." Farther on he says: "The twenty-two books of the Hebrews are the following: That which is called by us Genesis, but by the Hebrews, from the beginning of the book, Bresith, which means, 'In the beginning'; Exodus, Welesmoth, that is, 'These are the names'; Leviticus, Wikra, 'And he called'; Numbers, Ammesphekodeim; Deuteronomy, Eleaddebareim, 'These are the words'; Jesus, the son of Nave, Josoue ben Noun; Judges and Ruth, among them in one book, Saphateim; the First and Second of Kings, among them one, Samouel, that is, 'The called of God'; the Third and Fourth of Kings in one, Wammelch David, that is, 'The kingdom of David'; of the Chronicles, the First and Second in one, Dabreïamein, that is, 'Records of days'; Esdras, First and Second in one, Ezra, that is, 'An assistant'; the book of Psalms, Spharthelleim; the Proverbs of Solomon, Meloth; Ecclesiastes, Koelth; the Song of Songs (not, as some suppose, Songs of Songs), Sir Hassirim; Isaiah, Jessia; Jeremiah, with Lamentations and the epistle in one, Jeremia; Daniel, Daniel; Ezekiel, Iezekiel; Job, Job; Esther, Esther. And besides these there are the Maccabees, which are entitled Sarbeth Sabanaiel." He gives these in the above-mentioned work.[51]

---

books of Esther and Nehemiah—though many assume that these books were included in the book of Ezra. Origen, however, practically expands that list by his extensive quoting from the Apocrypha, as was common among the Greek fathers. Eusebius, *Ecclesiastical History* 6.40.

49. Origen, *Philocalia* 8.1.

50. Fairweather writes, "With Origen *apocryphal* means *secret* or *hidden*, and the pseudepigrapha as represented by the *Book of Enoch*, etc., are not included by him among the sacred writings." Fairweather, *Origen and Greek Patristic Theology*, 66.

51. Eusebius, *Ecclesiastical History* 6.25.

While Origen accepted the content and order found in the Septuagint, one should not assume that he did so uncritically. Instead, Origen's alignment with the Septuagint came because of his own extensive studies in the field of textual criticism.

Origen's New Testament Text

While benefiting greatly from the Jewish community's work with the Hebrew Scriptures, Origen also benefited from living at a time in which the Christian community had extensively debated the content of the New Testament. Thanks to the efforts of Christian leaders before him, Origen possessed Christian writings that, though lacking official ecclesiastical support, had settled into an orthopraxis of use in Christian churches.[52]

Alongside his account of Origen's Old Testament texts, Eusebius also records the Christian writings that Origen regarded as scriptural, bearing the same weight of the Old Testament Scriptures. Eusebius writes,

> Among the four Gospels, which are the only indisputable ones in the church of God under heaven, I have learned by tradition that the first was written by Matthew, who was once a publican, but afterwards an apostle of Jesus Christ, and it was prepared for the converts from Judaism, and published in the Hebrew language. The second is by Mark, who composed it according to the instructions of Peter, who in his catholic epistle acknowledges him as a son, saying, "The church that is at Babylon elected together with you, saluteth you, and so doth Marcus, my son." And the third by Luke, the Gospel commended by Paul, and composed for gentile converts. Last of all that by John. In the fifth book of his Expositions of John's Gospel, he speaks thus concerning the epistles of the apostles: "But he who was 'made sufficient to be a minister of the New Testament, not of the letter, but of the Spirit,' that is, Paul, who 'fully preached the Gospel from Jerusalem and round about even unto Illyricum,' did not write to all the churches which he had instructed and to those to which he wrote he sent but few lines. And Peter, on whom the church of Christ is built, 'against which the gates of hell shall not prevail,' has left one acknowledged epistle; perhaps also a second, but this is doubtful.

---

52. Metzger, *New Testament*, 274. Metzger notes, "During the course of the second century most churches came to possess and acknowledge a canon that included the present four Gospels, the Acts, thirteen letters of Paul, 1 Peter, and 1 John. Seven books still lacked general recognition: Hebrews, James, 2 Peter, 2 and 3 John, Jude, and Revelation."

Why need we speak of him who reclined upon the bosom of Jesus, John, who has left us one Gospel, though he confessed that he might write so many that the world could not contain them? And he wrote also the Apocalypse, but was commanded to keep silence and not to write the words of the seven thunders. He has left also an epistle of very few lines; perhaps also a second and third; but not all consider them genuine, and together they do not contain a hundred lines. In addition he makes the following statements in regard to the Epistle to the Hebrews in his Homilies upon it: "That the verbal style of the epistle entitled 'To the Hebrews,' is not rude like the language of the apostle, who acknowledged himself 'rude in speech' that is, in expression; but that its diction is purer Greek, any one who has the power to discern differences of phraseology will acknowledge. Moreover, that the thoughts of the epistle are admirable, and not inferior to the acknowledged apostolic writings, any one who carefully examines the apostolic text will admit."

Farther on he adds: "If I gave my opinion, I should say that the thoughts are those of the apostle, but the diction and phraseology are those of some one who remembered the apostolic teachings, and wrote down at his leisure what had been said by his teacher. Therefore if any church holds that this epistle is by Paul, let it be commended for this. For not without reason have the ancients handed it down as Paul's. But who wrote the epistle, in truth, God knows. The statement of some who have gone before us is that Clement, bishop of the Romans, wrote the epistle, and of others that Luke, the author of the Gospel and the Acts, wrote it." But let this suffice on these matters.[53]

Origen also believed that, while all Scripture was valuable, it was not equally valuable.[54] Fairweather notes that Origen held the Gospel of John in the highest regard as being the greatest of the Gospels. Additionally, Origen viewed the four Gospels to be greater in importance than the Epistles, which he regarded as having a "mixed" value.[55]

Origen on the Inspiration of Scripture

Origen's views on the mixed value of Scripture did not, however, mean that Origen held a low view of New Testament writings. Instead, Origen held

---

53. Eusebius, *Ecclesiastical History* 6.25.
54. Fairweather, *Origen and Greek Patristic Theology*, 67.
55. Fairweather, *Origen and Greek Patristic Theology*, 67.

that God verbally inspired all Scriptures of both Hebrew and Christian origins.[56] This position was not a new idea within Alexandrian philosophy, as Philo had argued that God also inspired the Jewish Scriptures. Considering the inspiration of the Jewish Scriptures, Philo writes, "for the prophet is the messenger of the Lord, who is the real speaker."[57] Origen applied Philo's view of the inspiration to both the Old and New Testaments, though he parted from Philo's philosophy in how the Scriptures were recorded. Philo held that God communicated the Scriptures to the evangelists via a dictation method in which the writers were little more than instruments in God's hand. However, Origen maintained that the human writers of Scripture maintained their faculties, as evidenced by nuances in writing styles.[58]

In the opening paragraphs of Origen's systematic examination of the Christian faith and practice, *On First Principles*, Origen introduces his view of the Scripture's inspiration:

> Then, finally, that the Scriptures were written by the Spirit of God, and have a meaning, not such only as is apparent at first sight, but also another, which escapes the notice of most. For those (words) which are written are the forms of certain mysteries, and the images of divine things.[59]

Later, in the last chapter of *On First Principles*, Origen further expands upon the inspiration of the Scriptures:

> But as it is not sufficient, in the discussion of matters of such importance, to entrust the decision to the human senses and to the human understanding, and to pronounce on things invisible as if they were seen by us, we must, in order to establish the positions which we have laid down, adduce the testimony of Holy Scripture. And that this testimony may produce a sure and unhesitating belief, either with regard to what we have still to advance, or to what has been already stated, it seems necessary to show, in the first place, that the Scriptures themselves are divine, i.e., were inspired by the Spirit of God.[60]

Thus, Origen once again asserts that the Scriptures themselves are inspired by God, and as such constitute the basis of the Christian's faith, doctrine, and practice. Further, according to the fragments of his homily of Jeremiah

---

56. Zöllig, *Inspirationslehre des Origenes*, 13.
57. Philo, *Complete Works of Philo*, fragment on Exodus 23:20.
58. Origen, *Fathers of the Church* 1.22.
59. Origen, *Origen*, preface, 8.
60. Origen, *Origen on First Principles* 4.1.

39, Origen's view on the inspiration of the Scriptures meant that every aspect of the Scriptures was valuable, down to the slightest mark and letter.[61]

Origen's belief in the verbal inspiration of the Scriptures also led him to hold other firm beliefs about the Scriptures. One position Origen took on the Scriptures was that they were without error. Once again, this position was not new to Origen. In fact, Philo had already advanced the position that the Jewish Scriptures were without error.[62] Origen's belief in the inerrancy of the Scriptures drove him to intentionally address difficult passages of Scripture[63] such as 1 Samuel 28 and Jeremiah 20,[64] though his solution for these difficult passages tended to be interpreting them allegorically or supposing a textual mistake.[65]

Another position predicated by Origen's view of the inspiration of the Scriptures is his belief in the inherent unity of the Scriptures. An argument inherent in gnostic belief was a strong disconnect between the Jewish Old Testament and the Christian New Testament. However, because both the Old and New Testament were inspired by the same Spirit, Origen held that they were one.[66] Origen writes,

> Those who do not know how to recognize this divine harmony of the Holy Books think sometimes that they can sense a dissonance between the Old Testament and the New . . . But . . . all of Scripture is a perfectly regulated divine instrument whose different sounds form a marvelous concert.[67]

While Origen sees a unity and harmony between the Old and New Testaments, he also acknowledges differences. Origen held that both contain

---

61. Origen, *Fathers of the Church* 277. Additionally, in his commentary on the book of Romans, Origen notes that he believes that within the letters of the Apostles, through whom Christ speaks, there is not one "superfluous jot or tittle."

62. Hanson, *Allegory and Event*, 192. It should be noted that Origen surmises that "none of the evangelists make mistakes or tell untruths," Origen, *Commentary on the Gospel according to John* 202.

63. Hanson, *Allegory and Event*, 192.

64. In his commentary on 1 Samuel, Origen maintains that the story of the Witch of Endor is true, though he struggled with the idea that a prophet could be summoned by a demon. Origen, *Homilies on Jeremiah, Homily on 1 Kings 28* 320. In his homily on Jeremiah, Origen was also disturbed by the prophet's claim that God had deceived him, leading Origen to suggest that Jeremiah may have been mistaken.

65. Martens, *Origen and Scripture*, 131.

66. Origen, *Fathers of the Church* 10.5.

67. Origen, *Philocalia* 6.2.

truth, though in the Old Testament the truth is seen as shadows, while it is seen in the substance of Christ in the New Testament.[68]

Origen's Allegorical Hermeneutic

Of Origen's various works, he is perhaps most remembered for his allegorical hermeneutic and remains among his most controversial practices to this day. In *Recherches sur le Symbolisme Funéraire des Romains*, Franz Cumont accuses Origen of "strange ramblings" in his homilies, arguing that Origen's allegory is little more than a "chimerical method based upon a false hermeneutic."[69] In *Allegory and Event*, Hanson echoes this criticism, noting that because Origen's hermeneutic did not follow any discernable methodology, it represents an "arbitrary fancy" in which only Origen could be seen as a proper interpreter of Scripture.[70] Despite the many critics of Origen's work, many have also rushed to his defense. Henri de Lubac's *History and Spirit: The Understanding of Scripture According to Origen* is largely dedicated to an apologetic for Origen's allegorical interpretation. De Lubac argues that Origen's attempt to make the Scriptures applicable to his hearers is laudable, even though his methodology is frustrating to scholars.[71] August Zöllig also attempts to justify Origen's use of allegory by noting that allegorical passages were present in Paul's works, and that virtually every early church father employed allegory.[72] Origen himself provides a justification to understand the Scriptures allegorically when he references Paul's first letter to the Corinthians. Paul writes of a wisdom of this world, the wisdom of princes, and the wisdom of God. Following from this passage, Origen writes,

> In this passage, wishing to describe the different kinds of wisdom, he points out that there is a wisdom of this world, and a wisdom of the princes of this world, and another wisdom of God. But when he uses the expression "wisdom of the princes of this world," I do not think that he means a wisdom common to all the princes of this world, but one rather that is peculiar to certain individuals among them . . . [W]e must inquire whether his meaning be, that this is the same wisdom of God which was hidden from other times and generations, and was not made

---

68. Fairweather, *Origen and Greek Patristic Theology*, 70.
69. Cumont, *Recherches sur le Symbolisme Funéraire des Romains*, 10.
70. Hanson, *Allegory and Event*, 257.
71. De Lubac, *History and Spirit*, 307.
72. Zöllig, *Inspirationslehre des Origenes*, 123.

known to the sons of men, as it has now been revealed to his holy apostles and prophets, and which was also that wisdom of God before the advent of the Savior.[73]

From this passage, among others,[74] Origen developed his three senses of the Scripture, in which, to be properly understood, one must seek out the literal, moral, and spiritual sense of the Scripture.[75]

Origen's Literal Sense of Scripture

While Origen favored a deeper understanding of the Scriptures than what the literal sense alone could provide, Origen never divorced the historical context of a passage from its allegorical meaning. Instead, Origen argued that the literal sense of a passage of Scripture represented the foundation needed to investigate that passage's spiritual and moral implications.[76] Origen noted that just as Christ came in both Spirit and in flesh, so too does the Word of Christ possess spiritual and physical connotations. As such, Origen argued that Scripture existed "not in fantasy, but in truth," and that all things happened as recorded in Scripture.[77]

While Origen maintained that the scriptural records were historically accurate and one should seek to understand the literal sense of Scripture, he also believed that to truly understand the depth of the biblical message one should seek to understand it allegorically. In the fourth book of his work *On First Principles*, Origen explains that heterodox theologies generally spawn from a misreading of the Scriptures. Regarding Jewish misreadings of the Scriptures, Origen argues that it is due to their strictly literal interpretations of the Scriptures. Origen writes, "Now the reason why all those we have mentioned hold false opinions and make impious or ignorant assertions about God appears to be nothing else but this, that Scripture is not

---

73. Jenkins, "Origen on 1 Corinthians," 231–47.

74. See also Origen's homilies on Genesis, Leviticus, Numbers, Joshua, and Psalms.

75. De Faye, *Origene: Sa Vie, son Oeuvre, sa Pensée*, 81. It should be noted that Origen did not believe that every passage of Scripture possessed all three senses. Origen contended that some passages should be taken in a strictly literal sense. In his homilies, Origen proposed a solely literal interpretation of passages from Genesis, Exodus, Numbers, Joshua, Jeremiah, and Ezra. Origen thought that other passages, such as the creation story in Genesis, were too impossible to be taken in any literal sense and should be strictly viewed allegorically. According to Origen, most passages of Scripture possessed at least two senses–the literal and a moral or spiritual sense.

76. Origen, *Homilies on Genesis and Exodus* 2.1.

77. Origen, *Homily on Jeremiah* 7.1.

understood in its spiritual sense, but is interpreted according to the bare letter."[78] Throughout the course of Origen's writings, he warns against a Jewish (i.e., strictly literal) understanding of the Scripture, as the literal meaning of a passage should be but a springboard to a deeper, spiritual understanding of God's word.[79]

Origen's Moral Sense of Scripture

Origen's moral sense of Scripture closely resembles the sense in which Philo had previously allegorized the Old Testament in seeking its ethical implications.[80] In his work titled *Origene*, Jean Daniélou refers to this moral sense as an "ecclesiastical" sense in that, in this sense of Scripture, Origen explains the piety and moral conduct which the Scriptures expect from Christians.[81] Equally, Lubac notes that Origen's moral sense of Scripture represented an entry into his "interior"[82] senses of the Scripture and consisted of more than simple moralisms for the Christian to follow, but rather an explanation of the full Christian life.[83] Because Origen's moral aspect of the Scriptures intersects with the daily lives of believers, it should not be surprising that Origen frequently focused upon the moral sense of the Scriptures in his homilies and public addresses to Christians.[84]

Origen himself explains this sense of the Scripture numerous times in his homiletical discourses. In *On First Principles*, Origen considers Paul's

---

78. Origen, *Origen on First Principles* 4.2.

79. Martens finds it odd that Origen would criticize a strictly literal reading of the Scriptures as a "Jewish error" for a number of reasons. First, while Origen criticized literal Jewish traditions, he also borrowed from their scriptural interpretations and from their hermeneutical principles in his own work. Also, Martens notes that Jewish allegorical interpretations of the Old Testament were quite common in Alexandria before and during Origen's lifetime. In fact, in several instances Origen acknowledges the presence of allegory in the Jewish tradition. As such, many such as Nicholas de Lange, Margureite Harl, and Guy Stroumsa have questioned if Origen's critique was an honest one, or simply an attempt to differentiate himself and Christianity from Jewish influences in Alexandria. Martens, *Origen and Scripture*, 139.

80. Zöllig, *Inspirationslehre des Origenes*, 110.

81. Daniélou, *Origene*, 166.

82. In his homily on Exodus, Origen suggests that the literal sense of Scripture offers the Christian little more than a surface understanding of God's word. He notes that to fully understand God's will, one must gravitate beyond the exterior word of Scripture to its interior meanings (i.e., the moral and spiritual sense of the Scriptures). Origen, *Homilies on Genesis and Exodus*, 4.

83. De Lubac, *History and Spirit*, 171.

84. Hanson, *Allegory and Event*, 242.

words to the Corinthian church in 1 Corinthians 9:9 when Paul, referring to the Old Testament passage of Deuteronomy 25:4, tells the Corinthians to "not muzzle the ox while he is threshing." Origen argues that while Moses wrote the passage in the literal sense—that one should provide food for their animals because their work provides food to the farmer and his family, Paul gravitated away from the literal sense to the moral. In 1 Corinthians, Origen notes that Paul uses this passage to encourage the Corinthian church to a proper Christian ethos; mainly, they should supply the apostles and their own pastors with the material resources needed to care for themselves and their families because they are providing the spiritual food of God's word to their congregants.[85]

Origen's Spiritual Sense of Scripture

While Origen viewed the literal sense of Scripture as an elementary reading of God's word and a moral understanding of the Bible to be an introduction to the interior sense of Scripture, Origen regarded the spiritual sense of Scripture as the allegorical sense *par excellence*.[86] Origen believed the spiritual sense of the Scripture to be its highest sense because it revealed the purpose and ministry of God through Jesus Christ. As such, to reach this spiritual sense of Scripture, Origen would often resort to typological interpretations of the Old Testament, arguing that events, people, and situations found in the Hebrew Scriptures were shadows that foresaw the ministry of Christ found in the New Testament.[87] While Origen frequently sought to understand the Old Testament as a shadow of things to come, Origen saw the Gospels as the culmination of the Hebrew Scriptures.[88] Origen notes that the Gospels are the "first fruits of all the Scriptures," as they reveal the Christ to which the Old Testament prophets could only allude.[89] However, even though the New Testament represented the Old Testament realized, Origen contended that the New Testament should also be interpreted in the spiritual sense because the same Spirit that inspired the writing of the Old Testament also inspired the writing of the New Testament. As such, Origen argues that one should expect the Spirit to operate in a similar fashion while inspiring New Testament authors as he did the Hebrew prophets.[90] Thus,

---

85. Origen, *Origen on First Principles* 4.2.
86. Zöllig, *Inspirationslehre des Origenes*, 108.
87. Hanson, *Allegory and Event*, 243.
88. de Lubac, *History and Spirit*, 223.
89. Origen, *Commentary on the Gospel according to John* 1.4.
90. Origen, *Origen on First Principles* 4.2.

Origen concludes that the New Testament will also contain typological elements that point to Christ that are not readily evident to the casual reader of the Scriptures.

In *On First Principles*, Origen defends his search to understand the spiritual sense of Scripture by quoting passages such as 1 Corinthians 10:1–11 which, after considering the Israelite's wilderness wanderings, concludes by saying, "These things happened to them as an example, and they were written for our instruction."[91] Origen also uses Hebrews 8:5 as an example of a biblical writer acknowledging that Scripture possesses a spiritual sense.[92] Origen also makes great usage of Paul's allegorical writings in his letters, such as his allusion to Sarah and Hagar in Galatians 4:24, in which Paul acknowledges that their examples were allegories that provided a shadow of things that were yet to come.[93]

Origen on the Purpose of Scripture

While Origen studied to understand the three senses of the Scriptures, he did not believe that a simple understanding of the Scripture was its goal. Origen did not believe that the chief end of biblical studies was to understand the literal context of a passage, nor was the Bible's purpose to bring a moral conformity. To an extent, Origen did not even believe that the Bible's purpose was to present to its readers true facts of God and Jesus Christ. In Origen's mind, the chief end of the Scriptures was to lead people to experience God's grace in his salvation offered through Jesus Christ. In *Origen and Scripture*, Peter Martens notes that, to Origen, "the Scriptures were composed with the intent of promoting the salvation of their interpreters by making the vast story of salvation their cardinal theme."[94]

According to Origen, the Scriptures were the efficacious cause that led to salvation and continued to guide believers on their path to sanctification. This is due, in large part, because of Origen's belief that God could only be encountered through a study of the Scriptures. In his argument against Celsus, Origen challenges Celsus to compare the writings of the greatest Greek poets and philosophers to the writings of Moses to see which of these writings had the power to change an individual "on the very spot."[95] Origen contends that Scripture begins this process of salvation by first calling

---

91. Origen, *Origen on First Principles* 4.2.
92. Origen, *Origen on First Principles* 4.2.
93. Origen, *Origen on First Principles* 4.2.
94. Martens, *Origen and Scripture*, 221.
95. Origen, *Contra Celsum* 1.18.

one away from his sin so that he might embrace Christ. In his homily on the book of Exodus, Origen interprets Moses's flight from Egypt as a foreshadowing of the Christian's flight from sin to find peace in Christ.[96] Once the Christian has abandoned the flesh and embraced Christ, he then experiences a spiritual metamorphosis, which reforms the individual at the fundamental level.[97] Once undergoing such a spiritual transformation, the Scriptures continue to guide the Christian in his spiritual walk. According to Origen, the Scriptures produce a yearning to know more of God and his word. In his homily on the book of Psalms, Origen exclaims,

> I too meditate on the words of the Lord and repeatedly train myself in them, but I do not know if I am the kind of person in the course of whose meditation fire comes forth from each and every word of God and sets my heart ablaze and inflames my soul to keep those things upon which I am meditating... If only now our hearts would burn within us, as we open the divine scriptures and a fire be kindled in our meditation; if only we might be roused to put what we hear and read into action![98]

Additionally, while giving the Christian a passion for God, Origen notes that the Scriptures are also designed to give the Christian a lasting joy in his relationship with God. Several times Origen notes that the Christian will read the Scriptures with enthusiasm.[99] In his commentary on the book of John, Origen considers Jesus' title of "the true vine." Origen reasons that since the Scriptures are the words of Christ, they, too, should be considered the true vine that, when one partakes of it, will produce the same effect as wine, making the reader to have "cheer and enthusiasm."[100]

ORIGEN'S USE OF SCRIPTURE IN AGAINST CELSUS

Written near the end of the reign of Marcus Aurelius,[101] Celsus's attack upon the Christian faith was initially ignored by Origen, who only took up the task of refuting it at the urging of his friend Ambrosius. Though lost today and preserved only through Origen's apology, Celsus's work *True Discourse*

---

96. Origen, *Homilies on Genesis and Exodus* 3.3.
97. Origen, *Contra Celsum* 7.10.
98. Origen, *Homélies sur les Psaumes 36 à 38* 342.3.
99. Origen, *Origen on First Principles* 4.1.
100. Origen, *Commentary on the Gospel according to John* 1.2.
101. Fairweather, *Origen and Greek Patristic Theology*, 105.

represents one of the first challenges to the Christian faith penned by a writer familiar with the actual claims and practices of Christianity.[102] Within his work Celsus demonstrates his knowledge of Greek Platonic philosophies, as well as Jewish writings and thought and Christian writings and theology. Celsus's understanding of Christianity is deep enough that he even appears to be able to differentiate between Orthodox Christianity and heretical expressions of the Christian faith,[103] though in his assault on the Christian faith Celsus accuses Christians of holding doctrines that were, in fact, only held by heretical sects.[104]

Celsus's arguments against Christians and Christianity were not new arguments against the young faith. What was different about Celsus's arguments against the Christians was that his criticisms used Christian practice and doctrine as proofs. When Celsus accused Christians of violating Roman law, he did not accuse them of sedition or murder or cannibalism or any other hyperbolic charge frequently seen from Roman critics of Christianity.[105] Instead, Celsus charged Christians with the crime of forming secret societies and meeting in secret, a charge that Origen admits to being true.[106] Celsus's primary and overarching criticism of Christianity, however, focuses upon the origins of Christianity. Like many of his predecessors, Celsus made the claim that Christianity is a new religion that borrowed its history and doctrine from other cultures and philosophies.[107] However, Celsus differs from his contemporaries in that he does not speak in broad terms when discussing his views on the origins of Christianity. Instead, Celsus relies upon his knowledge of both Judaism and Christianity to provide specific examples of practices and beliefs that he believes were borrowed from others. To debate Celsus's points, Origen looks to the Scriptures to demonstrate

---

102. Fairweather, *Origen and Greek Patristic Theology*, 106.

103. Fairweather, *Origen and Greek Patristic Theology*, 106.

104. In book 3 of *Against Celsus*, Origen charges Celsus with duplicity in his description of the Christian faith. Origen elucidates how Celsus mocks the divisions within Christianity. In these chapters, Origen quotes Celsus as noting that soon after the rise of Christianity, it began to fracture over practice and belief. Most of these divisions, Celsus says, originated in how the early Christians related to Judaism regarding whether Christians should keep the kosher laws, practice circumcision, observe feast days, etc. According to Celsus, these divisions prove that Christianity is an unstable system of belief. However, Origen points out that at other times Celsus accuses all Christians of heretical beliefs by saying "all the Christians were of one mind." Ibid. Origen looks at these two positions and argues that Celsus's complaints against Christianity should be dismissed because his arguments are inconsistent with each other.

105. Suetonius, *Lives of the Caesars* 6.16.

106. Origen, *Contra Celsum* 1.1.

107. Wilken, *Christians as the Romans Saw Them*, 50.

that the origin of Christianity did not lie in pagan philosophies, but in the revelation of God himself.

The Basis of Origen's Apology

Before considering the content of Origen's apologetic, one should first consider the logic that drove Origen to write. In the preface to *Against Celsus*, Origen argues that Celsus's polemic should be ignored, not refuted. Origen argues that just as Christ himself did not give an answer to those charging him, Christians should not concern themselves with those who would condemn Christianity, as Celsus's attack lacked "credibility or validity."[108] Furthermore, Origen contends that should one read the Scripture for themselves, their concern for Celsus's philosophy would disappear, as the truths contained in the Scripture are self-evident. In a similar manner, Origen argues that if he were to pen an apology to Celsus's attack, it would actually weaken the defense of Christianity as, unlike Origen's writings, the Scriptures rest upon the power of Jesus and Origen wished people to look to the Scriptures instead of his reasoning.[109]

Nevertheless, Origen was convinced to pen an apology against Celsus's criticism of Christianity. He was not, however, convinced to write it by Ambrosius's pleading or by the perplexing nature of Celsus's arguments. Instead, Origen was convinced to write *Against Celsus* by the Scriptures themselves. Origen reminds himself of Paul's admonition in Colossians 2:8 that Christians should "beware lest any man spoil you through philosophy and vain deceit, after the tradition of men, after the rudiments of the world, and not after Christ" (KJV). Origen reasoned that Celsus's criticisms were "vain deceits" designed to spoil one's faith in Christ and, as such, demanded a response.[110]

While Origen's preface did not advance a defense of the Christian faith, its explanation of his methodology reveals the foundation of his defense: the Scriptures themselves. In this preface, Origen demonstrates his belief in the self-attesting nature of the Scriptures and their ability to lead people to faith because they rest upon the power of Jesus Christ himself. This belief lays the foundation and tone of his apology that follows.

---

108. Origen, *Contra Celsum*, preface, 1.
109. Origen, *Contra Celsum*, preface, 3.
110. Origen, *Contra Celsum*, preface, 5.

Origen on the Christian and the Roman Social Order

The first criticism Origen addresses, and returns to a number of times through his work, is Celsus's charge that Christians do not follow the Roman law. Origen writes,

> The first point which Celsus brings forward, in his desire to throw discredit upon Christianity, is that the Christians entered into secret associations with each other contrary to law, saying, that "of associations some are public, and that these are in accordance with the laws; others, again, secret, and maintained in violation of the laws." And his wish is to bring into disrepute what are termed the "love-feasts" of the Christians, as if they had their origin in the common danger, and were more binding than any oaths. Since, then, he babbles about the public law, alleging that the associations of the Christians are in violation of it.[111]

While not directly alluding to Acts 4, Origen answers Celsus's charge the same way that John and Peter answered the chief priests and elders when they were ordered to stop teaching in the name of Jesus—that one must on occasion disobey the ruling powers in order to obey God. Origen reasons,

> that if a man were placed among Scythians, whose laws were unholy, and having no opportunity of escape, were compelled to live among them, such an one would with good reason, for the sake of the law of truth, which the Scythians would regard as wickedness, enter into associations contrary to their laws, with those like-minded with himself; so, if truth is to decide . . . it is not irrational, then, to form associations in opposition to existing laws, if done for the sake of the truth.[112]

At the core of Origen's defense of the Christian practice to ignore the Roman laws that forbade them from meeting and worshiping Christ was his belief that all men will be held accountable to Christ. As such, Origen reasons that it is better to disobey Rome and suffer its judgment than it is to disobey Christ and suffer his judgment. Origen writes,

> Probably those who embrace the views of Celsus will smile at us when we say, "At the name of Jesus every knee shall bow, of things in heaven, of things on earth, and of things under the

---

111. Origen, *Contra Celsum* 1.1.
112. Origen, *Contra Celsum* 1.1.

earth, and every tongue" is brought to "confess that Jesus Christ is Lord, to the glory of God the Father."[113]

Origen on the Origins of Christianity

The primary argument that Celsus makes against Christianity is that none of its doctrines originate from Christianity and that its beliefs are but poor copies stolen from other faiths and philosophies. The Christian's appropriation of other philosophies, according to Celsus, began with Judaism's theft of ideas from other faiths. Celsus lists a number of wise societies who have flourished through history, but did not include the Hebrews in his list, arguing that the Jews were a new race that rebelled against the Egyptians and bastardized the Egyptian religion to create Judaism.[114] Celsus continues this reasoning when he argues that the Christians then rebelled from Judaism as the Jews had from the Egyptians[115] and in so doing syncretized Judaism with a corrupted interpretation of Greek philosophy and mythology.[116]

Origen does not deny that Christianity and Judaism share lofty ideals with pagan philosophy. Origen does not, however, agree with Celsus that these beliefs originated outside Christianity. Instead, Origen argues that

---

113. Origen, *Contra Celsum* 8.59.

114. Origen, *Contra Celsum* 3.5 and 4.31. Origen records Celsus's argument as "Celsus, imagining that the Jews are Egyptians by descent, and had abandoned Egypt, after revolting against the Egyptian state, and despising the customs of that people in matters of worship." Again, Origen quotes Celsus in saying he asserts that the Jews were "fugitives from Egypt, who never performed anything worthy of note, and never were held in any reputation or account."

115. Origen, *Contra Celsum* 3.5. Continuing in his aforementioned train of thought, Origen writes, Celsus, imagining that the Jews are Egyptians by descent, and had abandoned Egypt, after revolting against the Egyptian state, and despising the customs of that people in matters of worship, says that "they suffered from the adherents of Jesus, who believed in him as the Christ, the same treatment which they had inflicted upon the Egyptians; and that the cause which led to the new state of things in either instance was rebellion against the state."

116. Origen, *Contra Celsum* 1.6. One area to which Celsus repeatedly returned was the person of Christ himself. Throughout the course of his work, Celsus would compare the work of Jesus to divine men found in Greek mythology or magicians found in the Roman Empire. Origen quotes Celsus as writing, "Celsus asserts that it is by the names of certain demons, and by the use of incantations, that the Christians appear to be possessed of (miraculous) power; hinting, I suppose, at the practices of those who expel evil spirits by incantations." Origen refuted Celsus's claim by reminding the Christian of Christ's own words in Matthew 7:22. Origen writes, "Jesus himself taught [that it] (would be the case), when he said: 'Many shall say to Me in that day, In Thy name we have cast out devils, and done many wonderful works.'"

these foundational ideals originated with the Christian God. Origen writes, "In my reply to Celsus I accepted the opinion of those philosophers who have affirmed the immortality or the survival of the soul. We have some ideas in common with them."[117] Origen answers Celsus's attacks upon the origins of the Christian faith by referencing Romans 2, arguing that whatever truth may be found among non-Christian philosophies exists because of God's general revelation, that God has spoken to all people in all places in ways that reveal his character and his moral law. Origen writes,

> It is not therefore matter of surprise that the same God should have sown in the hearts of all men those truths which he taught by the prophets and the Savior, in order that at the divine judgment every man may be without excuse, having the "requirements of the law written upon his heart"—a truth obscurely alluded to by the Bible in what the Greeks regard as a myth, where it represents God as having with his own finger written down the commandments, and giving them to Moses.[118]

Furthermore, contrary to Celsus's assertion that the most venerable ideals held by Christians originated outside of the faith, Origen argues that pagan philosophy was, in fact, dependent upon the revelation of God most perfectly seen in the Christian Scriptures. Origen argues that this pagan dependence upon God's revelation is possible because the writing of Moses, as inspired by God, existed prior to the writing of the Greek philosophers. Given the antiquity of the writings of Moses, Origen could confidently assert that if anyone appropriated ideas from another culture, it was the Greeks.

CONCLUSION

Celsus's polemic against Christianity represented the first attack upon the Christian faith that attempted to root its criticism in facts drawn from Christian beliefs as opposed to strawmen and conjecture. Origen responded to this attack upon the faith with the facts of the Scriptures. Origen's approach to his apology should not surprise his readers, as Origen was convinced that the same Spirit that inspired the writing of the Scriptures also empowered the Scriptures to authenticate the truth they contain and transform its reader. Origen states his conviction on the power and efficacy of the Scripture early in *Against Celsus* when he writes,

---

117. Origen, *Contra Celsum* 3.81.
118. Origen, *Contra Celsum* 1.4.

We have to say, moreover, that the gospel has a demonstration of its own, more divine than any established by Grecian dialectics. And this diviner method is called by the apostle the "manifestation of the Spirit and of power:" of "the Spirit," on account of the prophecies, which are sufficient to produce faith in any one who reads them, especially in those things which relate to Christ.[119]

---

119. Origen, *Contra Celsum* 1.2.

4

The Use of Scripture in the Evangelistic Writings of Athanasius

During the third century AD, the Roman Empire experienced its most tumultuous period. Between AD 235 and AD 285, there were twenty-six different Roman emperors, with only one of them dying a natural death, the rest being deposed by their successor or, many times, by their own soldiers.[1] During this period of Roman history, various factions within the Roman military formed juntas that struggled to install their own emperor to the throne, producing nearly a century of civil wars. During this time of internal strife, the Roman Empire experienced a season of decline. Because its military forces were busy quelling internal disputes, Rome was unable to respond to external threats to its borders, such as from the Saxons in the north, the Germans in Europe, and the Goths in the east. Rome's military decline during this period is perhaps best seen in Emperor Valerian's defeat and capture at the hands of the Persians.[2] Rome's culture and economy also did not escape the trouble of the third century AD. As Rome's military expanded, the cost to maintain it also increased, resulting in the steady rise of taxation through the third century.[3] Additionally, toward the end of the third century, as tax income could not keep pace with the debts owed by the Roman state, emperors began minting coinage from base metals such

---

1. Rostovtzeff, *Rome*, 269.
2. Rostovtzeff, *Rome*, 269.
3. Rostovtzeff, *Rome*, 275.

as copper and lead, leading to massive inflation that primarily affected the working-class members of the empire.[4]

The chaos that reigned in the third century finally began to subside during the reign of Diocletian and came to a head in the early fourth century as Constantine united the Eastern and Western portions of the empire in AD 324. During his reign, Constantine reestablished Roman military supremacy by winning victories over several Germanic tribes that had previously established themselves within Rome's borders by improving the Roman economy by introducing new gold and silver coinage, and, most importantly to the church, by legalizing Christianity in the empire. However, while the church emerged from the shadow of official persecution, there were still significant challenges to the faith from outside of the church and from within. Fortunately, the fourth-century church found a champion who could articulate "the faith once for all delivered to the saints" (Jude 3) to both the lost and to the heterodox in Athanasius of Alexandria.

ALEXANDRIAN THOUGHT IN THE TIME OF ATHANASIUS

The city of Alexandria was more than six hundred years old at the birth of Athanasius.[5] In the decades prior to Athanasius's birth, Alexandria had become one of the principal cities in the Roman Empire due to its numerous granaries filled by the Egyptian countryside, which fed much of the empire, particularly the cities of Rome and Constantinople.[6] Because of its vital role in the physical and economic wellbeing of the empire, the city of Alexandria was governed not by a proconsul, as was common among most territories, but by a prefect, appointed by the emperor himself to be his direct representative in the city.[7] Ecclesiastically, Alexandria held a prominent place within the oriental church, as it was the home of the Patriarch of Alexandria, who was responsible for overseeing and appointing bishops throughout Egypt and Libya.[8] As Alexandria served as a hub for learning, it is no surprise that the city also became a major center for the discussion of religious philosophy. The Alexandrian church produced a number of important Christian thinkers in the patristic era, including Clement of Alexandria and Origen.

---

4. Rostovtzeff, *Rome*, 276.
5. Hough, *Athanasius*, 30.
6. Bush, *St. Athanasius*, 7.
7. Anatolios, *Athanasius*, 1.
8. Tanner, *Decrees of the Ecumenical Councils*, 8.

However, the Alexandrian church was also the starting point of one of the most significant heresies within the early church: Arianism.

Born in Libya around AD 256, Arius served as a deacon in the Alexandrian church when, in AD 319, he delivered a letter to the bishop of Alexandria, Alexander, outlining his views on the person of Christ.[9] Arius explained that while he held that Christ was the chief of all creatures, he was, nonetheless, a created being and, as such, inferior to God himself.[10] It was also in this letter to Alexander that Arius first expressed his now famous mantra, "There was [a time] when he [Jesus] was not."[11] In his book *Athanasius*, Khaled Anatolios notes that early church historians were divided upon what precipitated Arius's letter to Alexander. Anatolios writes,

> Socrates seems to assign the initiative to Alexander, whom he describes as attempting "too ambitious a discourse" on the subject of Triune unity, to which Arius reacts out of a fear of Sabellianism, a modalist reduction of the Trinity into a singular unity. Sozomen, on the other hand, characterizes Arius as "a most expert logician" who initiated investigations into hitherto unexamined questions and thus came up with a novel doctrine which "no one before him had ever suggested."[12]

While Anatolios finds himself in agreement with Socrates, both were correct that Alexander and Arius found themselves debating a doctrine whose finer points had yet to be polished. Eventually, the dispute between Arius and Alexander became so pointed that Alexander called a council of Egyptian bishops who drafted a confession of faith.

When Arius refused to sign the confession, he was excommunicated and exiled with the hope that his expulsion would end the controversy. His exile, however, had the opposite effect. After leaving Egypt, Arius found himself under the patronage of Eusebius, bishop of Nicomedia, who accepted his position and began to spread it to the churches in Asia Minor.[13] Arius's error would serve as the backdrop behind Athanasius's life and ministry.

---

9. Arius, "Arius Letter."
10. Walker, *Great Men of the Christian Church*, 50.
11. Walker, *Great Men of the Christian Church*, 50.
12. Anatolios, *Athanasius*, 7.
13. Anatolios, *Athanasius*, 10.

BIOGRAPHY

Save for the few times Athanasius briefly mentioned his youth in his various writings, little is known about his early life, and much is hagiographical in nature. The hagiographical nature of his biographies should not surprise the contemporary reader, as Athanasius's life was one that tended to evoke extreme responses from the people around him. To his theological compatriots, Athanasius was viewed as a hero of the faith and contender for the truth. To his enemies, Athanasius was a constant source of irritation, which often led to false accusations and personal attacks. In *The Fathers of the Eastern Church*, Robert Payne notes,

> In the history of the early church no one was ever so implacable, so urgent in his demands upon himself or so derisive of his enemies. There was something in him of the temper of the modern dogmatic revolutionary: nothing stopped him. The Emperor Julian called him "hardly a man, only a little manikin." Gregory Nazianzen said he was "angelic in appearance, and still more angelic in mind." In a sense both were speaking the truth.[14]

Athanasius was born in Alexandria circa AD 299.[15] The nature of his upbringing, however, is a point of contention among historians. Tenth-century Egyptian bishop Severus Ibn al-Muqaffa records that Athanasius was raised in an affluent pagan household.[16] According to Bishop Severus, Athanasius came to Christ while his mother was consulting a magician to help her find a wife for Athanasius. Upon hearing that her son had become a Christian, Athanasius's mother took him to Alexander, the bishop of Alexandria, to be baptized. Following her death soon afterward, Alexander took Athanasius under his tutelage and, after a period of study, Athanasius became Alexander's scribe.[17] During Athanasius's service under Alexander,

---

14. Payne, *Holy Fire*, 67.

15. Jackson, *New Schaff-Herzog Encyclopedia*, 343.

16. Atiya, *Coptic Encyclopedia*, 137.

17. Hough recounts a more common, hagiographical account of Athanasius and Alexander's first meeting records that, while eating dinner and overlooking the sea, Alexander observed a group of boys "playing" church. In the course of their game, one of the boys baptized the others. Believing that the boys' game had ventured too close to the ordinances of the church, Alexander sent to have the boys brought to him. Slowly they confessed that one of the boys, Athanasius, had taken on the role of the bishop and, after catechizing the others, baptized them. After closely examining the boys, Alexander declared that everything had been done in proper order and that the baptisms he observed were valid. Alexander was so impressed by Athanasius that he invited the boy to receive formal ecclesiastical training and eventually enter into the service of the bishop himself. Hough, *Athanasius*, 37.

the Arian controversy began to spread, prompting Constantine to summon the first general council of churches to meet at Nicaea in AD 325.[18] Given his role as Alexander's secretary, it is safe to assume that Athanasius did attend the council meeting, though it is unlikely that he played any role in its deliberations.[19] Regardless, the Christological theology advocated there would have an indelible impact upon the rest of Athanasius's life.

Three years after Nicaea, Alexander died, and Athanasius became the bishop of Alexandria in AD 328.[20] After his election, Athanasius's bishopric was immediately mired in controversy. Many opposed his election due to the fact that he had not yet reached the canonical age of thirty required to become a bishop.[21] Athanasius's most strident opponents, however, were the Melitians. The Melitians were followers of bishop Melitius of Lycopolis who, like the Donatists, opposed the leniency showed to Egyptian Christians who lapsed under persecution.[22] The Melitians colluded with Arius's supporter Bishop Eusebius of Nicomedia to accuse Athanasius of a number of crimes, including bribery and murder.[23] Eventually a council was called at Tyre to try Athanasius of these crimes. The Council of Tyre found Athanasius guilty, accepted Arian theology, and accepted the Melitian faction back into communion with the church.[24] Athanasius immediately fled to Constantinople to appeal the decision to Constantine, who was initially supportive of Athanasius, though he eventually exiled him to Trier due to rumors that Athanasius was conspiring to disrupt grain shipments from Egypt.[25] Two years after his exile, Constantine died and divided the Roman Empire among his heirs. His son, Constans, a friend of Athanasius's, declared that Constantine had sent Athanasius into exile not because of any wrongdoing, but to protect him.[26] Constans also prevailed upon his brothers as fellow emperors to allow Athanasius to return to Alexandria.[27]

Despite the rejoicing of his congregants, however, Arians continued to conspire against Athanasius. Old criminal charges were once again brought against him with the additional charge that he was withholding grain from

18. Washburn, *Men of Conviction*, 32.
19. Weinandy, *Athanasius*, 2.
20. Betz et al., *Religion Past and Present*, 475.
21. Betz et al., *Religion Past and Present*, 475.
22. Weinandy, *Athanasius*, 2.
23. Weinandy, *Athanasius*, 3.
24. Weinandy, *Athanasius*, 2.
25. Weinandy, *Athanasius*, 2.
26. Robertson, "Athanasius: Select Works and Letters" 4:1.4.
27. Weinandy, *Athanasius*, 14.

Alexandrian widows for his own profit. Eventually, a council was held in Antioch where Athanasius was deposed from his position, forcing him to flee to Rome.[28] During his exile in Rome, Athanasius won the support of Julius and the western emperor Constantinus who convened a council that restored Athanasius to the bishopric.[29] When Constantinus died in AD 336, Athanasius's opponents sent five thousand soldiers to his church to arrest him, prompting his third exile, spent among Egypt's desert monks.[30] Athanasius was able to return to Alexandria in AD 336 when the pagan Emperor Julian, in an effort to weaken and sow discord in the church, declared that all church leaders in exile could return to their duties.[31] Athanasius's homecoming was short-lived, though, as Julian decided to send him into exile once again when Athanasius became critical of his religious policies.[32] Athanasius was able to return to Alexandria in AD 364, following Julian's death. Athanasius was again forced to flee the city when emperor Valens ordered all bishops exiled by Julian back into exile. However, this exile was short-lived as Valens was convinced to make an exception for Athanasius.[33] After his fifth exile, Athanasius was allowed to remain in Alexandria undisturbed until his death in AD 373.[34]

While Athanasius lived a very tumultuous life, his spiritual life was one of quiet piety and faithfulness. During his funeral sermon, Gregory Nazianzus, Archbishop of Constantinople, commemorated Athanasius by saying,

> But why should I paint for you the portrait of the man? St. Paul has sketched him by anticipation. This he does, when he sings the praises of the great High-priest . . . Let one praise him in his fastings and prayers as if he had been disembodied and immaterial, another his unweariedness and zeal for vigils and psalmody, another his patronage of the needy, another his dauntlessness towards the powerful, or his condescension to the lowly. Let the virgins celebrate the friend of the Bridegroom; those under the yoke their restrainer, hermits him who lent wings to their course, cenobites their lawgiver, simple folk their guide, contemplatives the divine, the joyous their bridle, the unfortunate their consolation, the hoary-headed their staff, youths their instructor, the poor their resource, the wealthy their steward.

28. Walker, *Great Men of the Christian Church*, 56–57.
29. Betz et al., *Religion Past and Present*, 476.
30. Jackson, *New Schaff-Herzog Encyclopedia*, 344.
31. Piper, *Contending for Our All*, 56.
32. Piper, *Contending for Our All*, 56.
33. Jackson, *New Schaff-Herzog Encyclopedia*, 344.
34. Jackson, *New Schaff-Herzog Encyclopedia*, 344.

> Even the widows will, methinks, praise their protector, even the orphans their father, even the poor their benefactor, strangers their entertainer, brethren the man of brotherly love, the sick their physician, in whatever sickness or treatment you will, the healthy the guard of health, yea all men him who made himself all things to all men that he might gain almost, if not quite, all.[35]

ATHANASIUS'S THEOLOGY OF SCRIPTURE

Like Justin Martyr and Origen, Athanasius lived in a time prior to the official canonization of the Scriptures at the Council of Carthage in AD 397. However, as Athanasius lived at the cusp of the Council of Carthage's deliberations, the content of both the Old Testament and the New Testament had largely been settled.[36] In Athanasius's own mind, the content of the Christian Bible had already been finalized, not due to an official council vote, but by the command of God. In fact, in his *Thirty-Ninth Festal Letter* published in AD 367, Athanasius provided a list of books that he believed to constitute the Christian Bible and referred to this collection as a canon.[37] As such, before considering Athanasius's overall theology of Scripture, one must ask, "What did Athanasius consider to be Scripture?"

Athanasius's Old Testament Text

While serving as bishop of Alexandria, Athanasius continued the practice of the bishops of Alexandria before him of issuing annual Festal Letters. These Festal Letters would be issued after Epiphany each year and were designed to announce the dates of Lent and Easter, which then also set the church's calendar for all other holidays. Athanasius's Festal Letters, rediscovered in 1842,[38] have garnered the most attention from scholars because in his thirty-ninth letter he becomes the first to list all of the books of the Bible as preserved to this day.[39] Regarding the Old Testament text of the Bible, Athanasius writes,

> In proceeding to make mention of these things, I shall adopt, to commend my undertaking, the pattern of Luke the Evangelist,

---

35. Nazianzus, "Oration 21" 7:1.10.
36. Martens, *Origen and Scripture*, 201.
37. Kirchhofer, *Quellensammlung zur Geschichte*, 9.
38. Athanasius, *Festal Letters*, lxi.
39. Livingstone, *Concise Oxford Dictionary*, 90.

saying on my own account: "Forasmuch as some have taken in hand," to reduce into order for themselves the books termed apocryphal, and to mix them up with the divinely inspired Scripture, concerning which we have been fully persuaded, as they who from the beginning were eyewitnesses and ministers of the word, delivered to the fathers; it seemed good to me also, having been urged thereto by true brethren, and having learned from the beginning to set before you the books included in the canon, and handed down, and accredited as divine; to the end that any one who has fallen into error may condemn those who have led him astray; and that he who has continued steadfast in purity may again rejoice, having these things brought to his remembrance.[40]

There are, then, of the Old Testament, twenty-two books in number; for, as I have heard, it is handed down that this is the number of the letters among the Hebrews; their respective order and names being as follows. The first is Genesis, then Exodus, next Leviticus, after that Numbers, and then Deuteronomy. Following these there is Joshua, the son of Nun, then Judges, then Ruth. And again, after these four books of Kings, the first and second being reckoned as one book, and so likewise the third and fourth as one book. And again, the first and second of the Chronicles are reckoned as one book. Again Ezra, the first and second are similarly one book. After these there is the book of Psalms, then the Proverbs, next Ecclesiastes, and the Song of Songs. Job follows, then the Prophets, the twelve [minor prophets] being reckoned as one book. Then Isaiah, one book, then Jeremiah with Baruch, Lamentations, and the epistle, one book; afterwards, Ezekiel and Daniel, each one book. Thus far constitutes the Old Testament.[41]

One interesting aspect of Athanasius's list is the fact that he actively decried any consideration of the Apocrypha as Christian Scripture. Athanasius writes,

But since we have made mention of heretics as dead, but of ourselves as possessing the divine Scriptures for salvation; and since I fear lest, as Paul wrote to the Corinthians, some few of the simple should be beguiled from their simplicity and purity, by the subtilty [sic] of certain men, and should henceforth read other books— those called apocryphal—led astray by the similarity of their names with the true books; I beseech you to bear

40. Athanasius, *Festal Letters* 1.3.
41. Athanasius, *Festal Letters* 1.4.

patiently, if I also write, by way of remembrance, of matters with which you are acquainted, influenced by the need and advantage of the church.[42]

Again, Athanasius argues,

But for the sake of greater exactness I add this also, writing under obligation, as it were. There are other books besides these, indeed not received as canonical but having been appointed by our fathers to be read to those just approaching and wishing to be instructed in the word of godliness: Wisdom of Solomon, Wisdom of Sirach, Esther, Judith, Tobit, and that which is called the Teaching of the Apostles, and the Shepherd. But the former, my brethren, are included in the canon, the latter being merely read; nor is there any place a mention of secret writings. But such are the invention of heretics, who indeed write them whenever they wish, bestowing upon them their approval, and assigning to them a date, that so, using them as if they were ancient writings, they find a means by which to lead astray the simple-minded.[43]

Athanasius's *Festal Letter* demonstrates that he maintained the traditional view of the Apocrypha—that while the intertestamental books had value and should be read they should not be considered Scripture.[44] However, some contemporaries of Athanasius felt differently about the Apocrypha, as evidenced by its inclusion by the Council of Carthage in AD 397.[45]

Athanasius's New Testament Text

Athanasius's *Festal Letter* is of particular interest to biblical historians as it is the first writing to list the books of the New Testament exactly as it is preserved today.[46] Athanasius writes,

---

42. Athanasius, *Festal Letters* 1.2.
43. Athanasius, *Festal Letters* 1.7.
44. Smith and Bennett, *How the Bible Was Built*, 26–27. When Jerome translated the Bible into Latin, he included the Apocrypha. However, he also included a note before each one noting that these books should not be considered Holy Scripture. Smith and Bennett note that "as time went by, though, scribes who copied Jerome's Bible grew careless about including these disclaimers. The books came to be seen as just books of the Old Testament, and people tended to accept them as part of holy Scripture."
45. Westcott, *General Survey*, 541.
46. Livingstone, *Concise Oxford Dictionary*, 90.

> Again, it is not tedious to speak of the [books] of the New Testament. These are the four Gospels, according to Matthew, Mark, Luke, and John. After these, the Acts of the Apostles, and the seven epistles called catholic: of James, one; of Peter, two, of John, three; after these, one of Jude. In addition, there are fourteen Epistles of Paul the apostle, written in this order: the first, to the Romans; then two to the Corinthians; after these, to the Galatians; next, to the Ephesians; then to the Philippians; then to the Colossians; after these, two to the Thessalonians; and that to the Hebrews; and again, two to Timothy; one to Titus; and lastly, that to Philemon. And besides, the Revelation of John.[47]

In his *Thirty-Ninth Festal Letter*, Athanasius provides a list of writings that he believed should be considered canonical. His New Testament list is identical to the twenty-seven writings still accepted as canonical today, and thus Athanasius has been regarded as the first to issue an authoritative statement on the canon of the New Testament.[48] Athanasius's view did not, however, gain universal acceptance. Some even in Alexandria rejected writings such as 2 and 3 John, while considering the Shepherd of Hermas and even the Didache as Scripture.[49] Despite objections, Athanasius held fast to the writings he considered to be Scripture, eventually being vindicated by the Codex Vaticanus and, eventually, by the church itself.

Athanasius on the Sufficiency of Scripture

In his *Systematic Theology*, Wayne Grudem defines the doctrine of the sufficiency of Scripture:

> The sufficiency of Scripture means that Scripture contained all the words of God he intended his people to have at each stage of redemptive history, and that it now contains everything we need God to tell us for salvation, for trusting him perfectly, and for obeying him perfectly.[50]

---

47. Athanasius, *Festal Letters* 1.5.
48. Thiede, "100 Most Important Events," 12.
49. Thiede, "100 Most Important Events," 12.
50. Grudem, *Systematic Theology*, 127. This definition is echoed in Akin, *A Theology for the Church*. While discussing the issue of worship and the regulative principle, the doctrine of the sufficiency of Scripture is defined as "the idea that the Scriptures sufficiently reveal everything God's people need for salvation, perfect trust, and perfect obedience," Akin, *Theology for the Church*, 810.

Following from this definition, one will see that the doctrine of the sufficiency of Scripture possesses both doctrinal and pastoral implications. Doctrinally speaking, the sufficiency of Scripture governs how one is to think of a particular doctrinal issue. The doctrine of the sufficiency of Scripture dictates that God has revealed himself through the Scriptures and that Christians should not believe anything about God or his nature that is not found in Scripture. This aspect of the doctrine of the sufficiency of Scripture becomes a primary focus of Athanasius in his various polemics against Arian theology. In these writings, Athanasius takes an almost exegetical approach to his arguments to demonstrate that the Arian understanding of Jesus is contrary to how God has revealed himself in the Scriptures. Pastorally, the doctrine of the sufficiency of Scripture dictates that Christians' spirituality and morality must reflect scriptural revelation; the Christian should be bound by the expectations of Scripture while being free of extrabiblical expectations. Athanasius often reflects upon the application of the doctrine of the sufficiency of Scripture in his various pastoral writings, such as *The Life of Anthony*.

As one considers the doctrine of the sufficiency of Scripture, one will find that it is a doctrine that enjoys considerable biblical support. In his letter to his young protégé, Paul encourages Timothy to remain focused upon the Scriptures, writing,

> continue in what you have learned and have become convinced of, because you know those from whom you learned it, and how from infancy you have known the Holy Scriptures, which are able to make you wise for salvation through faith in Christ Jesus. All Scripture is God-breathed and is useful for teaching, rebuking, correcting, and training in righteousness, so that the man of God may be thoroughly equipped for every good work (2 Tim 3:14–17, NIV).

In this passage Paul notes that a focus on the Scriptures will produce everything God requires of the Christian, including salvation, proper doctrine, and personal holiness. Given the Bible's strong support of the doctrine of the sufficiency of Scripture, it is not surprising that it held a central place in Athanasius's theology as Athanasius was, first and foremost, a Bible scholar.

Athanasius's inherent trust and reliance upon the Scriptures should not come as a surprise to his readers. Athanasius came under the tutelage of Alexander, the bishop of Alexandria, at a young age.[51] As such, Athanasius did not receive a classical education that included various Greek philosophies as did many of the early church fathers. Instead, Athanasius's

---

51. Atiya, *Coptic Encyclopedia*, 136.

education primarily focused upon memorizing the content of the Scriptures and how to interpret them.[52] Given his lifelong focus on the Scriptures, it is not surprising that Athanasius would look to them for guidance whether he was writing an apologetic treatise for non-Christians, encouraging the faithful to greater holiness, or penning a theological discourse arguing against Arian heretics.

During his ministry, Athanasius penned commentaries on the books of Psalms, Ecclesiastes, the Song of Songs, and Genesis. Unfortunately, history has only left fragments of these works, none of which have been translated into English. Because Athanasius left so few exegetical works, today's understanding of his hermeneutics is derived from a "hermeneutical sampler" of his didactic works.[53] As Christopher Hall notes in his *Reading Scripture with the Church Fathers*, "Athanasius's exegesis is generally scattered throughout his theological works, and writings focused solely on biblical exegesis itself are relatively rare."[54]

Despite the fact that the examples of Athanasius's exegesis are scattered throughout a variety of writings, address a multitude of issues, and were written at various stages of his life, there is one consistent theme: Athanasius was convinced that the Scriptures contained all that was needed for salvation and holiness. In his aforementioned *Thirty-Ninth Festal Letter*, after listing the writings he holds as canonical, Athanasius goes on to note,

> These are fountains of salvation, that they who thirst may be satisfied with the living words they contain. In these alone is proclaimed the doctrine of godliness. Let no man add to these, neither let him take ought from these. For concerning these the Lord put to shame the Sadducees, and said, "You do err, not knowing the Scriptures." And he reproved the Jews, saying, "Search the Scriptures, for these are they that testify of Me."[55]

In this passage Athanasius affirms his belief in the sufficiency of Scripture, noting that it is the "fountain of salvation" and that the Bible "alone is proclaimed the doctrine of godliness."

While Athanasius's exegetical works are, unfortunately, fragmented and unavailable to modern scholars, a letter written by Athanasius to his friend Marcellinus encourages Marcellinus in his devotion to the Bible, particularly the book of Psalms.

---

52. Atiya, *Coptic Encyclopedia*, 136.
53. Hall, *Reading Scripture with the Church Fathers*, 57.
54. Hall, *Reading Scripture with the Church Fathers*, 64.
55. Athanasius, *Festal Letters* 1.6.

Athanasius had written Marcellinus to encourage him following a serious illness and to express his gladness that Marcellinus had remained devoted to his daily Bible reading through the illness. Because it was reported to Athanasius that Marcellinus had a fondness for the book of Psalms, a fondness shared by Athanasius, Athanasius took the opportunity to share some of his insights from that book. In Athanasius's discussion of the book of Psalms, he also reaffirmed his belief in the sufficiency of the Scriptures.

From the outset of this letter, Athanasius assures Marcellinus that there is benefit to be found in the reading of the Scriptures. Echoing the words of Paul in his second letter to his friend Timothy, Athanasius writes, "*All Scripture of ours, my son— both ancient and new—is inspired by God and profitable for teaching*, as it is written."[56] Regarding the Scripture's power to lead one to salvation, Athanasius writes, "Of such a sort is the commandment to repent—for to repent is to cease from sin. Herein is prescribed also how to repent and what one must say in the circumstances of repentance."[57] Again, Athanasius affirms this belief by writing, "But you sinned, and being ashamed, you repent and you ask to be shown mercy. You have in Psalm 50 the words of confession and repentance."[58] Here, Athanasius contends that the Scriptures lead one to the point of repentance and then gives one the words needed to repent.

Athanasius does not believe, however, that the Scripture's profitability is limited to this first contact of repentance. Instead, Athanasius contends that the Scriptures continue to work in the life of the believer to affect holiness. Athanasius writes, "If the point needs to be put more forcefully, let us say that the entire Holy Scripture is a teacher of virtues and of the truths of faith."[59] Furthermore, he argues, "for Scripture did not seek out that which is pleasant and winning, but this also has been fashioned for the benefit of the soul, and for all number of reasons."[60] In these statements, Athanasius once again assures his friend Marcellinus that the Scriptures can be trusted to lead one to both salvation and holiness.

The theme that Scripture will lead one to a true faith in Christ is again found in Athanasius's apologetic *Against the Heathen*. As Athanasius argued that salvation is found in Christ, he also encouraged his lost readers to read the Scriptures for themselves because, in the words of Scripture, one will

---

56. Athanasius, *Life of Antony and Letter to Marcellinus* 1.2.
57. Athanasius, *Life of Antony and Letter to Marcellinus* 1.10.
58. Athanasius, *Life of Antony and Letter to Marcellinus* 1.20.
59. Athanasius, *Life of Antony and Letter to Marcellinus* 1.14.
60. Athanasius, *Life of Antony and Letter to Marcellinus* 1.27.

find salvation. Athanasius writes, "The sacred and inspired Scriptures are sufficient to declare the truth."[61]

Athanasius's faith in the sufficiency of the Bible is presented to his readers in many of his writings. In his *On the Incarnation of the Word*, Athanasius explains God's creation, man's fall, and thus their need for a redeemer. Athanasius argues that Jesus, as God's son, came into the world to redeem it, and then he offers several arguments for the incarnation and responds to several arguments against the incarnation. Athanasius argues that this is the only conclusion that one can reach from Scripture and that one should consult the Scriptures to better understand Jesus' relationship with the Father. He writes,

> Let this, then, Christ-loving man, be our offering to you, just for a rudimentary sketch and outline, in a short compass, of the faith of Christ and of his Divine appearing to usward. But you, taking occasion by this, if you light upon the text of the Scriptures, by genuinely applying your mind to them, will learn from them more completely and clearly the exact detail of what we have said. For they were spoken and written by God, through men who spoke of God. But we impart of what we have learned from inspired teachers who have been conversant with them, who have also become martyrs for the deity of Christ, to your zeal for learning, in turn.[62]

In his various writings against Arian theology and encouragements to embrace the Nicene formula, Athanasius repeatedly argues from the Scriptures and emphatically states this belief that the Scriptures are sufficient for faith and godliness. At the beginning of his third exile, Athanasius wrote to the bishops serving in Egypt to encourage them to stand firm upon the truths of Christ as stated in the Nicene Creed, even though their insistence upon the Nicene Creed would result in their expulsion from Egypt as well. In this letter, Athanasius writes,

> But since holy Scripture is of all things most sufficient for us, therefore recommending to those who desire to know more of these matters, to read the divine word, I now hasten to set before you that which most claims attention, and for the sake of which principally I have written these things.[63]

---

61. Thomson, *Athanasius* 1.1.3.
62. Thomson, *Athanasius* 5.6.
63. Robertson, "Athanasius" 1.4.

At the end of his third exile, Athanasius penned a brief history of the Nicene Council, titled "de Synodis," in which he affirmed this belief that the words of Scripture supersede all philosophies, including those of ecclesiastical councils. Athanasius argues,

> Vainly then do they run about with the pretext that they have demanded councils for the faith's sake; for divine Scripture is sufficient above all things; but if a council be needed on the point, there are the proceedings of the fathers, for the Nicene bishops did not neglect this matter, but stated the doctrine so exactly, that persons reading their words honestly cannot but be reminded by them of the religion towards Christ, announced in divine Scripture.[64]

Due to his belief in the sufficiency of Scripture, Athanasius held that Scripture would affect its readers by leading them to salvation, proper doctrine, and to personal holiness. In his biography of the desert monk Antony, Athanasius notes that, despite his simplicity, Antony maintained a great deal of spiritual maturity through his rudimentary knowledge of the Scriptures. Athanasius asserted that Antony himself agreed with him regarding the sufficiency of Scripture, as evidenced by the fact that a common theme of Antony's teachings was that the Scripture has the power to lead one to faith and holiness.[65] Additionally, Athanasius records that the fact of the Scripture's sufficiency is evidenced in Antony's conversion and his formative years in the faith. Athanasius writes, "For he paid such close attention to what was read that nothing from Scripture did he fail to take in—rather he grasped everything, and in him the memory took the place of books."[66] Athanasius argued that Antony was able to overcome temptation and maintain a high level of personal holiness due to his devotion to the Scriptures. Athanasius records,

> From the Scriptures Antony learned that the treacheries of the enemy are numerous, and he practiced the discipline with intensity, realizing that although his foe had not been powerful enough to beguile him with bodily pleasure, he would surely attempt to entrap him by some other method, for the demon is a lover of sin. More and more then he mortified the body and kept it under subjection, so that he would not, after conquering some challenges, trip up in others.[67]

---

64. Athanasius, "de Synodis" 1.6.
65. Athanasius, *Life of Antony and Letter to Marcellinus* 1.16.
66. Athanasius, *Life of Antony and Letter to Marcellinus* 1.3.
67. Athanasius, *Life of Antony and Letter to Marcellinus* 1.7.

From a brief survey of Athanasius's writings on the nature of the Scriptures it becomes obvious that Athanasius held the doctrine of the sufficiency of the Scriptures in high regard. Athanasius believed that the Scriptures had the power to teach proper doctrine, lead one to personal holiness, and, most importantly, lead one to faith in Jesus Christ.

ATHANASIUS'S USE OF SCRIPTURE IN HIS APOLOGETIC WRITINGS

While the bulk of Athanasius's writings was directed toward the heretical Arian sect, he took considerable care to address challenges to the faith that originated outside of Christianity as well. Athanasius's *Against the Pagans* and *On the Incarnation* are apologies in the traditional sense in that they were written to argue for the superiority of Christianity over pagan religions and philosophies. However, as Athanasius was writing during the age of Constantine, he did not need to address his writings to Roman emperors to urge them to cease Christian persecutions. Nor did Athanasius need to defend the faith from slander as Christianity had become a mainstream religion within Roman society. Instead, Athanasius wrote *Against the Pagans* and *On the Incarnation* to defend the faith against Jewish and pagan mockers, while also presenting an accurate portrait of the person and work of Jesus Christ. Athanasius's *Against the Pagans* and *On the Incarnation* have been referred to as "bookish" and "unoriginal" as his arguments so closely mirror those that preceded him—to the extent that Athanasius even denounces pagan practices that were common in the lives of his predecessors, but had ended by the time he penned his apologies.[68] Nevertheless, Athanasius's *Against the Pagans* and *On the Incarnation* stand as wonderful apologetics that reflect his reliance upon Scripture to point the lost to faith in Jesus Christ.

Athanasius's Use of Scripture in *Against the Pagans*

Athanasius begins his treatise *Against the Pagans* with an affirmation of the sufficiency of Scripture:

> As you nevertheless desire to hear about it, Macarius, come let us as we may be able set forth a few points of the faith of Christ: able though you are to find it out from the divine oracles, but yet generously desiring to hear from others as well. For although

---

68. Ernest, *Bible in Athanasius of Alexandria* 46.

the sacred and inspired Scriptures are sufficient to declare the truth . . . which a man will gain some knowledge of the interpretation of the Scriptures, and be able to learn what he wishes to know.[69]

After his initial affirmation of the sufficiency of Scripture, Athanasius then begins to explain the natural condition of man. Alluding to the creation narrative found in Genesis 1, Athanasius argues that "in the beginning wickedness did not exist," and quotes from Matthew 5:8 to demonstrate that Adam and Eve's purity of soul allowed them to have a perfect relationship with God.[70] Athanasius explains that humanity lost this sinless state when Adam and Eve were enticed by their lusts to follow their own desires. Quoting from 1 Corinthians 6:12, Athanasius argues that man is now mastered by their lusts and moving in a direction contrary to God's design.[71] Quoting Philippians 3:14, Athanasius defines sin as "missing the goal," arguing that the man of God will strive for the high mark of God's expectations.[72]

Following his explanation for the cause of evil according to the Christian faith, Athanasius works to refute the explanations for the reality of evil as found in Greek dualism. Quoting from Mark 12:29 and Matthew 11:25, Athanasius argues that a dualistic philosophy is impossible as Jesus asserts that there is only one God who is the creator of both the heavens and the earth.[73] Furthermore, he cites Ecclesiastes 7:29 as evidence that evil did not originate with a divine being, but with man.[74]

Following his brief refutation of dualism, Athanasius focuses his discourse on a refutation of idolatry. Athanasius quotes from Romans 1:25 to argue that idolatry is an elevation of "the creature rather than the Creator" and, from Proverbs 18:3, notes that this perversion of religion is despised of God.[75] In his effort to prove that idolatry is despised of God, Athanasius turns to the Scriptures themselves. He quotes Psalm 113:12–16 and Isaiah 44:9–20 to support his conclusion:

> How then can they fail to be judged godless by all, who even by the divine Scripture are accused of impiety? or how can they be anything but miserable, who are thus openly convicted of worshipping dead things instead of the truth? or what kind of

---

69. Thomson, *Athanasius* 1.1.
70. Thomson, *Athanasius* 1.2.
71. Thomson, *Athanasius* 1.4.
72. Thomson, *Athanasius* 1.5.
73. Thomson, *Athanasius* 1.6.
74. Thomson, *Athanasius* 1.7.
75. Thomson, *Athanasius* 1.8.

hope have they? or what kind of excuse could be made for them, trusting in things without sense or movement, which they reverence in place of the true God?[76]

After concluding that idolatry is despised of God, Athanasius uses Romans 1:26 to present the Christian understanding of pagan idolatry; that idolatry is an expression of a person's lust as opposed to an expression of one's piety.[77] According to Athanasius, this is the reason why paganism is subject to a wide variety of moral corruptions.[78] He further argues from Psalm 18:2 that, instead of worshiping the creation, true worship glorifies the creator of the created order.[79]

Following his refutation of paganism, Athanasius set out to offer several arguments for the existence of God. Athanasius's first argument for the existence of God comes from the existence of the human soul itself. He quotes Deuteronomy 30:14, noting Moses' words, "The word is within your heart," and Luke 17:21, "The kingdom of God is within you" to argue that one should be able to perceive God's existence because people have "in ourselves faith, and the kingdom of God."[80] Athanasius continues,

> For having in ourselves faith, and the kingdom of God, we shall be able quickly to see and perceive the King of the Universe, the saving Word of the Father. And let not the Greeks, who worship idols, make excuses, nor let anyone else simply deceive himself, professing to have no such road, and therefore finding a pretext for his godlessness. For we all have set foot upon it, and have it, even if not all are willing to travel by it, but rather to swerve from it and go wrong, because of the pleasures of life which attract them from without. And if one were to ask, what road is this? I say that it is the soul of each one of us, and the intelligence which resides there. For by it alone can God be contemplated and perceived. Unless, as they have denied God, the impious men will repudiate having a soul; which indeed is more plausible than the rest of what they say, for it is unlike men possessed of an intellect to deny God, its Maker and Artificer.[81]

Athanasius's second argument for the existence of God is derived from an examination of the cosmos itself. He cites Romans 1:20 and Acts 14:15

76. Thomson, *Athanasius* 1.14.
77. Thomson, *Athanasius* 1.19.
78. Thomson, *Athanasius* 1.26.
79. Thomson, *Athanasius* 1.27.
80. Thomson, *Athanasius* 2.30.
81. Thomson, *Athanasius* 2.30.

to argue that, just as an artist may be identified by a careful examination of his craft, so too can the existence of God be discerned by considering his creation.[82] Following the logic of a classical teleological argument,[83] Athanasius contends that the rationality and order of the universe proves that it is the work of the Christian God.[84] Athanasius cites John 1:1 to note that the cosmos point to the Christian God, as opposed to another spirit, because the reason found in it originates with a rational God, as worshiped by Christians.[85]

Following his denunciation of idolatry and argument for the existence of God from both the soul and the cosmos, Athanasius revisits these themes at length to provide scriptural support for the Christian view on sin, idolatry, creation, and salvation. In this lengthy dissertation, in which he explains a basic Christian worldview, Athanasius cites twenty-six passages of Scripture to explain why Christians believe as they do.[86] Following his explanation of the Christian worldview, Athanasius concludes *Against the Pagans* with a note on John 14:10 and Romans 1:25 to argue that if one wishes to overcome sin and be restored to a sinless condition, one must return to God through Jesus Christ.[87]

Athanasius's Use of Scripture in *On the Incarnation*

Written to the same person and reliant upon the information shared in *Against the Pagans*, Athanasius's *On the Incarnation* is, in many regards, a follow-up to his first apology. Despite this, *On the Incarnation* proved to be

82. Thomson, *Athanasius* 3.35.

83. The teleological argument is an argument for the existence of God based upon the apparent deliberate design that exists in the natural world. In his *Summa Theologiae*, Thomas Aquinas notes,

> The fifth way [the teleological argument] is taken from the governance of the world. We see that things which lack knowledge, such as natural bodies, act for an end, and this is evident from their acting always, or nearly always, in the same way, so as to obtain the best result. Hence it is plain that they achieve their end, not fortuitously, but designedly. Now whatever lacks knowledge cannot move towards an end, unless it be directed by some being endowed with knowledge and intelligence; as the arrow is directed by the archer. Therefore some intelligent being exists by whom all natural things are directed to their end; and this being we call God. (Elders, *Philosophical Theology of St. Thomas Aquinas*, 120.)

84. Thomson, *Athanasius* 3.40.

85. Thomson, *Athanasius* 3.40.

86. Ernest, *Bible in Athanasius of Alexandria*, 72.

87. Thomson, *Athanasius* 3.47.

more original and beneficial to those wishing to understand the work of Christ. Summarizing Charles Kannengiesser's study of *On the Incarnation*, James Ernest notes,

> *On the Incarnation* is the first description of the essence of Christianity for an educated Christian readership that consistently focuses on the gospel narratives of the crucifixion and the resurrection. The signal contribution of this work is its first (of two) explanations of the incarnation—a fresh, Pauline insertion in an otherwise mainly Origenian composition. In the latter part of this work, Athanasius follows traditional apologetic forms, but for his prooftexts he creatively blends testimonia collections known to us from Origen, Eusebius, and Cyprian.[88]

After a brief introduction in which Athanasius introduces the subject of his apology, "the Word's becoming Man, and to his divine Appearing among us,"[89] Athanasius turns to the subject of creation, refuting various pagan views of creation's origin. However, as Athanasius considers and refutes these pagan creation theories, it should be noted that he does not encourage his readers to reject them because they are philosophically inconsistent, but because they stand in contradiction to the Scriptures. Following his rejection of non-Christian creation theories, he endeavors to offer a biblical understanding of creation in which he cites generously from Genesis 1 and 2 while noting, from Hebrew 11, that it is through "faith we understand that the worlds have been framed by the word of God, so that what is seen has not been made out of things which do appear."[90]

Following his consideration of Christian and non-Christian views of creation, Athanasius delves into the primary subject of this treatise—why God put on flesh in Jesus Christ. Athanasius looks to fourteen passages of Scripture to argue that the first and primary reason for the incarnation is to overcome sin and death.[91] Following his initial argument for the incarnation, he references seven other passages of Scripture in support of his second reason for the incarnation: the renewal of the image of God.[92]

After his arguments in support of the incarnation of Jesus Christ, Athanasius turns to answering various challenges to the incarnation and crucifixion of Christ. Once again, he does not answer the philosophical objections of the lost with philosophical reasoning, but with reasoning

---

88. Ernest, *Bible in Athanasius of Alexandria*, 24.
89. Thomson, *Athanasius* 1.1.
90. Thomson, *Athanasius* 3.2.
91. Ernest, *Bible in Athanasius of Alexandria*, 73.
92. Ernest, *Bible in Athanasius of Alexandria*, 73.

from the Scriptures themselves. Athanasius uses ten scriptural references to answer pagan criticisms of the crucifixion and ninety-seven scriptural references to answer the criticism of the Jews.[93]

Following his discourse on the incarnation of Christ, Athanasius concludes *On the Incarnation* in the same manner in which he opened *Against the Pagans*—with an affirmation of the sufficiency of Scripture and an encouragement for his readers to investigate the Scriptures themselves. He writes,

> Let this, then, Christ-loving man, be our offering to you, just for a rudimentary sketch and outline, in a short compass, of the faith of Christ and of his divine appearing to usward. But you, taking occasion by this, if you light upon the text of the Scriptures, by genuinely applying your mind to them, will learn from them more completely and clearly the exact detail of what we have said. For they were spoken and written by God, through men who spoke of God.[94]

Again, Athanasius writes,

> But for the searching of the Scriptures and true knowledge of them, an honorable life is needed, and a pure soul, and that virtue which is according to Christ; so that the intellect guiding its path by it may be able to attain what it desires, and to comprehend it, in so far as it is accessible to human nature to learn concerning the word of God.[95]

CONCLUSION

Athanasius's apologetics, designed to demonstrate the foolishness of paganism and to establish the core doctrine of Christianity, offered his readers ideas that had been voiced by his predecessors Origen, Clement, and Eusebius. Athanasius's contribution in this genre of writing, however, was not his originality, but his reliance upon the Scriptures. Given Athanasius's high view of the sufficiency of Scripture, one should not be surprised that he used the Scriptures as the foundation of his arguments. Athanasius himself gives the reason why he relies so heavily upon the Scriptures in his apologetic writings when he writes, "These [Scriptures] are fountains of salvation, that

---

93. Ernest, *Bible in Athanasius of Alexandria*, 74.
94. Thomson, *Athanasius* 5.6.
95. Thomson, *Athanasius* 57.1.

they who thirst may be satisfied with the living words they contain. In these alone is proclaimed the doctrine of godliness."[96]

---

96. Athanasius, *Festal Letters* 1.6.

5

The Use of Scripture in the Evangelistic Writings of John Chrysostom

By the end of the fourth century, the Roman Empire was in a state of decline.

The empire had been officially split between western and eastern districts, with the economically poorer and militarily weaker western portion of the empire breaking down into its component parts; namely, Italy and its former provinces, which were increasingly coming under the influence of Germanic tribes.[1] In the east, the Roman Empire's decline was less pronounced. Benefiting from a stronger economy and military, the Eastern Roman Empire was able to maintain its previous traditions and influence.[2] While the decline of the Eastern Roman Empire was slower than that of its western counterpart, it still suffered from a distinct malaise. Scientific advances slowed to a standstill, agricultural methods became more primitive and produced lower yields, leading to social anxiety over the food supply, while lower birth rates led to a scarcity of laborers and an industrial slowdown.[3] As the economic and political strength of the Roman Empire began to sway, so too did its social identity experience a decay. The highest classes of society found in the government bureaucracy and military managed to

---

1 Rostovtzeff, *Rome*, 309.
2. Rostovtzeff, *Rome*, 309.
3. Rostovtzeff, *Rome*, 310.

maintain a relatively high standard of living, though the family structure of even the upper classes began to break down. The greatest decline was found in the once-large urban middle class who found their opportunities to better themselves dissipating. Slavery, though it continued as an established institution, had lost all economic importance as only the very elite could afford to maintain even a small slave workforce.[4]

While the Roman Empire was experiencing a period of decay, the Christian community within the empire was flourishing. At the dawn of the fourth century AD, the Christian church found itself suffering under the empire-wide persecution of Diocletian. By the end of the fourth century, Christianity had become the official religion of the empire, while pagan religions had been pushed to the fringes of society.[5] Rodney Stark estimates that by AD 300, merely 10 percent of people within the Roman Empire had claimed Christianity,[5] whereas by AD 399, more than 50 percent of the empire's residents had become Christians.[7] While the dramatic growth of the Christian church over the course of the fourth century represents a tremendous victory for Christianity, the church still faced a number of challenges. As Christianity became the dominant religion in the Roman Empire, it continued to attract criticism from rival pagan religions in its death throes. Additionally, as Christianity became an official, and even preferred, religion, it began to attract followers who did not maintain the discipline found among previous scholars. As such, the church found itself in need of a new champion that could articulate a theological defense of the faith to those outside of Christianity, while calling the saints to embrace a thoroughly Christian worldview. The church found this champion in John Chrysostom.

BIOGRAPHY

While the exact year of his birth is unknown, historians typically place John Chrysostom's birth between the years of AD 345 to 347.[8] Chrysostom was born in Antioch, Syria, to upper-class Christian parents.[9] John Chrysostom's father, Secundus, was an officer in the imperial army who achieved the rank of "magister militum,"[10] who sadly died soon after John's birth, leaving his

4. Rostovtzeff, *Rome*, 313.
5. Stark, *Cities of God*, 183.
6. Stark, *Triumph of Christianity*, 157.
7. Stark, *Rise of Christianity*, 13.
8. Jackson, *New Schaff-Herzog Encyclopedia*, 72.
9. Fahlbusch, *Encyclopedia of Christianity*, 475.
10. Stephens, *Saint John Chrysostom*, 10.

mother, Anthusa, a widow.[11] Depsite being widowed at a young age, Anthusa proved to be an able single parent who concerned herself with John's piety and education.[12] In her quest to further John's education, Anthusa sent her son to Antioch to study under distinguished pagan sophist Libanius.[13] Under Libanius, John excelled in his studies of rhetoric, literature, and philosophy, with a desire to become a lawyer serving the imperial courts.[14] John Chrysostom realized this dream of working in the legal profession for a short time where he excelled and gained notoriety, to the extent that his former teacher, Libanius, had planned on John succeeding him in his school.[15]

Libanius's desire to see John take on his academy after his retirement was, however, derailed at John's conversion to Christianity. At the age of eighteen, John Chrysostom became a Christian through the influence of a close friend named Basil, and he decided to abandon his pursuit of "vain verbosity."[16] Following his conversion to Christianity, John began to study under the guidance of Meletius, the bishop of Antioch, who baptized John on Easter of AD 368 and then advanced him to the office of reader within the church.[17] Very soon after John became a Christian he began to feel the call to monastic life and would have immediately taken up the practice of monasticism if it were not for his aging mother, who insisted that John remain with her.[18] Honoring her wishes, John stayed with his mother in her home, while observing a monastic discipline.[19]

During this time, John began to gain the respect of his fellow Christians to the degree that, around AD 370, John found himself and his friend Basil in consideration to fill a number of vacancies in Syria following the banishment of Bishop Meletius.[20] Knowing that, should they be elected to the positions against their wills, they would most likely be abducted and forced into the positions, John and Basil said that they would either accept the appointments together or resist them together, hoping that their combined efforts would be enough to avoid being forced into the positions. However, while Chrysostom agreed to the terms of this deal, he was

11. Jackson, *New Schaff-Herzog Encyclopedia*, 72.
12. Stephens, *Saint John Chrysostom*, 10.
13. Fahlbusch, *Encyclopedia of Christianity*, 475.
14. Stephens, *Saint John Chrysostom*, 16.
15. Stephens, *Saint John Chrysostom*, 16.
16. Kelly, *Golden Mouth*, 16.
17. Kelly, *Golden Mouth*, 18.
18. Cross and Livingstone, *Oxford Dictionary of the Christian Church*, 342.
19. Cross and Livingstone, *Oxford Dictionary of the Christian Church*, 342.
20. Stephens, *Saint John Chrysostom*, 40.

determined to not fulfill it, through what he regarded as a "pious fraud."[21] In *St. John Chrysostom: His Life and Times*, W. R. W. Stephens records the events that followed:

> He regarded himself as totally unworthy and incompetent to fill so sacred and responsible an office; but considering Basil to be far more advanced in learning and piety, he resolved that the church should not, through his own weakness, lose the services of his friend. Accordingly, when popular report proved correct, and some emissaries from the electing body were sent to carry off the young men (much, it would seem from Chrysostom's account, as policemen might arrest a prisoner), Chrysostom contrived to hide himself. Basil, less wary, was captured, and imagined that Chrysostom had already submitted; for the emissaries acted with subtlety when he tried to resist them. They affected surprise that he should make so violent a resistance, when his companion, who had the reputation of a hotter temper, had yielded so mildly to the decision of the fathers. Thus Basil was led to suppose that Chrysostom had already submitted; and when he discovered too late the artifice of his friend and his captors, he bitterly remonstrated with Chrysostom upon his treacherous conduct.[22]

Following his mother's death around AD 375, John was free to pursue this monastic calling. John spent his first four years under the tutelage of an unknown Syrian monk before departing to live alone in a cave for another two years.[23] After these two years of solitude, John Chrysostom's strict asceticism began to create severe health complications, forcing him to return to civilization for medical treatment and a return to clerical life.[24]

After John's return from the monastic life, he began to be given several responsibilities within the church. From AD 381 to AD 386, John served the church as a deacon.[25] During this time, be began to put a good deal of energy into writing, focusing on the defense and explanation of the ascetic lifestyle to pagans and Christians alike.[26] In February of AD 386, John was ordained as a presbyter by Flavian, bishop of Antioch.[27] During his tenure,

21. Stephens, *Saint John Chrysostom*, 40.
22. Stephens, *Saint John Chrysostom*, 40.
23. Jackson, *New Schaff-Herzog Encyclopedia*, 72.
24. Fahlbusch, *Encyclopedia of Christianity*, 476.
25. Betz et al., *Religion Past and Present*, 644.
26. Fahlbusch, *Encyclopedia of Christianity*, 476.
27. Betz et al., *Religion Past and Present*, 644.

John became well known for his impassioned hermeneutics that called the faithful to self-denial, holiness, and faithfulness. His sermon "On the Statues" following a local revolt was credited to bringing peace to his city. John defended the faith in a sermon series known as "Eight Speeches against Judaizing Christians," and he faithfully exposited a number of books of the Bible, such as Genesis, Matthew, and Paul's epistles.[28]

In AD 397, at the death of Nectarius, bishop of Constantinople, John Chrysostom was forcibly abducted and brought to Constantinople to be elected as its new bishop.[29] Arriving in Constantinople with the intention to see the capital city won to Christ,[30] John threw himself into the task of shepherding his church while also reforming it from within.[31] Among John's reforms was the end of the practice of the clergy having "spiritual sisters" with whom they lived within a nominally spiritual marriage, deposing a number of bishops who gained their office through simony, and a decrease in ecclesiastical expenses, with the savings applied to area hospitals.[32] While this caused a modest amount of concern from certain segments of the clergy, it posed no danger to John, who found favor with the imperial court. John's favored position, however, did not last long.

During one of his sermons, John forcefully preached against the style of luxurious clothing common among women of the aristocracy. The Empress Eudocia believed John's criticisms were leveled at her and, along with Theophilus, the bishop of Alexandria, and a number of John's critics, assembled a synod against him. At the conclusion of this synod, John was banished from Constantinople, though he was recalled to the city within a matter of days.[33] Two months after his return, John once again found himself drawing the ire of the empress. Constantinople's prefect erected a statue of Eudocia on the south side of the church that attracted a number of tourists and revelers. During one of his sermons, John complained of the noise that the statue drew and how it interrupted the church's worship. Empress Eudocia took this as a personal insult and once again convened a synod against John. Having been condemned by two synods, the emperor deposed John

---

28. Betz et al., *Religion Past and Present*, 644.
29. Eliade, ed., *Encyclopedia of Religion*, 466.
30. Betz et al., *Religion Past and Present*, 644.
31. Eliade, *Encyclopedia of Religion*, 466.
32. Jackson, *New Schaff-Herzog Encyclopedia*, 73.
33. Jackson, *New Schaff-Herzog Encyclopedia*, 73.

and banished him to Asia Minor.[34] In AD 407, John died while in transit to the place of his banishment.[35]

Following his death, John Chrysostom was quickly lauded by all, even his opponents, for his contributions to the faith. Thirty years after his death, John was praised by his successor, Proclus, who eventually received permission to have John's remains moved to Constantinople.[36] John became iconic for his preaching, and was eventually given the name "Chrysostom," or "golden-mouthed," in the sixth century.[37]

JOHN CHRYSOSTOM'S THEOLOGY OF SCRIPTURE

What Chrysostom Viewed as Scripture

While Chrysostom's predecessors, such as Justin Martyr and Athanasius, lived and ministered in a time before an official canonization of the Bible, an official statement of what writings constituted the Bible was made during his lifetime. Late in Chrysostom's life, a synod of bishops met in Carthage on August 28, 397, and declared,

> The canonical Scriptures are these: Genesis, Exodus, Leviticus, Numbers, Deuteronomy, Joshua the son of Nun, Judges, Ruth, four books of Kings, two books of Paraleipomena, Job, the Psalter, five books of Solomon, the books of the twelve Prophets, Isaiah, Jeremiah, Ezechiel, Daniel, Tobit, Judith, Esther, two books of Esdras, two books of the Maccabees. Of the New Testament: four books of the Gospels, one book of the Acts of the Apostles, thirteen Epistles of the Apostle Paul, one Epistle of the same [writer] to the Hebrews, two Epistles of the Apostle Peter, three of John, one of James, one of Jude, one book of the Apocalypse of John . . . Let this be made known also to our brother and fellow-priest Boniface, or to other bishops of those parts, for the purpose of confirming that canon, because we have received from our fathers that those books must be read in the church.[38]

Over the course of his writings, John gave no definitive list of what he considered Scripture and dedicated little time to discussions on biblical

---

34. Jackson, *New Schaff-Herzog Encyclopedia*, 73.
35. Eliade, *Encyclopedia of Religion*, 466.
36. Betz et al., *Religion Past and Present*, 644.
37. Eliade, *Encyclopedia of Religion*, 466.
38. Westcott, *General Survey*, 440.

canonicity.[39] However, given that he also did not argue against the Council of Carthage's declaration, it could be surmised that he agreed with it. In *Chrysostom: A Study in the History of Biblical Interpretation*, Frederic Henry Chase notes that, like many of the Greek fathers, Chrysostom lacked a working knowledge of the Hebrew language, leaving him entirely dependent upon the Septuagint for his studies of the Old Testament.[40] While he was aware of other Greek translations of the Hebrew Scriptures and did, on occasion, criticize the text of the Septuagint, Chrysostom nonetheless considered it a work of divine providence and accepted it as authoritative Scripture.[41] In addition, Chrysostom made use of each book found in the Apocrypha in his writings and homilies.[42]

Regarding the New Testament text, Chrysostom, again, offered no definitive statement on what he considered to be authoritative Scripture. Considering the body of literature that John Chrysostom authored during his life and ministry, it would be fair to argue that he accepted the list of works offered by the Council of Carthage as Scripture, given that he taught from each of the listed works from his pulpit.[43]

John Chrysostom on the Interpretation of Scripture

Bible students who find themselves uncomfortable with the allegorical tendencies found in Origen, Athanasius, and the Alexandrian school of thought will find relief in the Antiochene school, well represented by John Chrysostom. Though a spiritually diverse city,[44] Antioch maintained a thriving Christian population and was the birthplace of the moniker "Christian" to refer to those who followed Jesus Christ (Acts 11:19–26). A formally organized "School of Antioch" may be traced back to AD 269 and a series of councils that sought to ascertain whether or not their bishop, Paul, had fallen into heresy.[45] A man named Malchion, a church leader in Antioch who uncovered Paul's heresy, led the final council. Eusebius records that Malchion was a faithful presbyter who was wise, godly, and presided over a theological school in Antioch.[46] This brief notation of Malchion's life is important, as

39. Krupp, *Shepherding the Flock of God*, 74.
40. Chase, *Chrysostom*, 28.
41. Krupp, *Shepherding the Flock of God*, 75.
42. Krupp, *Saint John Chrysostom*, 94.
43. Krupp, *Saint John Chrysostom*, 101.
44. Metzger, "Antioch-on-the-Orontes," 75.
45. Chase, *Chrysostom*, 2.
46. Eusebius, *Ecclesiastical History* 29.1.

it demonstrates that a school meeting in Antioch was similar in nature to Alexandria's Catechetical School. This school continued to grow and flourish, and reached the zenith of its influence in "the late fourth and early fifth centuries" with expositors such as "Diodore of Tarsus, John Chrysostom, Theodore of Mopsuestia, and Theodoret of Cyrrhus."[47] While scholars still debate the nature and extent of the rift between Antioch and Alexandria,[48] it could be said that in many ways Antioch served as a foil to Alexandria's focus on the spiritual nature of the Scriptures. While the school at Antioch did not ignore allegorical and typological imagery in the Scriptures, it did focus upon understanding the Scriptures literally, in their historical context. In *Biblical Interpretation in the Early Church,* Karlfried Froehlich argues, "There can be little doubt that the hermeneutical theories of the Antiochene school were aimed at the excesses of Alexandrian spiritualism."[49] Froehlich adds that Antioch was a scholarly environment well known for producing interpreters versed in "careful textual criticism, philological and historical studies, and the cultivation of classical rhetoric."[50] "Froehlich warns, however, that to make a sharp distinction between Alexandrian and Antiochene exegesis, as though Alexandrian fathers were only allegorizers while Antiochene exegetes remained firmly planted in the literal meaning of the text,

---

47. Hall, *Reading Scripture with the Church Fathers*, 157. The history of the School of Antioch is frequently divided into three main epochs. While Eusebius notes that Malchion led a school at Antioch, scholars debate when a distinct Antiochene school of thought began. Chase suggests that it began as early as AD 240 with Lucian, who studied theology in Edessa and Caesarea and had significant contact with the school of Alexandria. Joseph W. Trigg identifies the emergence of a distinctive Antiochene approach with the work of Theophilus of Antioch, a scholar from the late second century. The School of Antioch's second period is marked by Christianity's legalization under Constantine. In this period, the work of the apologist was eclipsed by the work of the exegete. This is the period in which John Chrysostom lived and worked, though the School of Antioch was led by Diodore. Antioch's final period of decline began with the deaths of Diodore and Chrysostom. Due to the political and theological controversies that embroiled the school, few church leaders rose to follow in their footsteps, causing Antiochene thought to diffuse and be absorbed by other movements. Chase, *Chrysostom*, 1–27.

48. Pelikan, *Christian Tradition*. The Alexandrian and Antiochene schools found themselves in agreement with most major doctrines. The extent of their disagreements typically stemmed from their philosophical approach to the faith. The Alexandrian school of thought tended toward a Platonic metaphysical approach, which manifested itself in how they understood Scripture and sanctification. The Antiochene school of thought, however, tended toward an Aristotelian approach which focused on concrete realities. This led them to adopt a more literal approach to the Scriptures, as well as an intense focus on the historical accounts of Jesus' life.

49. Froehlich, *Biblical Interpretation in the Early Church*, 20.

50. Froehlich, *Biblical Interpretation in the Early Church*, 20.

is to simplify matters,"[51] as Alexandrian exegetes did frequently consider the literal meaning of the Scriptures, while Antiochenes also frequently allegorized texts.[52]

Though Chrysostom did speak of the typologies seen in the Scriptures, he was, in the vein of Antiochene thought, careful to avoid allegorizing the Scriptures. While summarizing the differences between Alexandrian and Antiochene exegesis, Johannes Quasten examines how John Chrysostom approached the Scriptures and said this of John:

> Always anxious to ascertain the literal sense and opposed to allegory, he combines great facility in discerning the spiritual meaning of the scriptural text with an equal ability for immediate, practical application to the guidance of those committed to his care. The depth of his thought and the soundness of his

51. Froehlich, *Biblical Interpretation in the Early Church*, 20.

52. Hall, *Reading Scripture with the Church Fathers*, 157. Trigg has been a leading scholar in the school of thought that sees the exegetical principles of Alexandria and Antioch to be in harmony with one another, with their differences being one of emphasis as opposed to principle. In his work *What Is the Difference between Contemplation and Allegory?* Diodore argued against allegory

> because it seemed to impose a foreign meaning upon the biblical text. In contrast to the allegorical approach, Diodore advocated "contemplation" or "theoria," which, as Joseph Trigg defines it, is an interpretive disposition and device that identifies "the spiritual meaning of a text which both inheres in the historical framework and also takes the mind of the reader of scripture to higher planes of contemplation. *Theoria* was the disposition of mind, the insight, which enabled prophets to receive their visions in the first place; it was thus both the necessary condition for scripture and its highest interpretation. Diodore then could acknowledge the typological interpretation of the Old Testament which had long been a standard reading in the church without accepting an allegorical reading. (Hall, *Reading Scripture with the Church Fathers*, 158)

Additionally, Froehlich notes,

> In Antioch, the Hellenistic rhetorical tradition, and therefore the rational analysis of biblical language, was stressed more than the philosophical tradition and its analysis of spiritual reality. Moreover, in Alexandria, history was subordinated to a higher meaning; the historical referent of the literal level took second place to the spiritual teaching intended by the divine author. In Antioch, the higher *theōria* remained subject to the foundational *historia*, the faithful (or sometimes even fictional) account of events; deeper truth for the guidance of the soul took second place to the scholarly interest in reconstructing human history and understanding the human language of the inspired writers. (Froehlich, *Biblical Interpretation in the Early Church*, 20–21)

Thus, it may be said that while there were varied approaches to the Scriptures in the Antiochene and Alexandrian schools of thought, those variances may amount to distinctions without a difference.

masterful exposition are unique and attract even modern readers. He is equally at home in the books of the Old and the New Testament and has the skill to use even the former for the conditions of the present and the problems of daily life.[53]

Chrysostom on the Truthfulness of the Scriptures

One primary tenet of the School of Antioch was its view that the Scriptures are the solely valid divine word of God.[54] As a leading figure within the School of Antioch, Chrysostom naturally held this view as well. In his first homily on the book of Matthew, Chrysostom notes,

> It were indeed meet for us not at all to require the aid of the written word, but to exhibit a life so pure that the grace of the Spirit should be instead of books to our souls, and that as these are inscribed with ink, even so should our hearts be with the Spirit. But, since we have utterly put away from us this grace, come, let us at any rate embrace the second best course.
>
> For that the former was better, God hath made manifest, both by his words and by his doings. Since unto Noah, and unto Abraham, and unto his offspring, and unto Job, and unto Moses too, he discoursed not by writings, but himself by himself, finding their mind pure. But after the whole people of the Hebrews had fallen into the very pit of wickedness, then and thereafter was a written word, and tables, and the admonition which is given by these.
>
> And this one may perceive was the case, not of the saints in the Old Testament only, but also of those in the New. For neither to the apostles did God give anything in writing, but instead of written words he promised that he would give them the grace of the Spirit: for "*He*," says our Lord, "*shall bring all things to your remembrance*," John 14:26. And that you may learn that this was far better, hear what he says by the Prophet: "*I will make a new covenant with you, putting my laws into their mind, and in their heart I will write them*," and, "*they shall be all taught of God.*" And Paul too, pointing out the same superiority, said, that they had received a law "*not in tables of stone, but in fleshy tables of the heart.*"
>
> But since in process of time they made shipwreck, some with regard to doctrines, others as to life and manners, there

---

53. Quasten, *Patrology*, 433.
54. Hovhanessian, *School of Antioch*, 8.

> was again need that they should be put in remembrance by the written word.
>
> 2. Reflect then how great an evil it is for us, who ought to live so purely as not even to need written words, but to yield up our hearts, as books, to the Spirit; now that we have lost that honor, and have come to have need of these, to fail again in duly employing even this second remedy. For if it be a blame to stand in need of written words, and not to have brought down on ourselves the grace of the Spirit; consider how heavy the charge of not choosing to profit even after this assistance, but rather treating what is written with neglect, as if it were cast forth without purpose, and at random, and so bringing down upon ourselves our punishment with increase. But that no such effect may ensue, let us give strict heed unto the things that are written; and let us learn how the Old Law was given on the one hand, how on the other the New Covenant.[55]

Thus, Chrysostom argues that since people are unable to follow the Spirit of God who writes the law of God upon their hearts, they should devote themselves to the study of the Scriptures, as they are a reliable record of the truth of God.

Chrysostom defends this belief in the truthfulness of the Scriptures by considering the number of prophecies made in the Old Testament that were then realized in the New Testament. Looking at the birth of Jesus, and the precise way in which it came about, leads John to conclude that the Scriptures are entirely accurate and trustworthy:

> But mark also the exactness of the prophecy. For it does not say, "*He will abide*" in Bethlehem, but "*He will come out*" thence. So that this too was a subject of prophecy, his being simply born there.
>
> Some of them, however, being past shame, say that these things were spoken of Zerubbabel. But how can they be right? For surely "*his goings forth*" were not "*from of old, from everlasting*," Micah 5:2. And how can that suit him which is said at the beginning, "*Out of you shall he come forth*": Zorobabel not having been born in Judæa, but in Babylon, whence also he was called Zorobabel, because he had his origin there? And as many as know the Syrians' language know what I say.
>
> And together with what has been said, all the time also since these things is sufficient to establish the testimony.[56]

---

55. Chrysostom, "Homily 1 on Matthew."
56. Chrysostom, "Homily 7 on Matthew."

John Chrysostom maintained his trust in the complete truthfulness of the Scriptures even when confronted with a difficult passage of Scripture or different passages that appeared to be contradictory in nature. When confronted with passages of Scripture that appeared contradictory, Chrysostom faulted readers for their lack of understanding as opposed to the Scriptures for their lack of clarity. This is seen in his homily on the creation account found in the book of Genesis, where Chrysostom resolved difficulties in the creation account by attributing them to the results of the fall. He writes,

> The fact that now we have fear and dread of the wild animals and have lost control of them, I personally don't dispute: but this doesn't betray a false promise on God's part. From the beginning, you see, things weren't like this; instead, the wild beasts were in fear and trembling, and responded to direction. But when through disobedience human beings forfeited their position of trust, their control was also lost. As evidence, after all, that everything was placed under the human being's control, listen to Scripture saying, "He brought the wild animals and all the brute beasts to Adam to see what he would call them." And seeing the animals near him, he didn't shrink back, but like a master giving names to slaves in his service, he gave them all names; the text says, "They each bore the name Adam gave them," this being a symbol of his dominion. Hence God was wanting to teach him through this the dignity of his authority, so he entrusted to him the giving of names.[57]

Likewise, John was prone to harmonize the gospel accounts, especially the apparent difficulties in their genealogical records.[58]

Chrysostom on the Condescension of Scripture

Chrysostom's view on the condescension of Scripture has led some to contend that he saw flaws and inaccuracies in the scriptural text.[59] However, as previously seen, when Chrysostom considered apparent discrepancies in the scriptural record, he was inclined to see such possible flaws as the responsibility of the reader as opposed to the text. As such, Chrysostom's view on the Condescension of Scripture is similar in nature to the modern Protestant view that, in the Scriptures, God used language in such a way as

---

57. Chrysostom, "Homily 9," 121–22.
58. Chrysostom, "Homily 9," 121–22.
59. Congar, *Lay People in the Church*, 55.

to accommodate human understanding. In his *Institutes of Christian Religion*, John Calvin notes,

> Indeed, that they dared abuse certain testimonies of Scripture was due to base ignorance; just as the error itself sprang from execrable madness. The Anthropomorphites, also, who imagined a corporeal God from the fact that Scripture often ascribes to him a mouth, ears, eyes, hands, and feet, are easily refuted. For who even of slight intelligence does not understand that, as nurses commonly do with infants, God is wont in a measure to "lisp" in speaking to us? Thus such forms of speaking do not so much express clearly what God is like as accommodate the knowledge of him to our slight capacity. To do this he must descend far beneath his loftiness.[60]

Robert C. Hill agrees with the notion that Chrysostom's understanding of the Condescension of Scripture is analogous with the modern understanding of scriptural accommodation, arguing that John's use of the term could be better translated and understood as "considerateness" or "graciousness" of divine activity toward humanity.[61] John argued that the progressive nature of Scripture demonstrates that God condescends to human understanding to communicate with men.[62] John notes that in Genesis God graciously revealed himself to Adam and Eve first, then progressively revealed himself to more people through the law of Moses, the history of Israel, and, finally, through Jesus Christ himself. In this process, God described himself through knowable, special terms, such as the phrase "Only-Begotten" in

---

60. Calvin, *Institutes of the Christian Religion* 1.13.1. In addition to Calvin's first expression of this principle of accommodation, others have sought to define the idea better. Other definitions of the principle of accommodation include: "Accommodation is God's adoption in inscripturation of the human audience's finite and fallen perspective. Its underlying conceptual assumption is that in many cases God does not correct our mistaken human viewpoints but merely assumes them in order to communicate with us." Sparks, *God's Word in Human Words*, 230–31. Considering this view, Richard Muller writes,

> The Reformers and their scholastic followers all recognized that God must in some way condescend or accommodate himself to human ways of knowing in order to reveal himself. This *accommodatio* occurs specifically in the use of human words and concepts for the communication of the law and the gospel, but it in no way implies the loss of truth or the lessening of scriptural authority. (Muller, *Dictionary of Latin and Greek Theological Terms*, 19.)

61. Chrysostom, "Chrysostom and Scripture," 17.
62. Chrysostom, "Chrysostom and Scripture," 17.

John 3, so that man's condition was not a hindrance in God's task of redeeming men to himself.[63]

God's condescension in Scripture is an important component in Chrysostom's *On Wealth and Poverty*, where he contrasts the philosophers of the age to the Apostles. He writes,

> But the apostles and prophets always did the very opposite; they, as the common instructors of the world, made all that they delivered plain to all men, in order that every one, even unaided, might be able to learn by the mere reading. Thus also the prophet spake before, when he said, "All shall be taught of God," (Isa 54:13). "And they shall no more say, every one to his neighbour, Know the Lord, for they shall all know me from the least to the greatest," (Jer 31:34). St. Paul also says, "And I, brethren, when I came to you, came not with excellency of speech, or of wisdom, declaring unto you the mystery of God" (1 Cor 2:1). And again, "My speech and my preaching was not with enticing words of man's wisdom, but in demonstration of the Spirit and of power" (1 Cor. 2:4). And again, "We speak wisdom," it is said, "but not the wisdom of this world, nor of the princes of this world that come to naught" (1 Cor 2:6). For to whom is not the gospel plain? Who is it that hears, "Blessed are the meek; blessed are the merciful; blessed are the pure in heart," and such things as these, and needs a teacher in order to understand any of the things spoken?[64]

Chrysostom on the Practical Application of Scripture

John Chrysostom worked and thought primarily as a pastor as opposed to a theologian. As such, it should come as no surprise that John sought to teach the Scriptures in a practical, rather than philosophical, manner. Chrysostom sought to connect the Scriptures to the lives of his congregation so that they may provide the Christian with practical guidance for their lives. Chrysostom believed that the Scriptures were sufficient to provide Christians with guidance in their quest for salvation and growth in their faith.

---

63. Chrysostom. "Homily 3 on the Gospel of John."
64. Chrysostom. *On Wealth and Poverty*, 3.

Chrysostom on the Scripture's Role in Salvation

Chrysostom's position was that God created man to be a social creature.[65] As a part of that social nature, man was also created to have a perfect relationship with his creator, God.[66] However, at the fall, the communion that man and God had together was shattered, resulting in both physical and spiritual death.[67] In order to regain the communion lost through the Fall, Chrysostom argued that one must be saved through an act of synergism in which God called the sinner to faith and the sinner freely accepted the faith offered by God.[68] According to John Chrysostom, one of the primary ways in which God calls the sinner to faith is through the Scriptures.

---

65. Krupp, *Shepherding the Flock of God*, 90.

66. When considering the relationship that man and God shared with each other prior to the fall, Chrysostom looks back to the Genesis narrative and argues,

> And their work is what was Adam's also at the beginning and before his sin, when he was clothed with the glory, and conversed freely with God, and dwelt in that place that was full of great blessedness. For in what respect are they in a worse state than he, when before his disobedience he was set to till the garden? Had he no worldly care? But neither have these. Did he talk to God with a pure conscience? (Chrysostom, "Homily 68 on Matthew.")

67. In the course of preaching on Ephesians 2:1–3, John considers the consequences of the fall when he writes,

> There is, we know, a corporal, and there is also a spiritual, dying. Of the first it is no crime to partake, nor is there any peril in it, inasmuch as there is no blame attached to it, for it is a matter of nature, not of deliberate choice. It had its origin in the transgression of the first-created man, and thenceforward in its issue it passed into a nature, and, at all events, will quickly be brought to a termination; whereas this spiritual dying, being a matter of deliberate choice, has criminality, and has no termination. (Chrysostom, "Homily 4 on Ephesians.")

In this passage, John notes that the results of Adam's disobedience are a physical death which all people— Christian and non-Christian—will experience. Another consequence of the fall is a spiritual death that the lost will experience due to their failure to place their faith in Christ.

68. Krupp, *Shepherding the Flock of God*, 89. While Chrysostom was often inconsistent in how this synergistic work of God and man transpired, it is obvious that he held to this synergistic theology in his seventh homily on John when he explained how God revealed himself to man, and a number of ways in which man might respond. John notes,

> Knowing therefore this, let us continue steadfastly to hold what "they have delivered unto us, which from the beginning were eye-witnesses, and ministers of the word." Luke 1:2. And let us not be curious beyond: for two evils will attend those who are sick of this disease, (curiosity,) the wearying themselves in vain by seeking what it is impossible to find, and the provoking God by their endeavors to overturn the bounds set by him. Now what anger this excites,

In "Homily 7 on the Gospel of John," a passage usually seen as Chrysostom's clearest explanation of how God and man work together to effect salvation, he notes that God begins the process by exposing the lost to Scripture. John begins his explanation by considering the nature of God and Christ, and then notes, "Knowing therefore this, let us continue steadfastly to hold what 'they have delivered unto us, which from the beginning were eye-witnesses, and ministers of the word.'"[69] This theme is repeated a number of times throughout the course of John's ministry. Again, in "Homily 59 on the Gospel of John," while considering John 10:1 and following, John alludes to God making himself known to the lost for their salvation through the Scriptures when he preaches,

> And with good cause he calls the Scriptures "a door," for they bring us to God, and open to us the knowledge of God, they make the sheep, they guard them, and suffer not the wolves to come in after them. For Scripture, like some sure door, bars the passage against the heretics, placing us in a state of safety as to all that we desire, and not allowing us to wander; and if we undo it not, we shall not easily be conquered by our foes. By it we can know all, both those who are, and those who are not, shepherds. But what is "into the fold"? It refers to the sheep,

---

it needs not that you who know should learn from us. Abstaining therefore from their madness, let us tremble at his words, that he may continually build us up. For, "upon whom shall I look," Isaiah 66:2, Septuagint, says he, "but upon the lowly, and quiet, and who fears my words?" Let us then leave this pernicious curiosity, and bruise our hearts, let us mourn for our sins as Christ commanded, let us be pricked at heart for our transgressions, let us reckon up exactly all the wicked deeds, which in time past we have dared, and let us earnestly strive to wipe them off in all kinds of ways. Now to this end God has opened to us many ways. For, "'Tell thou first,' says he, 'your sins, that you may be justified,'" Isaiah 43:26; and again, "I said, I have declared mine iniquity unto You, and You have taken away the unrighteousness of my heart," Psalm 32:5, Septuagint; since a continual accusation and remembrance of sins contributes not a little to lessen their magnitude. But there is another more prevailing way than this; to bear malice against none of those who have offended against us, to forgive their trespasses to all those who have trespassed against us. Will you learn a third? Hear Daniel, saying, "Redeem your sins by almsdeeds, and your iniquities by showing mercy to the poor," Daniel 4:27, Septuagint. And there is another besides this; constancy in prayer, and persevering attendance on the intercessions made with God. In like manner fasting brings to us some, and that not small comfort and release from sins committed, provided it be attended with kindness to others, and quenches the vehemence of the wrath of God, 1 Timothy 2:1. For "water will quench a blazing fire, and by almsdeeds sins are purged away." (Chrysostom, "Homily 7 on the Gospel of John.")

69. Chrysostom, "Homily 7 on the Gospel of John."

and the care of them. For he that uses not the Scriptures, but "climbs up some other way," that is, who cuts out for himself another and an unusual way, "the same is a thief." Do you see from this too that Christ agrees with the Father, in that he brings forward the Scriptures? On which account also he said to the Jews, "Search the Scriptures," John 5:39; and brought forward Moses, and called him and all the Prophets witnesses, for "all," says he, "who hear the Prophets shall come to Me"; and, "Had ye believed Moses, you would have believed Me."[70]

While considering the narrative of Lazarus and the Rich Man, Chrysostom again considers the act of God revealing himself through the Scriptures when he argues, "We must thoroughly quench the darts of the devil and beat them off by continual reading of the divine Scriptures. For it is not possible, not possible for anyone to be saved without continually taking advantage of spiritual reading."[71] In *Four Discourses*, John considers the example of the Ethiopian Eunuch, and how he was made wise to salvation through the ardent study of the Scriptures. He writes,

> Remember the eunuch of the queen of Ethiopia. Being a man of a barbarous nation, occupied with numerous cares, and surrounded on all sides by manifold business, he was unable to understand that which he read. Still, however, as he was seated in the chariot, he was reading. If he showed such diligence on a journey, think how diligent he must have been at home: if while on the road he did not let an opportunity pass without reading, much more must this have been the case when seated in his house; if when he did not fully understand the things he read, he did not cease from reading, much more would he not cease when able to understand. To show that he did not understand the things which he read, hear that which Philip said to him: "Understandest thou what thou readest?" (Acts 8:30). Hearing this question he did not show provocation or shame: but confessed his ignorance, and said: "How can I, except some man should guide me?" (ver. 31). Since, therefore, while he had no man to guide him, he was thus reading; for this reason, he quickly received an instructor. God knew his willingness, he acknowledged his zeal, and forthwith sent him a teacher.
>
> But, you say, Philip is not present with us now. Still, the Spirit that moved Philip is present with us. Let us not, beloved, neglect our own salvation! "All these things are written for our

---

70. Chrysostom, "Homily 59 on the Gospel of John."
71. Chrysostom, *On Wealth and Poverty*, 2.

admonition upon whom the ends of the world are come" (1 Cor. 10:11). The reading of the Scriptures is a great safeguard against sin; ignorance of the Scriptures is a great precipice and a deep gulf; to know nothing of the Scriptures is a great betrayal of our salvation.[72]

In "Homily 53: John 8.20–30," Chrysostom makes a very clear statement concerning his view of Scripture's role in salvation as he comments on John 8:31: "Now if we are willing to examine the Scriptures in this way, carefully and systematically, we shall be able to obtain our salvation. If we unceasingly are preoccupied with them, we shall learn both correctness of doctrine and an upright way of life."[73] After a thorough reading of John Chrysostom's writings, it becomes apparent that he believed that an exposure to the Scriptures was a necessary and vital component that God used to effect salvation in the lost.

Chrysostom on Scripture's Role in Sanctification

Just as John believed an exposure to Scripture was a necessary component to salvation, he also held that it was a necessary component to one's sanctification. In his thirty-second homily on the Gospel of John, Chrysostom overtly declared that being exposed to the Scriptures was a vital part of one's growth as a Christian:

> Moreover, if the devil does not dare to enter into the house where the gospel lies, much less will he ever seize upon the soul which contains such thoughts as these, and no evil spirit will approach it, nor will the nature of sin come near. Well, then, sanctify your soul, sanctify your body by having these thoughts always in your heart and on your tongue. For if foul language is defiling and evokes evil spirits, it is evident that spiritual reading sanctifies the reader and attracts the grace of the Spirit.[74]

Chrysostom believed that, while persons are not saved by their works, once a person was saved he or she would produce works in accordance with God's will. In his fifty-fifth homily on the book of Matthew, Chrysostom takes up this idea as he considers Christ's call that "if anyone wishes to come

---

72. Allen, *Four Discourses on Chrysostom*, 67.

73. Chrysostom, "Homily 53 (John 8.20–30)," 61.

74. Constantincu, "Select Quotes from St. John Chrysostom on the Benefits and Importance of Scripture Reading for Christians."

after Me, he must deny himself, and take up his cross and follow Me" (Matt 16:24). He writes,

> Wherefore Christ compels not, but urges, sparing us. For since they seemed to be murmuring much, being secretly disturbed at the saying, he says, "No need of disturbance or of trouble. If you do not account what I have mentioned to be a cause of innumerable blessings, even when befalling yourselves, I use no force, nor do I compel, but if any be willing to follow, him I call.
>
> "For do not by any means imagine that this is your following of me; I mean, what ye now do attending upon me. You have need of many toils, many dangers, if ye are to come after me. For you ought not, O Peter, because you have confessed me Son of God, therefore only to expect crowns, and to suppose this enough for your salvation, and for the future to enjoy security, as having done all. For although it be in my power, as Son of God, to hinder you from having any trial at all of those hardships; yet such is not my will, for your sake, that you may yourself too contribute something, and be more approved." For so, if one were a judge at the games, and had a friend in the lists, he would not wish to crown him by favor only, but also for his own toils; and for this reason especially, because he loves him. Even so Christ also; whom he most loves, those he most of all will have to approve themselves by their own means also, and not from his help alone.
>
> But see how at the same time he makes his saying not a grievous one. For he does by no means compass them only with his terror, but he also puts forth the doctrine generally to the world, saying, "If any one will," be it woman or man, ruler or subject, let him come this way.[75]

Here, John argues that a person may come to Christ and be justified freely, but once that person freely chooses to follow Christ, he takes on a responsibility to live according to Christ's commands. Chrysostom revisits this theme once again in "Homily 7 on the Gospel of John." As he considered the implications of the phrase, "that was the true Light, which lighteth every man that cometh into the world" (John 1:9 KJV), he wrote,

> Knowing therefore this, let us continue steadfastly to hold what "they have delivered unto us, which from the beginning were eye-witnesses, and ministers of the word," Luke 1:2. And let us not be curious beyond: for two evils will attend those who are sick of this disease, (curiosity,) the wearying themselves in vain

75. Chrysostom, "Homily 55 on Matthew."

by seeking what it is impossible to find, and the provoking God by their endeavors to overturn the bounds set by him. Now what anger this excites, it needs not that you who know should learn from us. Abstaining therefore from their madness, let us tremble at his words, that He may continually build us up. For, "upon whom shall I look," Isaiah 66:2, Septuagint, says he, "but upon the lowly, and quiet, and who fears my words?" Let us then leave this pernicious curiosity, and bruise our hearts, let us mourn for our sins as Christ commanded, let us be pricked at heart for our transgressions, let us reckon up exactly all the wicked deeds, which in time past we have dared, and let us earnestly strive to wipe them off in all kinds of ways.

Now to this end God has opened to us many ways. For, "'Tell thou first,' says he, 'your sins, that you may be justified,'" Isaiah 43:26; and again, "I said, I have declared mine iniquity unto You; and You have taken away the unrighteousness of my heart,' Psalm 32:5, Septuagint; since a continual accusation and remembrance of sins contributes not a little to lessen their magnitude. But there is another more prevailing way than this; to bear malice against none of those who have offended against us, to forgive their trespasses to all those who have trespassed against us. Will you learn a third? Hear Daniel, saying, "Redeem your sins by almsdeeds, and your iniquities by showing mercy to the poor," Daniel 4:27, Septuagint. And there is another besides this; constancy in prayer, and persevering attendance on the intercessions made with God. In like manner fasting brings to us some, and that not small comfort and release from sins committed, provided it be attended with kindness to others, and quenches the vehemence of the wrath of God. 1 Timothy 2:1. For "water will quench a blazing fire, and by almsdeeds sins are purged away."

Let us then travel along all these ways; for if we give ourselves wholly to these employments, if on them we spend our time, not only shall we wash off our bygone transgressions, but shall gain very great profit for the future. For we shall not allow the devil to assault us with leisure either for slothful living, or for pernicious curiosity, since by these among other means, and in consequence of these, he leads us to foolish questions and hurtful disputations, from seeing us at leisure, and idle, and taking no forethought for excellency of living. But let us block up this approach against him, let us watch, let us be sober, that having in this short time toiled a little, we may obtain eternal goods in endless ages, by the grace and lovingkindness of our Lord Jesus

Christ; by whom and with whom to the Father and the Holy Ghost, be glory for ever and ever. Amen.[76]

Here, Chrysostom encourages his congregants to continue to push forward in their sanctification because they have been justified by Christ. John argues that the Christian's justification is the motivation for acts such as generosity, prayer, fasting, and forgiving those who have offended them. In effect, John contends that once one gains the position of righteousness, one is then obligated to obtain a practical righteousness. But how can one gain such a practical righteousness? According to Chrysostom, this practical righteousness was obtainable by following the directions God has provided through the Scriptures.

In "Homily 7 on the Gospel of John," as mentioned, Chrysostom notes that humanity's rebelliousness pushes people to cross the boundaries God establishes through his word.[77] The only solution to this rebelliousness is to embrace the Scriptures so that one does not exceed the limits placed upon them. As Chrysostom writes,

> Now what anger this excites, it needs not that you who know should learn from us. Abstaining therefore from their madness, let us tremble at his words, that he may continually build us up. For, "upon whom shall I look," says he, "but upon the lowly, and quiet, and who fears my words?"[78]

Here, quoting from Isaiah 66:2, John argues that adherence to the words of God invites God's favor upon the Christian and gives him the guidance he needs to navigate the Christian life successfully.

While John Chrysostom's teachings were primarily expositional in nature, he often addressed issues with which many in his congregation were struggling. As he addressed these issues, he sought to bring the scriptural admonitions into the discussion, encouraging his congregants to look at their lives through a biblical lens. This is especially true when John sought to instruct his hearers on how to raise their children to be Christians.

In his short book *On Vainglory and the Education of Children*, Chrysostom aimed to instruct parents how they might raise their children to be Christians through early Christian training in the home.[79] Chrysostom encouraged Christian parents to instruct their children to be moral through stories, as was common in the culture. However, Chrysostom contended

---

76. Chrysostom, "Homily 7 on the Gospel of John."
77. Chrysostom, "Homily 7 on the Gospel of John."
78. Chrysostom, "Homily 7 on the Gospel of John."
79. Liebeschuetz, *Ambrose and John Chrysostom*, 199.

that the stories shared by Christians should come from the Scriptures as opposed to mythology or history.[80] Chrysostom's admonition to use the Scriptures as the foundation of a child's training is due to his belief that the Scriptures are able to lead a child to both salvation and sanctification. Chrysostom notes that there are several benefits from such an education. On the benefit of learning the story of Cain and Abel, Chrysostom writes,

> The soul indeed, as it receives the story within itself before thou hast elaborated it, is aware that it will benefit. Nevertheless, do thou say hereafter: "Thou dost see how great a sin is greed, how great a sin it is to envy a brother. Thou dost see how great a sin it is to think that thou canst hide aught from God; for he sees all things, even those that are done in secret." If only thou sowest the seed of this teaching in the child, he will not need his tutor, since this fear that comes from God, this complete fear has possessed the boy instead and shakes his soul. This is not all. Go, leading him by the hand in church and pay heed particularly when this tale is read aloud. Thou wilt see him rejoice and leap with pleasure because he knows what the other children do not know, as he anticipates the story, recognizes it, and derives great gain from it. And hereafter the episode is fixed in his memory. He can profit in other ways from the story. So let him learn from thee: "There is no reason for grief in adversity. God shows this from the very first in the example of this boy, seeing that he received one who was righteous through death into heaven."[81]

In a similar fashion, John argues that children will find value in the story of Jacob and Esau:

> First, children learn to reverence and honor their fathers, when they see so keen a rivalry for the father's blessing. And they will sooner suffer a myriad stripes than to hear their parents curse them. If a story can so master the children's soul that it is thought worthy of belief, the veritable truth, it will surely enthrall them and fill them with great awe. Again, they must learn to despise the belly; for the story must also show them that he gained nothing by being first-born and the elder. Because of the greed of his belly he belayed the advantage of his birthright.[82]

---

80. Liebeschuetz, *Ambrose and John Chrysostom*, 199.

81. Chrysostom, "An Address on Vainglory and the Right Way for Parents to Bring Up Their Children."

82. Chrysostom, "An Address on Vainglory and the Right Way for Parents to Bring Up Their Children."

John also considers the responsibility that parents have to expose their children to the Scriptures over the course of several homilies. While preaching on Colossians 3:16, Chrysostom notes,

> But now your children will utter songs and dances of Satan, like cooks, and caterers, and musicians; no one knows any psalm, but it seems a thing to be ashamed of even, a mockery, and a joke. There is the treasury house of all these evils. For whatsoever soil the plant stands in, such is the fruit it bears; if in a sandy and salty soil, of like nature is its fruit; if in a sweet and rich one, it is again similar. So the matter of instruction is a sort of fountain. Teach him to sing those psalms which are so full of the love of wisdom ... When in these you have led him on from childhood, by little and little you will lead him forward even to the higher things.[83]

Chrysostom again revisits this theme while considering Ephesians 6:4:

> Do you wish your son to be obedient? From the very first, "Bring him up in the chastening and admonition of the Lord." Never deem it an unnecessary thing that he should be a diligent hearer of the divine Scriptures. For there the first thing he hears will be this: "Honor thy father and thy mother"; so that this makes for you. Never say, this is the business of monks. Am I making a monk of him? No. There is no need he should become a monk. Why be so afraid of a thing so replete with so much advantage? Make him a Christian. For it is of all things necessary for laymen to be acquainted with the lessons derived from this source; but especially for children. For theirs is an age full of folly; and to this folly are superadded the bad examples derived from the heathen tales, where they are made acquainted with those heroes so admired amongst them ... [A child] requires therefore the remedies against these things. How is it not absurd to send children out to trades, and to school, and to do all you can for these objects, and yet not to "bring them up in the chastening and admonition of the Lord?" And for this reason truly we are the first to reap the fruits, because we bring up our children to be insolent and profligate, disobedient, and mere vulgar fellows. Let us not then do this; no, let us listen to this blessed Apostle's admonition. "Let us bring them up in the chastening and admonition of the Lord." Let us give them a pattern. Let us make them from the earliest age apply themselves to the reading of the Scriptures ... Study not to make him an orator, but train him up

---

83. Chrysostom, "Homily 9 on Colossians."

to be a [Christian] philosopher. In the want of the one there will be no harm whatever; in the absence of the other, all the rhetoric in the world will be of no advantage. Tempers are wanted, not talking; character, not cleverness; deeds, not word. These gain a man the kingdom. These confer what are benefits indeed. Whet not his tongue, but cleanse his soul. I do not say this to prevent your teaching him these things, but to prevent your attending to them exclusively. Do not imagine that the monk alone stands in need of these lessons from Scripture. Of all others, the children just about to enter into the world specially need them.[84]

When considering the often-difficult interpersonal relationships within a family, Chrysostom once again directs people to find guidance through the Scriptures. In his work *On Wealth and Poverty*, Chrysostom writes,

This, also, I am ever urging, and shall not cease to urge, that you give attention, not only to the words spoken, but that also, when at home in your house, you exercise yourselves constantly in reading the Divine Scriptures. This, also, I have never ceased to press upon those who come to me privately. Let not any one say to me that these exhortations are vain and irrelevant, for "I am constantly busy in the courts," (suppose him to say;) "I am discharging public duties; I am engaged in some art or handiwork; I have a wife; I am bringing up my children; I have to manage a household; I am full of worldly business; it is not for me to read the Scriptures, but for those who have bid adieu to the world, for those who dwell on the summit of the hills; those who constantly lead a secluded life." What dost thou say, O man? Is it not for thee to attend to the Scriptures, because thou art involved in numerous cares? It is thy duty even more than theirs, for they do not so much need the aid to be derived from the Holy Scriptures as they do who are engaged in much business.[85]

In *On Wealth and Poverty*, John notes that one encounters a myriad of struggles as a husband and father and that each of these struggles can be overcome through the direction provided through the Scriptures. When considering the Christian's sanctification, Chrysostom frequently employed athletic metaphors, similar in nature to those used in Pauline writings.[86] John compared the life of a catechumen to that of an athlete in training, who

---

84. Chrysostom, "Homily 21 on Ephesians."
85. Allen, *Four Discourses on Chrysostom*, 60–62.
86. Sawhill, "Use of Athletic Metaphors," 10.

then enters into competition once he is baptized.[87] To prepare for the trials of competition, John prescribes the Scriptures to train and encourage the Christian to remain true to his calling. He argues,

> Great is the profit to be derived from the sacred Scriptures and their assistance is sufficient for every need. Paul was pointing this out when he said, "Whatever things have been written have been written for our instruction, upon whom the final age of the world has come, that through the patience and the consolation afforded by the Scriptures we may have hope." The divine words, indeed, are a treasury containing every sort of remedy, so that, whether one needs to put down senseless pride, or to quench the fire of concupiscence or to trample on the love of riches, or to despise pain, or to cultivate cheerfulness and acquire patience— in them one may find in abundance the means to do so.[88]

From a brief survey of John Chrysostom's writings it becomes evident that Chrysostom believed that the Scriptures should be considered a priority in the life of the Christian. Based upon his contention that knowledge of the Scriptures is a necessary component to one's salvation and sanctification, Chrysostom regularly implored his hearers to take note of the words of the Scriptures in both their corporate and private times of worship.

JOHN CHRYSOSTOM'S USE OF SCRIPTURE IN HIS APOLOGETIC WRITINGS

While Christianity had gained a favored position within the Roman Empire by the beginning of the fourth century, challenges to the faith from the lost remained. During the years that encompass the end of the fourth and beginning of the fifth centuries, paganism experienced a number of minor renaissances. In AD 361, the last openly pagan emperor, Julian, came to power in Rome. Believing that the empire's decline was due to Christian influences and a rejection of the old gods, Julian sought to restore paganism within the ruling classes of the empire.[89] Writing at the beginning of the fourth century, Porphyry sought to exemplify pagan worship and denigrate Christian worship philosophically. His fifteen books, *Against Christians*, are regarded as "the most extensive and scholarly work composed against

---

87. Sawhill, "Use of Athletic Metaphors," 10.
88. Chrysostom, "Homily 37 (John 5.7–13)," 359.
89. Athanassiadi, *Julian: An Intellectual Biography*, 88.

Christianity in antiquity."[90] Refuting Porphyry's works occupied Christian apologists through the fourth and fifth centuries. It is estimated that by AD 400 more than 50 percent of the Roman Empire's citizens were Christians, meaning that there was still a tremendous need for evangelism.[91] Seeing the need for evangelism, Chrysostom frequently targeted Gothic soldiers and administrators brought to Constantinople for evangelism.[92] John also frequently encouraged his congregants to consider the eternal destinies of those who worked for them and he sought to send clergymen, especially ascetics, out to engage in missionary endeavors.[93] John himself sought to reach the lost through his preaching, personal evangelism, and by writing a series of apologetics aimed at defending the Christian faith and encouraging his readers to adopt the faith themselves. While Chrysostom does employ logic in his apologetic works as proof of the legitimacy of the Christian faith, it is so closely tied to scriptural references that he seemed to see rational arguments as supplements for his arguments from Scripture. Given his position that an exposure to God's word is a necessary component to producing faith, it should come as no surprise that he would give the Scriptures a position of priority in his apologetical works.

"Discourse on Blessed Babylas and against the Greeks"

In "Discourse on Blessed Babylas and against the Greeks," written in approximately AD 378,[94] Chrysostom responds to specific attacks on Chris-

90. Von Harnack, *Porphyrius*, "Gegen die Christen," 1, 3.
91. Stark, *Cities of God*, 183.
92. Momigliano, *Conflict between Paganism and Christianity*, 57.
93. While considering the crowd's response to Peter's Pentecost sermon, Chrysostom remarks on the individual's responsibility to evangelize those around them:

> Suppose an emperor had ordered thee to build a house that he might lodge there, wouldest thou not have done everything to please him? And here now it is palace of Christ, the church which thou buildest. Look not at the cost, but calculate the profit. Thy people yonder cultivate thy field: cultivate thou their souls: they bring to thee thy fruits, raise thou them to heaven. He that makes the beginning is the cause of all the rest: and thou wilt be the cause that the people are brought under Christian teaching both there, and in the neighboring estates. (Schaff, "Homily XVIII: Acts VII. 54," 118.)

In various homilies on the book of Ephesians, John criticizes ascetics who have chosen to live as hermits, completely disconnected from the world. John notes that if one completely abandons the world, it is impossible to influence others to become Christians. As such, it would be better for ascetics to seek to abstain from worldly pleasures, but remain among people for the purpose of evangelism.

94. In *Apologist*, it is noted that the date of "Discourse on Blessed Babylas and

tianity by such philosophers as Porphyry, Heraclitus, and Julian by using historical narratives and the arguments of fulfilled prophecies to prove Christ's divinity.[95] Chrysostom relates the story of St. Babylas, the bishop of Antioch, who was martyred during the Decian persecution and whose relics were believed to supernaturally suppress the worship at Daphne and silence the oracle of Apollo, as the backdrop for his apologetical argument for Christianity.

Chrysostom demonstrates his reliance upon the Scriptures as a means to salvation and sanctification as he begins his first apologetic by immediately turning to the Scriptures. Chrysostom begins his argument that Christianity is superior to paganism by quoting Christ, who promised his disciples that "he who believes in Me, the works that I do, he will do also; and greater works than these he will do" (John 14:12). John argues that, based upon this promise, Christianity is superior to other religions because it offers what no other religion can offer: a genuine change of life.[96] Furthermore, he argues that while pagan religions typically only concern themselves, Christianity demonstrates God's concern for all of humanity. Quoting from John 1:11, John argues that while Christ came to the Jewish people, he was rejected by his own people, yet continued his ministry for the

---

against the Greeks" authorship must be after AD 363 because the peace treaty between Persia and the Roman Empire made on the occasion of Emperor Julian's death is mentioned. It also must be written before AD 380, as it contains no reference to the martyr's shrine built for Babylas in Antioch, constructed by Bishop Meletius, which was completed in AD 380. In this work, Chrysostom notes that the relics of Babylas had been returned to their original resting place in the Christian cemetery in Antioch. In this writing, Chrysostom notes that twenty years had passed since the burning of the temple at Daphne, making AD 378 the approximate time of its composition. Chrysostom, "Discourse on Blessed Babylas and against the Greeks," 15–16.

95. While Chrysostom addressed the major criticisms of Christianity present in most pagan apologetics, it appears that "Discourse on Blessed Babylas and against the Greeks" was mostly inspired by Julian's philosophical and social attacks upon Christianity. Philosophically, Julian attacked the Christian faith in his *Three Treatises against the Christians*. In these works, Julian's primary criticism focused upon his claims that Christian history is fictitious, Jesus' teachings were inferior to those of pagan philosophers, and Christianity is harmful to society. Socially, Julian spent some time in Antioch and wished to revive the worship of Apollo there in the temple of Daphne. To that end, Julian ordered that the bones of St. Babylas be removed from the area, which provoked a number of protests from the city's Christian population.

Given that his "Discourse on Blessed Babylas and against the Greeks" considered the life of Babylas as an exemplar of Christian virtue and that Chrysostom defended the veracity of the apostle's writings, the indestructibility of the gospel, and the growth of the church, Chrysostom's primary purpose in penning this work was to argue against Julian's criticisms of Christianity.

96. Chrysostom, "Discourse on Blessed Babylas and against the Greeks," 1.

good of all people.⁹⁷ Continuing in this argument, Chrysostom also looks to the book of Acts, particularly Acts 19:12, to demonstrate that God's regard for all of humanity allowed people to be healed through the ministry of the apostles.⁹⁸

In his introduction to "Discourse on Blessed Babylas and against the Greeks," Chrysostom argues that pagan religions are the result of demonic attempts to subvert the gospel.⁹⁹ Chrysostom, however, argues from 1 Esdras 4:35 and Psalms 63:8 that these attempts to undermine the gospel are doomed to fail as the gospel is truth and, as such, indestructible.¹⁰⁰ Noting Luke 10:19, Chrysostom writes that because the gospel is truth, it enables Christians to endure persecution because they realize that the persecutions are, in fact, attempts by Satan to suppress the gospel.¹⁰¹

Another argument employed by Chrysostom to demonstrate the truth of Christianity is the personalities of the apostles who transmitted the gospel message. Chrysostom notes Acts 18 to remind his readers that Paul was a tentmaker, and Acts 22 to recall his place of birth. From Matthew 4, John writes that Peter was a fisherman. John also notes their simple nature by referencing Acts 4 to note that they could not even read or write. Chrysostom argues that if these simple men had been the progenitors of the gospel message, then the Christian religion would have failed. However, Christianity has thrived because the gospel message was not based on these men, but on the power of Christ working inside of them.¹⁰²

Following his initial argument that Christianity is superior to pagan religions because it offers a legitimate life change, Chrysostom then considers the life of Babylas as a case study. Babylas was the third-century bishop of Antioch who maintained his faith in Christ during the Decian persecution. Because of his confession of Christ, Babylas was imprisoned and died during his incarceration. Chrysostom recounts Babylas's life, giving particular attention to his high moral character. During his discussion of Babylas's life, Chrysostom makes numerous references to the Scriptures to demonstrate that Babylas's morality was not due to his upbringing or

97. Chrysostom, "Discourse on Blessed Babylas and against the Greeks, 8.

98. Chrysostom, "Discourse on Blessed Babylas and against the Greeks," 9.

99. Chrysostom, "Discourse on Blessed Babylas and against the Greeks," 2.

100. Chrysostom, "Discourse on Blessed Babylas and against the Greeks," 11.

101. Chrysostom continues this argument for a significant portion of his introduction. During this time, he also quotes Ephesians 6:12, noting that Christians are persecuted because they resist "against the principalities and the powers, against the world-rulers of the darkness of this age, against the spiritual forces of wickedness." Chrysostom, "Discourse on Blessed Babylas and against the Greeks," 12.

102. Chrysostom, "Discourse on Blessed Babylas and against the Greeks, 16.

philosophical enlightenment, but his faith. By continually comparing Babylas's moral character to that outlined in the Scriptures, Chrysostom seeks to demonstrate that it was God who shaped Babylas's character.

Chrysostom begins his biography of Babylas by recounting the crimes of an unknown political leader who he likens to the evil kings Ahab and Herod Antipas, who, historically, lived their lives in opposition to God.[103] In contrast to these men, John noted that Babylas maintained his dignity, even in the face of adversity, because he knew from the Scriptures that this world was but a temporary home.[104] However, while knowing that his time in this world was short, he maintained a "gentleness and sound judgment" with this leader because his "soul was seasoned with spiritual salt."[105] Chrysostom makes a special note of Babylas's boldness, tempered by gentleness, arguing that its rarity should cause others to take note. Chrysostom quotes 2 Samuel 16:7 to demonstrate that many have boldness without gentleness, which is a trait of godlessness.[106] Chrysostom argues that Babylas was able to maintain both the boldness of his convictions and his gentleness because of his faith, thus further demonstrating the superior nature of Christianity.

In his introductory remarks on the life of Babylas, Chrysostom references Romans 14:10, 2 Corinthians 5:10, Matthew 13:42, and Sirach 4:22 to note that the understanding of a future judgment was a driving force in Babylas's desire to maintain his convictions.[107] As John continued to recount the life, trials, and aftermath of Babylas's life, he quoted or alluded to the Scriptures more than forty times to demonstrate that Babylas's morality and perseverance during his persecution was based upon his faith in God. After considering Babylas's example, Chrysostom concludes that Christianity is superior to the pagan religions, as the Christian God fulfills the promises he makes in the Christian Scriptures. Chrysostom writes,

---

103. Chrysostom, "Discourse on Blessed Babylas and against the Greeks," 30. In his description of this leader, John argues that his generally immoral nature proves that those who sin are slaves to sin, thus proving the truth of Jesus' words in John 8:34.

104. Chrysostom, "Discourse on Blessed Babylas and against the Greeks," 34. John echoes 1 Chronicles 29:15, Job 8:9, and Psalms 143:4 that this earth is but a "shadow," and Job 20:8 that it is a "dream."

105. Chrysostom, "Discourse on Blessed Babylas and against the Greeks," 36. Referencing Colossians 4:5–6, "Conduct yourselves with wisdom toward outsiders, making the most of the opportunity. Let your speech always be with grace, as though seasoned with salt, so that you will know how you should respond to each person."

106. Chrysostom, "Discourse on Blessed Babylas and against the Greeks," 38. This refers to David's encounter with Shimei during his flight from Saul. Shimei demonstrated boldness by taunting David, but lacked sound judgment because he overstepped his bounds by cursing a man anointed by God.

107. Chrysostom, "Discourse on Blessed Babylas and against the Greeks," 51.

Such is the power of the martyrs during life, after death, when they are present in a place, and again when they leave it behind. The fact is that from beginning to end his accomplishments were joined together in a continuous sequence. Observe: he defended the outraged laws of God; exacted proper punishment in behalf of the deceased; showed the great gulf between priesthood and kingly office; put an end to all mundane vanity and trampled underfoot the fantasy of existence; taught emperors not to carry their authority beyond the measure given them by God; and showed bishops how they ought to exercise this office. These accomplishments and more than these were his when he was in the flesh; when he died and departed, he put an end to the strength of the demon; utterly refuted the deceit of the Greeks; exposed the nonsense of divination, shattered its mask, and displayed all its hypocrisy laid bare, having silenced and defeated by main force the one who seemed to be its master. Even now the walls of the temple are standing, proclaiming to all the shame, ridicule, and weakness of the demon; the crowns, victory, and strength of the martyr. So great is the power of the saints, so invincible and fearsome, both to emperors, and to demons, and to the chief of the demon himself.[108]

"Demonstration against the Pagans That Christ Is God"

The "Demonstration against the Pagans That Christ Is God" is one of Chrysostom's earlier works and represents his basic contribution to apologetics. Chrysostom argues for Christ's divinity in the fulfillment of Old Testament prophecies and in Christ's own prophecies, particularly those on the phenomenal growth of the church, to provide proof that Christianity gives its followers access to a power that can only be divine.

Chrysostom begins his apologetic by considering a fact that the pagans in Roman society could not dispute—the exponential growth of the Christian religion.[109] Chrysostom notes that the Christian faith has spread across the known world without force of arms, despite its humble beginnings from "only eleven men to start with, men who were undistinguished, without learning, ill-informed, destitute, poorly clad, without weapons, or sandals, men who had but a single tunic to wear."[110] Chrysostom notes that Christ:

108. Chrysostom, "Discourse on Blessed Babylas and against the Greeks," 127.
109. John Chrysostom, "Demonstration against the Pagans," 48.
110. John Chrysostom, "Demonstration against the Pagans That Christ Is God" 1.7.

succeeded in winning over these men to drag down their ancestral laws, to tear out their ancient customs, long and deeply rooted as they were, and to plant in their place other ways, which led them from the easygoing life to his own program of austerity. And he succeeded in doing this when the whole world was waging war against him, when they jeered at him and forced him to endure the most shameful death on a cross.[111]

Chrysostom lays the foundation that Christ is indeed divine, and that non-Christians should consider the accounts of Christ found in the Scriptures.

Once Chrysostom has asserted the fact that Christianity was indeed spreading throughout the known world, he used that truth as a bridge to invite his readers to consider the biblical evidence of Christianity. Chrysostom turns to an argument that was common for patristic apologists—analyzing Old Testament prophecies to prove that Jesus was the expected Jewish Messiah. In the course of his argument, Chrysostom draws primarily from the books of Isaiah and Psalms to prove it was predicted that Jesus would be born of a virgin,[112] come from Davidic lineage,[113] come to bring peace,[114] and be born in Bethlehem[115] during a time that Israel was under Roman control.[116] Furthermore, he noted that it was predicted that Herod would seek to kill Christ,[117] causing him to spend time in Egypt.[118] Then, as a man, it was foretold that Jesus would perform miracles[119] and preach

---

In his description of the apostles, John alludes to Matthew 10:10, Mark 6:8, and Luke 9:3, demonstrating his view that it was a reliable source of information that was able to change the hearts and minds of the pagans he was addressing.

111. John Chrysostom, "Demonstration against the Pagans That Christ Is God" 1.8.

112. Chrysostom, "Demonstration against the Pagans" 2.4. Here, Chrysostom quotes from Isaiah 7:14.

113. Chrysostom, "Demonstration against the Pagans" 2.5. Here, Chrysostom quotes from Isaiah 11:1–3 to reference Jesus' decent from Jesse.

114. Chrysostom, "Demonstration against the Pagans" 2.8. Here, Chrysostom quotes from Isaiah 9:7.

115. Chrysostom, "Demonstration against the Pagans" 3.3. Here, Chrysostom quotes from Micah 5:1.

116. Chrysostom, "Demonstration against the Pagans" 3.6. Here, Chrysostom quotes from Genesis 49:10.

117. Chrysostom, "Demonstration against the Pagans" 3.7. Here, Chrysostom quotes from Jeremiah 31:15.

118. Chrysostom, "Demonstration against the Pagans." Here, Chrysostom quotes from Hosea 11:1.

119. Chrysostom, "Demonstration against the Pagans" 3.8. Here, Chrysostom quotes from Isaiah 8:23.

to the poor.[120] Chrysostom also writes that Jesus' betrayal,[121] execution,[122] burial,[123] and resurrection[124] were all predicted in the Old Testament Scriptures. John also notes that the Old Testament predicted the success of the Christian church[125] and Jesus' imminent return to judge the living and the dead.[126] These predictions presented in the Old Testament and fulfilled by Jesus in the New Testament led Chrysostom to conclude that Christianity is the one and only true religion. Chrysostom concludes,

> Do you not see how precisely the prophets took up each point and predicted what was going to happen? How, then, can you have the boldness to refuse to believe, even though you have been given such proofs of his power, even though you hear the words which foretold it so long beforehand, even though you see that events did occur to match the predictions and that everything which the prophets foretold has been fulfilled to the last detail?[127]

Once Chrysostom had established that Jesus fulfilled the predictions of the Jewish Messiah as predicted in the Old Testament, he then turns his attention to the words of Christ himself concerning the church and the Jewish temple. Regarding the church, Chrysostom focuses upon Christ's promise that the church will succeed, as predicted in Matthew 16:18:

> When only twelve disciples followed him, neither the reality nor even the name of a church occurred to anyone. The synagogue was still flourishing. Why, then, did he speak of the church and predict it at a time when practically the whole world was in the grip of godlessness? "Upon this rock I shall build my church, and the gates of hell shall not prevail against it." Put this prediction

---

120. Chrysostom, "Demonstration against the Pagans" 4.1. Here, Chrysostom quotes from Psalm 77:2, Psalm 44:3, Isaiah 52:13, and Isaiah 61:1.

121. Chrysostom, "Demonstration against the Pagans" 4.4. Here, Chrysostom quotes from Psalm 40:10.

122. Chrysostom, "Demonstration against the Pagans" 4.6. Here, Chrysostom quotes from Psalm 2:1–3.

123. Chrysostom, "Demonstration against the Pagans" 4.12. Here, Chrysostom quotes from Psalm 87:7.

124. Chrysostom, "Demonstration against the Pagans" 4.15. Here, Chrysostom quotes from Psalm 46:5.

125. Chrysostom, "Demonstration against the Pagans" 5.1. Here, Chrysostom quotes from Psalm 67:11.

126. Chrysostom, "Demonstration against the Pagans" 8.1. Here, Chrysostom quotes from Malachi 3:2 and Psalm 49:3.

127. Chrysostom, "Demonstration against the Pagans" 1.4.

of Christ to whatever test you wish and you will see that its truth shines brightly forth. For it is a marvel not only that he built the church throughout the world but that he kept it unconquered even though it was harassed by so many assaults. The words: "The gates of hell shall not prevail against it," mean the dangers which beget death, the dangers which lead us down to hell. Do you not see that this prediction came true? Do you not see the strength of its fulfillment? Do you not see the words shining forth as proved in the light of the facts?[128]

Concerning the fate of the temple, John notes that Jesus predicted that the Jewish temple would be destroyed in Matthew 24:2:

One day he entered the Jewish temple area, which at that time was flourishing. On every side its magnificent structures shone with gold and beauty. No expense had been spared on its workmanship or materials. His disciples were amazed. But what did he say to them? "Do you see all these things? Amen I say to you, there will not be left here one stone upon another." He was revealing the future destruction of the temple, the utter ruin, the desolation, the wreckage which now exists in Jerusalem. For all those glorious and splendid buildings are now in ruins.[129]

In these closing chapters of "Demonstration against the Pagans That Christ Is God," Chrysostom seeks to use the words of Christ in the same fashion that he used the words of the Old Testament. He contends that the fulfillment of the Old Testament prophecies point to Jesus being the foretold Messiah—a fact then confirmed by the realization of Jesus' own prophecies.

CONCLUSION

John Chrysostom wrote his apologetical works relatively late in the patristic era and following a similar pattern to his predecessors, despite the fact that he wrote in a period when Christianity had been normalized in Roman society. Unlike his predecessors, Chrysostom did not find himself in a spiritual minority. While those who wrote prior to him found themselves arguing to people steeped in paganism, John wrote to a society familiar with Christianity that was seeking to revive the pagan faiths. Even though Chrysostom was writing to a vastly different audience making very different counterclaims to Christianity, he continued to rely on Scripture as his

---

128. Chrysostom, "Demonstration against the Pagans" 12.1.
129. Chrysostom, "Demonstration against the Pagans" 16.4.

primary source to convince the lost of the truth of the Christian faith. This is due to his conviction that the Scriptures were a necessary component of evangelism that led people to faith in Christ and then instructed them toward a practical righteousness.

6

The Use of Scripture in the Evangelistic Writings of John of Damascus

Following the division of the Roman Empire between eastern and western halves, the empire began to decay at an accelerated pace. This decay was most evident in the less prosperous Roman west. As soon as the early fifth century, the western portion of the Roman Empire began breaking down into its constituent states, which began to reassert their own regional independence or began to fall under the control of Germanic tribes.[1] Throughout the fifth century, all of the Western Roman Empire was conquered by Germanic invaders, including the city of Rome itself in AD 476 at the hands of a Germanic Roman general named Odoacer, which is the event most historians see as the official end of the Roman Empire.[2]

The decline of the Eastern Roman Empire was less pronounced than the collapse of the West. In many respects, the Roman Empire was remade in the city of Byzantium, where a mirror government was established. Like in the west, the eastern empire was ruled by an emperor with a senate, and it maintained many of its traditions, though it became heavily influenced by the political theories of the east.[3] While the eastern Byzantine Empire persisted for another millennium after the fall of the West, it persisted in the

---

1. Rostovtzeff, *Rome*, 309.
2. Cameron, *Oi Buzantinoi*, 52.
3. Rostovtzeff, *Rome*, 309.

face of a number of challenges. One of the more persistent challenges the Byzantines faced was the rise of Islam and the Caliphates.

Islam began in the early seventh century with the preaching of Muhammad ibn-Abdullah, who was born in AD 570.[4] As a youth, Muhammad participated in the polytheistic pagan worship common in the Arabian Peninsula until confronted by his monotheistic uncle who refused to eat with him, as the food he was eating was sacrificed to a false god, and his uncle would only eat food dedicated to the "one true god."[5] After this encounter, Muhammad stopped practicing pagan sacrifices and began his own path to monotheism.[6] This path continued until AD 610, when Muhammad claimed to have received "the first revelations of the Quran in Mecca" and began preaching in Mecca soon thereafter.[7] In *The History of Islam*, Robert Payne recounts Muhammad's story of his first revelation from Allah while waiting out a storm in a cave just outside of Mecca:

> He was lying asleep or in a trance, wrapped in his cloak, when he heard a voice saying: "Read!" He answered: "I cannot read." The voice said again: "Read!" He answered: "I do not know how to read." Once more, this time with terrible force, the voice said: "Read!" He answered: "What can I read?" The voice thundered:
>
> Read in the name of your Lord, the Creator, Who created man from a clot of blood!
>
> Read! Your Lord is most merciful, For he has taught men by the pen And revealed the mysteries to them!
>
> He was shown a scroll, which seemed to be of silk with letters of fire written on it. He read the words, though he had never read before, and when he awoke, he remembered them, for they were "as though written upon his heart." Trembling, he went out of the cave onto the hillside, not knowing what had happened to him . . . and then he heard a voice from heaven saying: "O Muhammad! You are Allah's messenger, and I am Gabriel!" Lifting up his eyes he saw "about two bowshots away" the figure of an angel standing in the sky.[8]

When Muhammad began preaching his new faith in Mecca, he soon found himself at odds with the Meccan establishment. When Muhammad began his preaching, his few followers were subjected to mockery for their

4. Aslan, *No god but God*, 18.
5. Aslan, *No god but God*, 16.
6. Aslan, *No god but God*, 16.
7. Armstrong, *Islam*, xiii.
8. Payne, *History of Islam*, 14.

beliefs, but as Muhammad's followers increased, so too did the resistance against the new religion.[9] Eventually, Muslims among Mecca's lower classes began to be subjected to torture for their adherence to Islam.[10] As Muhammad's relationship with Mecca's leadership deteriorated, Arabs from Yathrib (later Medina) reached out to Muhammad and offered him a place where he and his followers could live in peace. This offer of asylum led to the AD 622 *Hijrah*, or migration, of Muslims from Mecca to Yathrib and is typically seen as the event that marks the beginning of the Muslim era.[11]

While his relocation to Yathrib provided Muhammad and his followers some respite, it did not end his hostile relationship with the people of Mecca. Between AD 624 and 630, Muhammad and his growing confederacy of tribal allies won a series of battles against the Meccans, leading to the eventual surrender of Mecca to Muhammad.[12] Two years after his conquest of Mecca, Muhammad died, leaving his close companion Abu Bakr to consolidate Muhammad's conquests, resulting in the Riddah wars.[13] After a brief two-year rule, Abu Bakr died and was succeeded by Umar ibn al-Khattab.[14] After his ascendance to the position of Caliph, Umar began his campaigns into both the Byzantine and Persian empires. Umar's armies pushed into Jerusalem, Egypt, and Syria, where the city of Damascus fell under Islamic control in AD 635.[15]

The rapid expansion of the Islamic Caliphate did, however, present several challenges. One challenge was that many leaders who had learned to govern in a tribal setting were ill-equipped to govern in an imperial setting. As such, Islamic governors frequently employed former Byzantine officials to help them in the administration of their new holdings. One such official retained from the Byzantine era was Mansour ibn Sarjun, who had been responsible for the taxes of the region during the reign of Emperor Heraclius, and was later given the task of surrendering Damascus to Khalid ibn al-Walid.[16] Eventually, Mansour would become the chief financial officer in the city of Damascus.[17] Mansour's son succeeded his position and

---

9. Najeebabadi, *History of Islam*, 107.
10. Najeebabadi, *History of Islam*, 109.
11. Armstrong, *Islam*, xiii.
12. Armstrong, *Islam*, xiv.
13. Najeebabadi, *History of Islam*, 265.
14. Armstrong, *Islam*, xiv.
15. Aslan, *No god but God*, 124.
16. Janosik, *John of Damascus*, 25.
17. Janosik, *John of Damascus*, 26.

continued to serve the Caliphs, as did his grandson, John of Damascus.[18] Not only was John a skilled administrator within the Islamic government; he was also a devoted Christian thinker. His unique position within both Islamic and Christian circles enabled him to powerfully proclaim the gospel of Jesus Christ to his Muslim neighbors.

BIOGRAPHY

Beyond the basic facts of John of Damascus's life, little is known of his personal background. Traditionally, the primary source of John of Damascus's biography was found in an eleventh-century writing attributed to John, the Patriarch of Jerusalem.[19] While modern scholars doubt the historicity of the *Life* of John of Damascus, regarding it as a hagiography, the influence it has had upon the understanding of John's life is considerable and worthy of mention.[20]

The *Life* of John of Damascus records that John came from a devout Christian family employed as administrators in the Syrian Caliphate. John's father, who often sought to purchase and liberate Christian slaves, met an Italian monk named Comas who had been taken as a slave during the Islamic expansion.[21] After discovering that Comas was well educated, John's father secured his release so that he could tutor John.[22] Under Comas's direction, John excelled in his studies of geometry, astronomy, and theology until he exhausted Comas's knowledge. After deciding that there was no more that he could teach John, Comas tenured his resignation to John's father and retired to the monastery of St. Sabas near Jerusalem.[23]

After his father's death, John was summonsed to court, where he was named the chief councilor.[24] As John of Damascus was assuming his duties in the Syrian Caliphate, the iconoclastic controversy occurred after Emperor Leo III issued his first edict against the use of icons in worship.[25] John of Damascus responded to Leo's edict with a series of circular letters supporting the use of icons in worship. Leo sought to silence John's dissent, but

---

18. Janosik, *John of Damascus*, 27.
19. Chase, *Saint John of Damascus: Writings*, v.
20. Chase, *Saint John of Damascus: Writings*, vi.
21. Lupton, *St. John of Damascus*, 26.
22. Lupton, *St. John of Damascus*, 27.
23. Lupton, *St. John of Damascus*, 27.
24. Lupton, *St. John of Damascus*, 27.
25. Encylopaedia Britannica, "Iconoclastic Controversy."

could not do so by force because John was outside of the Roman Empire.[26] Because he could not take John by force, Leo instead had his scribes forge a letter from John offering the surrender of Damascus to Leo.[27] In response to his suppose sedition, the Caliph ordered that John's right hand be cut off and hung in the marketplace.[28] After being reunited with his hand, John spent the night praying to the Virgin Mary that his hand would be restored to him. After he fell asleep, the *Life* of John of Damascus purports that Mary visited him in a dream, and upon awaking, John discovered that his hand had been reattached to his body.[29] Following this miracle that perplexed the Muslims around him, John of Damascus chose to resign his position within the Syrian Caliphate and retire to the monastery of St. Sabas with his old teacher Cosmas.[30] While in the monastery of St. Sabas, John of Damascus endured a number of trials until his death.[31]

While the Patriarch of Jerusalem's *Life* of John of Damascus reflects a hagiographical version of John's biography, it does follow the basic outline of what is known of John of Damascus's life. While John of Damascus's birth date is unknown, it is generally agreed that he was born in the last quarter of the seventh century AD.[32] Additionally, John of Damascus did come from an influential Christian family. His grandfather, Mansour ibn Sarjun, was a financial officer in the city of Damascus when it was conquered by Khalid ibn al-Walid in AD 635.[33] Mansour maintained this position within the new Syrian Caliphate and passed the position down to his son and grandson.[34]

It is also true that John of Damascus did defend the use of icons in worship in opposition to the edicts made by Leo III. His three treatises against Leo in defense of iconography are still today lauded as "such a complete defense of the veneration of sacred images based upon Scripture, tradition, and reason that in subsequent ages and down to the present day there is no need to add to it."[35] However, while John of Damascus received a number of anathemas due to his position on iconography, there is no evidence that it caused him trouble within the Caliphate.

26. Lupton, *St. John of Damascus*, 28.
27. Lupton, *St. John of Damascus*, 28.
28. Lupton, *St. John of Damascus*, 29.
29 Lupton, *St. John of Damascus*, 29.
30. Lupton, *St. John of Damascus*, 30.
31. Lupton, *St. John of Damascus*, 35.
32. Janosik, *John of Damascus*, 23.
33. Chase, *Saint John of Damascus*, ix.
34. Chase, *Saint John of Damascus*, ix.
35. Chase, *Saint John of Damascus*, xiii.

Furthermore, John did retire to the monastery of St. Sabas after retiring from public service. This transition to the ascetic life, however, was not spurred on by any miraculous recovery. Instead, John of Damascus transitioned away from government service when the Caliph al-Walid changed the Caliphate's recordkeeping from Greek to Arabic, making John's service unnecessary in al-Walid's government.[36] It does not appear that the monks at St. Sabas were particularly harsh toward John during his time at the monastery. John was frequently referred to as both a "priest and a monk" during this period of his life, and as a "presbyter of the Holy Resurrection of Christ our God," suggesting that he was ordained to the ministry during this time and perhaps ventured into Muslim-controlled Jerusalem to minister to the Christian population still living there.[37] John also dedicated much of his time at St. Sabas to studying and writing; in fact, it is believed that the vast majority of John's writings were composed during his time at the monastery.[38] John of Damascus remained at St. Sabas until his death on November 4, 749.[39] After his death, he was buried at St. Sabas, but his relics were later moved to Constantinople in the fourteenth century.[40]

JOHN OF DAMASCUS'S THEOLOGY OF SCRIPTURE

What John of Damascus Viewed as Scripture

Born in the late seventh century, John of Damascus lived and ministered after the Synod of Carthage had met in 397. By this time, the question of what constituted the canon of Scripture was largely settled. The Synod of Carthage decreed,

> The canonical Scriptures are these: Genesis, Exodus, Leviticus, Numbers, Deuteronomy, Joshua the son of Nun, Judges, Ruth, four books of Kings, two books of Paraleipomena, Job, the Psalter, five books of Solomon, the books of the twelve Prophets, Isaiah, Jeremiah, Ezechiel, Daniel, Tobit, Judith, Esther, two books of Esdras, two books of the Maccabees. Of the New Testament: four books of the Gospels, one book of the Acts of the Apostles, thirteen Epistles of the Apostle Paul, one Epistle of the same

36. Louth, *St. John Damascene*, 6.
37. Louth, *St. John Damascene*, 6.
38. Louth, *St. John Damascene*, 7.
39. Chase, *Saint John of Damascus*, xvii.
40. Chase, *Saint John of Damascus*, xvii.

[writer] to the Hebrews, two Epistles of the Apostle Peter, three of John, one of James, one of Jude, one book of the Apocalypse of John . . . Let this be made known also to our brother and fellow-priest Boniface, or to other bishops of those parts, for the purpose of confirming that canon, because we have received from our fathers that those books must be read in the church.[41]

While the list of works generated by the Synod of Carthage established a baseline of what writings were considered canonical in the west, one can see that John of Damascus, ministering in the east, had a slightly different view of what constituted authoritative Scripture. In the third book of his magnum opus, *Fount of Wisdom*, John discusses the nature and value of the Scriptures and then concludes his chapter with a list of works he considers to be canon:

> Observe, further, that there are two and twenty books of the Old Testament, one for each letter of the Hebrew tongue. For there are twenty-two letters of which five are double, and so they come to be twenty-seven. For the letters Caph, Mere, Nun, Pe, Sade are double. And thus the number of the books in this way is twenty-two, but is found to be twenty-seven because of the double character of five. For Ruth is joined on to Judges, and the Hebrews count them one book: the first and second books of Kings are counted one: and so are the third and fourth books of Kings: and also the first and second of Paraleipomena: and the first and second of Esdra. In this way, then, the books are collected together in four Pentateuchs and two others remain over, to form thus the canonical books. Five of them are of the Law, viz. Genesis, Exodus, Leviticus, Numbers, Deuteronomy. This which is the code of the Law, constitutes the first Pentateuch. Then comes another Pentateuch, the so-called Grapheia, or as they are called by some, the Hagiographa, which are the following: Jesus the Son of Nave, Judges along with Ruth, first and second Kings, which are one book, third and fourth Kings, which are one book, and the two books of the Paraleipomena which are one book. This is the second Pentateuch. The third Pentateuch is the books in verse, viz. Job, Psalms, Proverbs of Solomon, Ecclesiastes of Solomon, and the Song of Songs of Solomon. The fourth Pentateuch is the Prophetical books, viz the twelve prophets constituting one book, Isaiah, Jeremiah, Ezekiel, Daniel. Then come the two books of Esdra made into one, and Esther. There are also the Panaretus, that is the Wisdom of Solomon, and the Wisdom of Jesus, which

---

41. Westcott, *General Survey*, 408.

> was published in Hebrew by the father of Sirach, and afterwards translated into Greek by his grandson, Jesus, the Son of Sirach. These are virtuous and noble, but are not counted nor were they placed in the ark.
>
> The New Testament contains four gospels, that according to Matthew, that according to Mark, that according to Luke, that according to John: the Acts of the Holy Apostles by Luke the Evangelist: seven catholic epistles, viz. one of James, two of Peter, three of John, one of Jude: fourteen letters of the Apostle Paul: the Revelation of John the Evangelist: the canons of the holy apostles, by Clement.[42]

While John is largely in agreement with the eastern church concerning the Scriptures, he does deviate from the Byzantine church in that he refers to the Wisdom of Solomon and the Wisdom of Jesus as "virtuous and noble" but then argues that they "are not counted nor were they placed in the ark."[43] While John considered these to not be Scripture, the Byzantine church did consider these works to be Scripture.[44] Furthermore, John lists the Catholic Epistles before the Pauline, following the eastern order of the New Testament.[45] Also, John of Damascus oddly lists "the canons of the holy apostles by Clement" as a part of his New Testament. While this is certainly an aberration this late in the patristic period, John is not the first to argue that Clement's writings should be considered Scripture.[46]

John of Damascus on the Authorship of Scripture

While John largely accepted the Synod of Carthage's pronouncement on what writings should be considered Scripture, he did not believe that the Bible was a product of human endeavor. Instead, John of Damascus believed that the Bible was authored by God himself. In his chapter "On Scripture" in *Fount of Wisdom*, John quotes from Hebrews 1 when he notes,

> And again . . . and the Apostle too, says: "God, who, at sundry times and in diverse manners, spoke in times past to the fathers by the prophets, last of all, in these days, hath spoken to us by

---

42. John of Damascus, *Fount of Wisdom* 3:17, in Chase, *Saint John of Damascus*, 376.
43. John of Damascus, *Fount of Wisdom* 3:17, in Chase, *Saint John of Damascus*, 376.
44. Louth, *St. John Damascene*, 186.
45. Louth, *St. John Damascene*, 186.
46. Louth, *St. John Damascene*, 186.

his Son." Through the Holy Ghost, then, both the Law and the Prophets, the evangelists, apostles, pastors, and teachers spoke.[47]

Here, John acknowledges the fact that God used human agents to produce the texts of Scripture and yet the texts they produced accurately record the words of God because these human authors wrote through the inspiration of the Holy Spirit. Thus, using contemporary terminology, one could say that John of Damascus held to the verbal theory of scriptural interpretation.[48]

John of Damascus on the Purpose of Scripture

In *Fount of Wisdom*, John of Damascus briefly presents his views of the Scriptures. In his section dedicated to the Scriptures, John argues that the Scriptures were authored by God and were valuable in that they could lead a person to salvation and sanctification. Therefore, the Christian should read the Scriptures with enthusiasm.

John of Damascus on the Scriptures' Role in Salvation

John of Damascus begins his treatise on the Scriptures by noting that the Scriptures point to God. Referencing Matthew 5:17, John writes, "The God proclaimed by the Old Testament and the New is one he who is celebrated and glorified in Trinity, for the Lord said: 'I am not come to destroy the law, but to fulfill.'"[49] John begins his discussion of the Scriptures by arguing that God himself is the lead character in the Bible and that the Scriptures all point to him and his redemptive work in Christ. Thus, because all Scripture points to God, one can find a salvific relationship with God by studying the Scriptures. Echoing John 5:39, John notes, "For he worked our salvation, for the sake of which all Scripture and every mystery has been revealed. And again: 'Search the Scriptures: for these give testimony of me.'"[50]

One should note what John of Damascus sees as the primary purpose of the Scriptures. He argues that the reason why all "Scripture and mystery" has been revealed to mankind was to work salvation within them. It is John

---

47. John of Damascus, *Fount of Wisdom* 3:17, in Chase, *Saint John of Damascus*, 376.

48. Erickson, *Christian Theology*, 232. According to Erickson, The *verbal* theory insists that the Holy Spirit's influence extends beyond the direction of thoughts to the selection of words used to convey the message. The work of the Holy Spirit is so intense that each word is the exact word God wants used at that point to express the message. Ordinarily, great care is taken to insist that this is not dictation, however.

49. John of Damascus, *Fount of Wisdom* 3:17, in Chase, *Saint John of Damascus*, 376.

50. John of Damascus, *Fount of Wisdom* 3:17, in Chase, *Saint John of Damascus*, 376.

of Damascus's contention that the Scriptures are, then, a necessary component for one to find salvation in Christ. This argument hinges upon several basic assumptions. First, it assumes that one must look to Christ in faith to be saved. Second, to put one's faith in Christ one must have an accurate account of Christ's work to secure salvation for the lost. Third, the Scriptures themselves are an accurate account of Christ's work to secure salvation for the lost. Thus, the conclusion is that a knowledge of the Scriptures is a necessary component to lead one to faith in Christ.

John of Damascus on the Scriptures' Role in Sanctification

While John of Damascus contended that the Scriptures were a vital part of effecting the salvation of the lost, he did not believe the Scriptures were limited to that role alone. Instead, John contended that the Scriptures were a vital component to the Christian's sanctification. He believed that just as the Scriptures instructed the lost in how to find salvation, they also instructed the saints in how to live a life worthy of their calling.

After making a brief argument contending that the Scriptures were authored by God himself, John of Damascus then alludes to 2 Timothy 3:16 and Psalms 1:3 to conclude,

> Therefore, "all scripture, inspired of God, is quite profitable," so that to search the sacred Scripture is very good and most profitable for the soul. For, "like a tree which is planted near the running waters," so does the soul watered by sacred Scripture also grow fat and bear fruit in due season.[51]

Following his assertion that the Scriptures are a necessary component to the Christian's sanctification, John of Damascus then identifies four primary areas in which the Scriptures aid in one's sanctification.

First, John argues that the Scriptures are necessary to develop a proper doctrine. John asserts that one of the fruits that develop in a Christian's life from reading the Scriptures is "the orthodox faith, and so is it adorned with its evergreen leaves."[52] An examination of John's writings demonstrates that John of Damascus was not a theological innovator, but saw himself as one who faithfully conveyed the true faith handed down to him from those who came before him to those who would follow after him. His adherence to the orthodox faith is perhaps best seen in the 103 treatises addressing various heresies, ranging from those who held to the Stoic philosophy to the

---

51. John of Damascus, *Fount of Wisdom* 3:17, in Chase, *Saint John of Damascus*, 376.
52. John of Damascus, *Fount of Wisdom* 3:17, in Chase, *Saint John of Damascus*, 376.

Essenes. In each of these writings John demonstrated the failings of these heresies by comparing their teachings to the Scriptures and then encouraging his readers to embrace an orthodox faith as defined by the Scriptures.

The second area in which John believed the Scriptures would aid in one's sanctification was in one's development of a practical holiness. In *Fount of Wisdom*, John notes that one of the fruits gained through the reading of the Scriptures is "actions pleasing to God, I mean. And thus we are disposed to virtuous action and untroubled contemplation by the sacred Scriptures. In them we find exhortation to every virtue and dissuasion from every vice."[53] Here, John of Damascus contends that a knowledge of the Scriptures is a necessary component to the development of a practical holiness in the life of a Christian. It is John's contention that, due to one's innate sinful nature, one cannot come to know the expectations God places upon the believer outside of a direct revelation from God himself. John's position reflects that of Paul's when he asks, in Romans 7:7, "I would not have come to know sin except through the law; for I would not have known about coveting if the law had not said, 'YOU SHALL NOT COVET.'" Just as food nourishes and strengthens one's physical body, so too does the bread of life—the Scriptures—nourish and strengthen one's spiritual body. By feasting upon God's word, the Christian's sin is exposed and direction toward holiness is discovered.

A third area in which John of Damascus felt that the Scriptures were a vital component in one's sanctification was that the Scriptures were needed in the pursuit of knowledge. Alluding to Luke 11, he writes, "Therefore, if we are eager for knowledge, we shall also be rich in knowledge, for by diligence, toil, and the grace of God who grants it, all things succeed. 'For he that asketh receiveth: and he that seeketh findeth: and to him that knocketh it shall be opened.'"[54] The ancient world highly valued knowledge and learning, and here John notes that if one were to desire true knowledge, one must look to the Scriptures. John's position echoes that of James who, in James 1, admonishes his readers, "If any of you lacks wisdom, you should ask God, who gives generously to all without finding fault, and it will be given to him" (James 1:5 NIV). God is the source of all true knowledge and, as such, if individuals seek to possess that knowledge they can only find it in God's word, the Scriptures.

A final way in which the Scriptures aid in one's sanctification is by providing comfort in the midst of trials. John notes,

---

53. John of Damascus, *Fount of Wisdom* 3:17, in Chase, *Saint John of Damascus*, 376.
54. John of Damascus, *Fount of Wisdom* 3:17, in Chase, *Saint John of Damascus*, 376.

> So let us knock at the very beautiful paradise of the Scriptures, the fragrant, most sweet and lovely paradise which fills our ears with the varied songs of inspired spiritual birds, which touches our heart, comforting it when grieving, calming it when angry, and filling it with everlasting joy, and which lifts our mind onto the back of the sacred dove, gleaming with gold and most brilliant, who bears us with his most bright wings to the only begotten Son.[55]

Living as a servant in the government of an occupying force, John of Damascus was painfully aware that the Christian community around him felt oppressed and marginalized. Whether their concern was national or personal, John affirmed the fact that one could turn to the Scriptures to find encouragement and perseverance in the most difficult situations. The comfort provided by the Scriptures was certain because they ultimately pointed people to place their hope in Jesus Christ, as opposed to any temporal comfort.

John of Damascus on Reading the Scriptures

After demonstrating that a knowledge of the Scriptures was necessary for one's salvation and sanctification, John of Damascus then concludes that the Christian should read the Scriptures deeply and often. John writes,

> Let us not knock casually, but with eagerness and persistence, and let us not lose heart while knocking, for so it will be opened to us. Should we read once and then a second time and still not understand what we are reading, let us not be discouraged. Rather, let us persist, let us meditate and inquire, for it is written: "Ask thy father, and he will declare to thee: thy elders and they will tell thee" . . . From the fountain of paradise let us draw ever-flowing and most pure waters springing up into life everlasting. Let us revel in them, let us revel greedily in them to satiety, for they contain the grace which cannot be exhausted.[56]

If the Scriptures really were necessary for one's salvation and sanctification, then it should only follow that an individual seeking those things should become an avid reader of the Scriptures. Because of his conviction of the Scriptures' usefulness in the Christian's life, John of Damascus exhorted his fellow believers to study the Scriptures regularly and deeply. John believed

---

55. John of Damascus, *Fount of Wisdom* 3:17, in Chase, *Saint John of Damascus*, 376.
56. John of Damascus, *Fount of Wisdom* 3:17, in Chase, *Saint John of Damascus*, 376.

that if a Christian were to search out the Scriptures, godly knowledge would be gained and the person's life would be changed.

JOHN OF DAMASCUS'S USE OF SCRIPTURE IN HIS APOLOGETIC WRITINGS

Roughly 12 percent of John of Damascus's *Fount of Wisdom* is dedicated to apologetic arguments. This section of John's work is titled *On Heresies*, but one should be cautious to understand that this section is meant to address a number of worldviews outside of Christian orthodoxy. As he does, John is careful to define non-Christian religions as "heresies" and non-orthodox Christian religions as "schisms." Thus, John addresses distinctively non-Christian religions such as Judaism and Hellenism alongside heterodox understandings of Christianity such as Arianism and Nestorianism. No matter what ideology John addressed, however, he did so from a decidedly biblical prospective.

When addressing non-Christian beliefs, such as the Hellenistic worldview, John of Damascus's discussion is largely descriptive in nature, but is described within the context of Scripture. John notes that the Hellenistic period was a time when people had developed a civil way of life while maintaining the idolatrous worship system that began with Abraham's grandfather Sarug.[57] In a similar vein, John describes the failure of Judaism by describing the religion within the background of the Gospels.[58]

In a similar fashion, John addresses heterodox Christian beliefs in a descriptive manner, demonstrating how these schisms depart from Scripture. When discussing the Arians, John simply notes that Arians "are they who say that the Son of God is a creature and that the Holy Ghost is the creature of a creature. They assert that Christ did not receive his soul from Mary, but only his body."[59] Equally, John also gives the Nestorians only a cursory description when he writes,

> The Nestorians hold that God the Word exists by himself and separately, and that his humanity exists by itself. And the more humble of the Lord's actions during his sojourn among us they attribute to his humanity alone, whereas the more noble and

---

57. John of Damascus, *Fount of Wisdom* 2:3, in Chase, *Saint John of Damascus*, 111.
58. John of Damascus, *Fount of Wisdom* 2:4 in Chase, *Saint John of Damascus*, 115.
59. John of Damascus, *Fount of Wisdom* 2:69 in Chase, *Saint John of Damascus*, 127.

those befitting the divinity they ascribe to God the Word alone. But they do not attribute them both to the same Person.[60]

In many respects, John of Damascus's works, including his apologetics, followed in the established footsteps of the church leaders who went before him. Because John saw himself continuing in the tradition of the church, his works against heterodox groups were frequently short and only demonstrated where their teachings departed from a biblical Orthodoxy.

John of Damascus's Muslim Apologetic

In the centuries following the legalization of Christianity in the Roman Empire, the Christian faith transitioned from an outlawed, persecuted religion to a religion that was both legal and favored by the empire. As Christianity ascended and pagan religions were pushed to the fringes of society, Christian apologetics became stagnant, often resembling detached philosophical treatises as opposed to practical answers to the lost. As Christians and Muslims began to interact with one another, Christian writings against Islam reflected a traditional polemical style, especially among Christian scholars who lived outside of Muslim-controlled territories.[61]

As a Syrian resident within an Islamic government, however, John of Damascus could not afford simply to make such an impassioned case for Christianity. While other faiths were at first tolerated by the new Islamic government, in time the new regime began to first favor Muslim citizens and then, in time, become hostile toward those outside of the Islamic faith.[62] As Islam became a favored religion and Christianity became a restricted faith in Syria, many people began converting to Islam for the sake of advancing or surviving in their new society. In an effort "to stem this flow of Christians converting to Islam," John of Damascus penned two apologies against Islam that sought to accurately describe the Islamic faith and refute it with the gospel.[63]

John of Damascus and the Heresy of the Ishmaelites

In *John of Damascus: First Apologist to the Muslims*, Daniel Janosik argues that John of Damascus's apologetic approach in *The Heresy of the Ishmaelites*

---

60. John of Damascus, *Fount of Wisdom* 2:81, in Chase, *Saint John of Damascus*, 138.
61. Meyendorff, "Byzantine Views of Islam," 113–32.
62. Lamoreaux, "Early Eastern Christian Responses to Islam," 25.
63. Janosik, *John of Damascus*, 199.

can be categorized along the following three lines. First, John states what the Ishmaelites believe. He then counters those beliefs with Christian Scripture and doctrine guided by reason. Finally, he refutes the Muslim beliefs and argues that they are inferior and irrational in comparison to Christian doctrine.[64]

I will use this framework in understanding John's *The Heresy of the Ishmaelites*.

John of Damascus on What Muslims Believe

Because of the differences between Christianity and Islam, early Christian scholars were frequently ignorant of Islamic beliefs and, thus, how adequately to refute them.[65] Perhaps an extreme example of how difficult it was for Christians to understand Islam is found in the life of ninth-century scholar Nicetas Byzantinos, who resided in Constantinople. Nicetas erred on basic facts of Islam "even though he had several translations of the Qur'an" available to him.[66] John Meyendorff concludes that Nicetas's example, along with others, "illustrate[s] the permanent misunderstanding between the two cultures and the two religious mentalities."[67]

As a Christian theologian and government employee living in Muslim-dominated Syria, John was in a unique situation to both accurately know what Muslims believed and refute those beliefs with a robust Christian worldview. John began his apologetic by bridging a gap with Muslims by accurately portraying their beliefs. He begins *The Heresy of the Ishmaelites* by briefly describing the history of those now called Muslims. He notes that, before Mohammad, the Arabic people were idolaters and followed a number of pagan religions.[68] John also writes that Mohammad created Islam by amalgamating Judaism, Arian Christianity, and indigenous religions into one worldview.[69] John pays careful attention to record the Islamic understanding of Jesus, noting,

> He [Mohammad] says that there is one God, creator of all things, who has neither been begotten nor has begotten. He says

---

64. Janosik, *John of Damascus*, 203.
65. Daniel, *Islam and the West*, 336.
66. Janosik, *John of Damascus*, 200.
67. Meyendorff, "Byzantine Views of Islam," 122.
68. John of Damascus, *Fount of Wisdom* 2:101, in Chase, *Saint John of Damascus*, 153.
69. John of Damascus, *Fount of Wisdom* 2:101, in Chase, *Saint John of Damascus*, 153. John is perhaps the first to argue that Islam is a syncretization of Judaism, Arian Christianity, and indigenous Arabic religions. This theory of Islam's origin remains popular to this day, being the explanation typically embraced by secular scholars.

that the Christ is the Word of God and his Spirit, but a creature and a servant, and that he was begotten, without seed, of Mary the sister of Moses and Aaron.[70]

John's Use of Scripture to Refute Islamic Beliefs

In his refutation of Islamic beliefs, John does so in the form of a hypothetical dialogue between a Christian and a Muslim. John's refutation of Islamic claims takes a classical form of looking to the Old Testament and using its prophecies as proof against Islamic claims.

John of Damascus begins his critique of Islam by refuting the Islamic claim that Mohammad was a prophet of God and that God spoke through him. To refute this claim, John asks two simple questions: "And who is there to testify that God gave him the book? And which of the prophets foretold that such a prophet would rise up?"[71] After asking these questions, he refers to the book of Exodus and notes that when "Moses received the law on Mount Sinai," God himself appeared and the people were able to testify to God's presence with Moses.[72] Furthermore, John notes that throughout the course of the Old Testament the prophets "foretold the coming of Christ and how Christ God (and incarnate Son of God) was to come and to be crucified and die and rise again, and how he was to be the judge of the living and the dead."[73] After considering God's presence with Moses while delivering the law and the numerous prophecies concerning Christ, John of Damascus then ponders why God was not present during the formation of the Quran and why the Old Testament prophets were silent about any prophet coming after the incarnation of Christ. He then asserts that these questions leave Muslim apologists silent and ashamed.[74]

After briefly considering the logical inconsistency of the Quran, John of Damascus then seeks to refute Islam's Christology. He notes that Muslims have, at times, referred to Christians as "Hetaeriasts" or "Associators" because they claim that Christians "introduce an associate with God by declaring Christ to the Son of God and God."[75] John refutes this by once again referring to the prophets who foretold of Christ's coming. In addition

---

70. John of Damascus, *Fount of Wisdom* 2:101, in Chase, *Saint John of Damascus*, 153.
71. John of Damascus, *Fount of Wisdom* 2:101, in Chase, *Saint John of Damascus*, 153.
72. John of Damascus, *Fount of Wisdom* 2:101, in Chase, *Saint John of Damascus*, 153.
73. John of Damascus, *Fount of Wisdom* 2:101, in Chase, *Saint John of Damascus*, 153.
74. John of Damascus, *Fount of Wisdom* 2:101, in Chase, *Saint John of Damascus*, 153.
75. John of Damascus, *Fount of Wisdom* 2:101, in Chase, *Saint John of Damascus*, 155.

to his reference to the prophets, he alludes to the Gospel of John 1, when he asserts that because Muslims consider Christ the "Word of God and Spirit," they should also accept Christ as God because "the word, and the spirit, is inseparable from that in which it naturally has existence. Therefore, if the Word of God is in God, then it is obvious that he is God."[76]

Finally, John of Damascus confronts the Islamic claim that Christians are idolaters because of the Christian veneration of the cross. In this case he does not use Scripture to support veneration of the cross but, instead, uses Scripture to undermine Islam's veneration of the Ka'ba.[77] John notes that Muslims believe that the Ka'ba sits on the site where Abraham was tested by God and almost sacrificed his son Isaac. He contends, however, that this is not possible, as the Genesis account records that Abraham and Isaac went up on a mountain that would have been wooded, so that Abraham could have cut the wood for the sacrifice.[78] If the Genesis account is true, then the Ka'ba could not have been the location of Abraham's testing because the Ka'ba is located in a desert plain instead of a wooded mountain.

CONCLUSION

Writing late in the patristic period and primarily addressing issues that had been considered by his predecessors, John of Damascus's contribution to the apologetic endeavor is, nonetheless, unique and valuable. He was the first to offer a serious Christian response to the theological challenges presented by the rise of Islam in the East. As John responded to Islamic beliefs, he did so through the use of Christian Scriptures due to his belief that within the word of God one might find both salvation and sanctification.

---

76. John of Damascus, *Fount of Wisdom* 2:101, in Chase, *Saint John of Damascus*, 155.

77. Armstrong, *Islam*, 10–12. The Ka'ba is the holiest site in Islam, and is the focus of the annual *hajj*, or pilgrimage, every Muslim is expected to participate in at least once in their lives. Before the rise of Islam, it was the center of pagan worship in Arabia. When Mohammad captured Mecca, he "cleansed" the site and dedicated it as a Muslim shrine, believing that the stone contained in the Ka'ba was the stone on which Abraham almost sacrificed his son Isaac.

78. John of Damascus, *Fount of Wisdom* 2:101, in Chase, *Saint John of Damascus*, 156.

7

Conclusion

In this concluding chapter, I will posit some of the results of my research. First, I consider some of the opportunities and challenges facing Evangelical Christianity in the terms of its evangelistic enterprise. Second, I consider how the Greek fathers addressed similar issues in their context. Third, I explore how the principles of evangelism developed by the Greek fathers may assist modern Evangelicals respond to the evangelistic challenges they currently face. Finally, I consider additional avenues for future research and study.

STATUS OF CONTEMPORARY EVANGELICAL EVANGELISM

In many respects, American Christianity is in a time of crisis. Observance of Christian worship in the United States has declined steadily in the twenty-first century. In its 2015 study titled "America's Changing Religious Landscape," the Pew Research Group notes,

> The United States remains home to more Christians than any other country in the world, and a large majority of Americans—roughly seven in ten—continue to identify with some branch of the Christian faith. But the major new survey of more than 35,000 Americans by the Pew Research Center finds that the percentage of adults (ages eighteen and older) who describe themselves as Christians has dropped by nearly eight percentage

points in just seven years, from 78.4 percent in an equally massive Pew Research survey in 2007 to 70.6 percent in 2014. Over the same period, the percentage of Americans who are religiously unaffiliated—describing themselves as atheist, agnostic or "nothing in particular"—has jumped more than six points, from 16.1 percent to 22.8 percent. And the share of Americans who identify with non-Christian faiths also has inched up, rising 1.2 percentage points, from 4.7 percent in 2007 to 5.9 percent in 2014.[1]

In this same period, non-Christian religions, while still accounting for a small number of people, are on the rise in the United States. Pew Research explains that the population of practitioners of Islam has grown by nearly a third,[2] and represent the fastest growing religion in the world.[3] At the same time, America's Hindu population is on pace to double in the near future.[4] While several non-Christian religions in the United States have seen a statistical rise in numbers in the twenty-first century, the greatest increase in religious affiliation in the United States is among the religiously unaffiliated, or "nones." Regarding the nones, Thom Rainer writes,

> Mark Chaves, in his wonderful book on church trends, *American Religion*, does a good job of helping us understand the importance of the nones. Since 1972, the General Social Survey has asked a plethora of questions every one to two years to representative samplings of Americans. One question that has been consistent is: "What is your religious preference? Is it Protestant, Catholic, Jewish, some other religion, or no religion?"
>
> From the inception of the study in 1972 to 1990, people who self-identified as nones stayed consistent in the 5 percent to 8 percent range. From 1990 to today, the number has increased significantly. The nones now represent 17% of all of our population, nearly one in five Americans. That statistical trend may be one of the most significant changes in the religious and moral landscape of our nation.[5]

---

1. Pew Research Center, "America's Changing Religious Landscape."
2. Mohamed, "New Estimates Show US Muslim Population Continues to Grow."
3. Zein, "The List: The World's Fastest-Growing Religions."
4. Pew Research Center, "Hindus."
5. Rainer, "The Rise of the Religious 'Nones.'"

Pew Research Group notes that as of 2015, the category of nones now includes approximately 56 million adults and represents the second-largest religious category behind evangelical Protestants.[6]

While the Catholic church and mainline Protestant denominations have represented the bulk of the decline of members in the United States, recent research shows that evangelical Protestant groups are beginning to see a loss in numbers as well. In its 2017 report titled "America's Changing Religious Identity," the Public Religion Research Institute states,

> White evangelical Protestants are in decline—along with white mainline Protestants and white Catholics. White evangelical Protestants were once thought to be bucking a longer trend, but over the past decade their numbers have dropped substantially. Fewer than one in five (17%) Americans are white evangelical Protestant, but they accounted for nearly one-quarter (23%) in 2006. Over the same period, white Catholics dropped five percentage points from 16% to 11%, as have white mainline Protestants, from 18% to 13%.[7]

This decline has even begun to be felt among the Southern Baptist Convention, which reports that its "310,000 baptisms in 2013 represented the lowest number among Southern Baptists since 1948."[8] Along with the general decline of Christian worship in the West's post-Christian era, Christian thinkers also find themselves faced with a rising hostility toward the faith, especially when practiced in the public sphere. D. A. Carson writes,

> In much of the Western world, despite the fact that Christianity was one of the forces that shaped what the West became (along with the Enlightenment, and a host of less dominant powers), culture is not only moving away from Christianity, it is frequently openly hostile toward it. Christianity can be tolerated, provided it is entirely private: Christian belief that intrudes itself into the public square, especially if it is trying to influence public policy, is most often taken, without examination, as *prima facie* evidence for bigotry and intolerance. In most of the Western world, this sneering condescension has become dominant in many public organs only within the last quarter-century or so—though obviously it advanced farther, faster, and earlier in deeply anti-clerical countries like France and in distinctly secular countries like Australia than in countries with a once-strong

---

6. Pew Research Center, "America's Changing Religious Landscape."
7. Cox and Jones, "America's Changing Religious Identity."
8. Chandler, "Personal Soul-Winning, Evangelism Task Force Named."

national church like England or with a pronounced Bible belt like America.[9]

Faced with the decline of Christian adherence, the rise of irreligion, and the hostility frequently expressed toward Christianity in the marketplace, many Christians find themselves looking for a way to respond to the now largely pluralistic culture found in the United States.

Classic Christian Schema for Relating to One's Culture

In *Christ and Culture*, H. Richard Niebuhr formulates a schema to help Christians better understand how to relate to the culture around them.[10] Niebuhr's study has become a leading theory among many Christians as they wrestle with this issue. Niebuhr argues that, throughout history, Christians have typically responded to their culture in one of three primary ways. The first way Christians may respond to their culture is by rejecting that culture entirely and retreating from it. A second response Christians may have to their surrounding culture is by accepting it and accommodating their beliefs and practices to their culture. Niebuhr notes that the final primary way Christians tend to relate to their culture is by seeking to redeem it through the gospel of Jesus Christ. Niebuhr further subdivides this trend into three responses—a synthetic relationship with the culture, a dualistic relationship with the culture, and a transforming relationship with the culture.

Christ against Culture

The first category of Niebuhr's typology is "Christ against culture," in which the surrounding culture is seen as being adversarial to the Christian and to Christianity.

Niebuhr defines this position as "one that uncompromisingly affirms the sole authority of Christ over the Christian and resolutely rejects culture's

---

9. Carson, *Christ and Culture Revisited*, 6.
10. For this dissertation I use Kroeber and Kluckhohn's definition of culture:

> Culture consists of patterns, explicit and implicit, of and for behavior acquired and transmitted by symbols, constituting the distinctive achievement of human groups, including their embodiment in artifacts; the essential core of culture consists of traditional (i.e., historically derived and selected) ideas and especially their attached values; culture systems may, on the one hand, be considered as products of action, on the other hand as conditioning elements of further action. (Kroeber and Kluckhohn, *Culture*, 357.)

claims to loyalty."[11] To adherents of this idea, Niebuhr writes that "the world appears as a realm under the power of evil; it is the region of darkness, into which the citizens of the kingdom of light must not enter."[12] Christians who follow this philosophy typically retreat in the face of their culture seeking to establish a Christian culture that is entirely separate from the surrounding culture. Niebuhr notes that this philosophy has been practiced throughout the history of the church, beginning with the early church, as seen in the writings of Tertullian[13] and the monastic movement,[14] and can still be found in Mennonite communities[15] and among sectarian Protestants.[16]

The Christ of Culture

The second method Christians frequently use when relating to their culture is what Niebuhr refers to as "the Christ of Culture." Niebuhr describes this idea as follows:

> These men are Christians not only in the sense that they count themselves believers in the Lord but also in the sense that they seek to maintain community with all other believers. Yet they seem equally at home in the community of culture. They feel no great tension between church and world . . . the ethics of salvation and the ethics of social conservation or progress. On the one hand they interpret culture through Christ, regarding those elements in it as most important which are most accordant with his work and person; on the other hand the understand Christ through culture, selecting from his teaching and action as well as from the Christian doctrine about him such points as seem to agree with what is best in civilization.[17]

Christians who hold this philosophy tend to syncretize Christianity with their culture and engage their surrounding culture at every level. Niebuhr notes that, once again, this practice has been observed throughout the

---

11. Niebuhr, *Christ and Culture*, 45.
12. Niebuhr, *Christ and Culture*, 48.
13. Niebuhr, *Christ and Culture*, 49.
14. Niebuhr, *Christ and Culture*, 56.
15. Niebuhr, *Christ and Culture*, 56.
16. Niebuhr, *Christ and Culture*, 64.
17. Niebuhr, *Christ and Culture*, 83.

history of the church. Niebuhr counts the gnostic heresy,[18] Abelard,[19] and modern Christian liberalism[20] as practitioners of this ideology.

Christ above Culture

Niebuhr's final category for the Christian's response to its culture is "Christ above culture." Niebuhr notes that the "Christ above culture" position is the majority position held throughout church history.[21] Niebuhr notes that those who hold to this position maintain a conviction of the radical, universal nature of sin,[22] a common view on the grace and law of God,[23] and a focus upon obedience to Christ.[24] Niebuhr further subdivides the "Christ above culture" position into three groups. The first is a synthetic position, which Carson defines as "a 'both-and' solution. They maintain the gap between Christ and culture that the cultural Christian never takes seriously and that the radical does not even try to breech—yet they insist that Christ is as sovereign over the culture as over the church."[25] Niebuhr's second subcategory on the "Christ above culture" position is the dualist subcategory. Explaining this position, Carson writes,

> For the dualists, the fundamental issue in life is not the line that must be drawn between Christians and the pagan or secular world, but between God and all humankind—or, "since the dualist is an existential thinker—between God and us; the issue lies between the righteousness of God and the righteousness of self."[26]

Niebuhr's final subgroup is the conversionist. Niebuhr writes,

> The men who offer what we are calling the conversionist answer to the problem of Christ and culture evidently belong to the great central tradition of the church. Though they hold fast to the radical distinction between God's work in Christ and man's work in culture, they do not take the road of exclusive Christianity into isolation from civilization, or reject its institutions . . . though

---

18. Niebuhr, *Christ and Culture*, 85.
19. Niebuhr, *Christ and Culture*, 91.
20. Niebuhr, *Christ and Culture*, 84.
21. Niebuhr, *Christ and Culture*, 117.
22. Niebuhr, *Christ and Culture*, 118.
23. Niebuhr, *Christ and Culture*, 119.
24. Niebuhr, *Christ and Culture*, 118.
25. Carson, *Christ and Culture Revisited*, 21.
26. Carson, *Christ and Culture Revisited*, 22–23.

they accept their station in society with its duties in obedience to their Lord, they do not seek to modify Jesus Christ's sharp judgment of the world and all its ways. In their Christology they are like synthesists and dualists; they refer to the Redeemer more than to the giver of a new law, and to the God whom men encounter more than to the representative of the best spiritual resources in humanity . . . What distinguishes conversionists from dualists is their more positive and hopeful attitude toward culture.[27]

Evangelical Christianity's Place in Niebuhr's Schema

As Niebuhr describes the theological convictions that characterize conversionists, one might assume that he is describing evangelical Christians.[28] Niebuhr also cites several Christian scholars such as Calvin, Wesley, and Edwards, whose theologies have helped shape modern evangelicalism as influential leaders who held to the conversionist position.[29]

As the Southern Baptist Convention seeks solutions to reverse its downward trend of baptisms and impact its society with the gospel, one finds that its response falls within the conversionist wing of the "Christ above culture" category. To become more effective in sharing the gospel, the Southern Baptist Convention convened a number of task forces with the goal of considering its evangelistic approach in an effort to make it more effective in reaching the lost. In 2013, in response to the 2012 Annual Church Profile (ACP) report that total baptisms had dropped by 5.52 percent, the North American Mission Board formed a national "Pastors' Task Force on Evangelistic Impact and Declining Baptisms" with the purpose of addressing the baptismal decline of the Southern Baptist Convention.[30] Later in 2017, the President of the Southern Baptist Convention created an Evangelism Task Force in an effort to reverse the decline in evangelism among Southern Baptist churches.[31] At their 2018 meeting, the Southern Baptist Convention received reports from several of these task forces. A disciple-making task force that was a joint effort between the North American Mission Board and LifeWay Christian Resources made three recommendations for churches seeking to improve their evangelistic efforts: "Increase efforts

27. Niebuhr, *Christ and Culture*, 190–91.
28. Niebuhr, *Christ and Culture*, 190.
29. Niebuhr, *Christ and Culture*, 217–19.
30. Conway, "Pastors' Task Force to Address Declining SBC Baptism Trend."
31. Chandler, "Personal Soul-Winning, Evangelism Task Force Named."

toward Bible engagement, examine the connection between salvation decisions and group involvement, and examine the number of groups that multiply on a regular basis."[32] Similarly, the Evangelism Task Force issued a report consisting of a list of affirmations and denials, along with a number of recommendations for how churches may act upon them. In their second affirmation, the Evangelism Task Force noted, "WE AFFIRM that the Scriptures teach that gospel conversations should seek to include both clear presentations of the 'good news' of salvation and genuine invitations for all people to receive Jesus Christ as Savior and Lord."[33]

As the Southern Baptist Convention has sought to counteract the rise of secularism in society and address declining baptism reports within their ranks, they have done so by seeking to engage individuals within their culture with a Scripture-educated outreach. The Southern Baptist Convention has recognized that while individual methods of evangelism may vary, effective evangelism and discipleship must have a robust biblical foundation.

GREEK PATRISTIC EVANGELISM IN THE MIDST OF TRIALS

Christianity was born into a pluralistic society that presented a number of challenges to the faith. In *Religions of Rome*, Mary Beard, John North, and Simon Price write,

> from the foundation of the city to its rise to world empire and its conversion to Christianity, religion was central to Roman culture; it was part of the fabric of politics and warfare, imperial power and its opponents, domestic life and philosophical theorizing.[34]

Rome's founding itself was steeped in religious symbolism and remembered through religious observances. Beard notes,

> Roman writers, from poets to philosophers, gave detailed accounts of the founding of Rome by the first king Romulus (the date they came to agree was—on our system of reckoning—753 BC): he consulted the gods for divine approval of the new foundation, carefully laying out the sacred boundary (the *pomerium*) around the city; he built the very first temple in the city (to Jupiter Feretrius, where he dedicated the spoils of his military

---

32. Elrod, "Disciple-Making Task Force Report."
33. Roach, "Evangelism Task Force Releases Report."
34. Beard et al., *Religions of Rome*, i.

victories); and he established some of the major festivals that were still being celebrated a thousand years later.[35]

One hallmark of the Roman religion was that it was exceptionally porous, giving room for other religious expressions and beliefs. These alien religions would be accepted into Roman society, but the Romans would put their own unique twist on them to make them subservient to Roman identity. This synchronistic tendency is perhaps best seen in the Roman adoption of the Greek pantheon of gods, albeit with a distinctly Roman understanding.[36] In the late republican era, religion continued to be intertwined with Roman legal and political traditions,[37] a trend that continued into the early imperial era, in which religion was used as a foundation in understanding Roman identity.[38]

As Christianity was introduced to the Roman Empire in the first century AD, there was a rise of spirituality among Romans, particularly among those in the middle classes of society.[39] However, due to its exclusivistic claims, Christianity could not be molded by Roman thought, and Christians began to face both social and legal ostracization. However, despite its entrance into a hostile pluralistic society, Christianity flourished. Paul writes in 1 Corinthians 15:5-8:

> He [Christ] appeared to Cephas, then to the twelve. After that he appeared to more than five hundred brethren at one time, most of whom remain until now, but some have fallen asleep; then he appeared to James, then to all the apostles; and last of all, as to one untimely born, He appeared to me also.

From this passage it is estimated that there were approximately five hundred Christians at the time of Christ's resurrection. According to Acts 2, after the ascension of Christ, three thousand more converts were added to the church. These converts were members of the Jewish Diaspora, and as they returned to their homes they were instrumental in the spread of Christianity across the Roman Empire, which saw the start of approximately forty-five Christian churches in the empire by AD 100.[40] It is difficult to determine exactly how many people converted to Christianity in the patristic period, though some suggest that the church's pace of growth increased throughout

---

35. Beard et al., *Religions of Rome*, 1.
36. Beard et al., *Religions of Rome*, 21.
37. Beard et al., *Religions of Rome*, 59.
38. Beard et al., *Religions of Rome*, 98.
39. Rostovtzeff, *Rome*, 292.
40. Van der Meer and Mohrmann, *Atlas of the Early Christian World*, 2.

the period.[41] Erwin R. Goodenough argues that by the fourth century AD, there were over six million Christians in the Roman Empire, constituting 10 percent of the general population,[42] which suggests that the early church grew at the rate of 40 percent per decade.[43] Perhaps the greatest estimation of the number of Christians in the Roman Empire by the fourth century is L. von Hertling's figure of fifteen million,[44] though this figure is considered high by most historians.[45]

Christianity's exponential growth in the first five centuries can be, in part, attributed to the evangelistic impulse of the patristic fathers. According to Niebuhr, the Greek patristic fathers primarily held to the "Christ above culture" philosophy. Niebuhr specifically identifies Justin Martyr as an early adherent to the "Christ above culture" motif within the synthesis subgroup.[46] Niebuhr also refers to Clement of Alexandria as a synthesist.[47] Considering that Clement was the founder of the Alexandrian school of thought, it can be argued that later Alexandrian thinkers such as Origen and Athanasius should be included among those that held to the "Christ above culture" position. The Greek patristic fathers sought to engage their surrounding culture around them while maintaining a Christian distinctiveness, including a radical understanding of man's sinfulness and God's graciousness through Christ. As they engaged their culture, they used several approaches, each of which was solidly educated by the Scriptures.

THE GREEK PATRISTIC FATHERS' APPROACH TO MODERN EVANGELISM

In many respects, the Greek fathers would find much of today's pluralistic society familiar. Their example of engaging their culture with a scripturally-educated apologetic is one that should be considered by modern evangelists. The Greek patristic fathers believed that the Scriptures would accomplish every task God had assigned to them, including the task of evangelism. Justin Martyr perhaps best summarizes why the Scriptures should take the forefront of one's evangelism when he argues, "For they possess a terrible power in themselves, and are sufficient to inspire those who turn aside from

41. Wilken, *First Thousand Years*, 65–66.
42. Goodenough, *Church in the Roman Empire*, 87.
43. Stark, *Rise of Christianity*, 7.
44. Von Hertling, "Die Zahl," 245–64.
45. Grant, *History of Rome*, 241.
46. Niebuhr, *Christ and Culture*, 123.
47. Niebuhr, *Christ and Culture*, 123.

the path of rectitude with awe; while the sweetest rest is afforded those who make a diligent practice of them."[48] Throughout the course of their ministries, the Greek patristic fathers demonstrated that the best evangelistic practice was to engage one's surrounding culture with a scripturally-educated apologetic, because such an approach is used by God to evoke salvation in the lost.

AREAS OF FUTURE RESEARCH AND STUDY

One obvious stream of further consideration would be whether the fathers from the Latin tradition held to the same practice and belief. A survey of evangelistic literature from the Latin church such as Tertullian's *Apologeticus*, Jerome's *Apology against Rufinus,* and Augustine's *City of God* to determine the Latin father's use of Scripture in their evangelistic writings would be a valuable contribution to patristic studies and would help scholars determine if the findings of this dissertation were widespread in early Christianity or if they were limited to the eastern church. Considering Niebur placed Tertullian in the "Christ against culture" camp, a thorough examination of his evangelistic writings may be of particular interest.[49] A cursory study of the Latin fathers' view of Scripture uncovered a suggestion that it is highly likely that the Latin church's view of the use of Scripture in evangelism may mirror that found in this dissertation. In his "Against Heresies," Irenaeus argues that "the Scriptures are indeed perfect,"[50] while Augustine contends that "every sickness of the soul hath in Scripture its proper remedy."[51] While far from a comprehensive survey, these quoted do at least suggest that the Scriptures also took a central position in the ministry of the Latin fathers.

In *Rediscovering the Church Fathers*, Michael Haykin notes, "Too many modern-day evangelicals are either ignorant of or quite uncomfortable with the church fathers."[52] This discomfort has led to a large portion of Evangelicals to disregard the ministry of the church fathers, to their detriment As I have studied the Greek fathers, I have discovered a group of men devoted to serving Christ and growing his church. I believe that the patristic era is a time period in the church's history that is now ripe to be mined in search of practical ministry wisdom.

   48. Justin Martyr, *Dialogue* 8.
   49. Niebuhr, *Christ and Culture* 45.
   50. Irenaeus, "Against Heresies" 2.28.
   51. Augustine, 'Discourse on Psalm 37," 332.
   52. Haykin, *Rediscovering the Church Fathers*, 13.

CONCLUSION

In *Evangelism in the Early Church,* Michael Green takes a pessimistic view of the church father's contribution to the evangelistic enterprise, arguing that the fathers' writings were unnecessarily pugnacious and counterproductive to the evangelistic pursuit. Green writes,

> But unfortunately tendencies which were already beginning to make themselves felt in the New Testament documents became heightened in the Apologists. It has long been recognized that there is a strong anti-Jewish element in parts of St. Matthew's Gospel, and in St. John too, where "the Jews" are always mentioned in contradistinction, if not open opposition, to Christian believers . . . At all events, in most of the second-century pieces of apologetic that we possess there is a hardness of approach which could hardly have been calculated to win the friendship and goodwill of the non-Christian readers. There is acrimony about Justin's *Dialogue* with the Jew, Trypho, a biting scorn for the pagan gods among Apologists like Tatian and Tertullian, which almost certainly frustrated the genuine evangelistic concern these men undoubtedly possessed. To launch a full-scale and at times bitter assault on someone's cherished beliefs is not the best way of inducing him to change them . . . The love must have been there, as is clear from the way in which these Apologists lived and died; but it is to a large extent masked in their writings, and to that extent one may well imagine that not many pagans or Jews were won to the faith through these documents, if in fact they read them . . . Were they written more perhaps in the interests of Christian readership than for external consumption? There is, to my knowledge, no example of an outsider being converted to Christianity by reading an apologetic writing.[53]

This dissertation demonstrates, however, that the apologetic writing of the church fathers represents a valuable contribution to Christianity's evangelistic effort. Instead of being acrimonious, they reflect a genuine concern for the lost and for the wellbeing of their own Christian community. This concern for non-Christians and the desire for their conversion to Christianity was demonstrated by their use of Scripture in their evangelistic works, as they believed that only the Scriptures had the power to move a person to faith in Jesus Christ.

---

53. Green, *Evangelism in the Early Church,* 350–51.

Bibliography

Abbott, Frank Frost. *The Common People of Ancient Rome: Studies of Roman Life and Literature*. New York: Charles Scribners' Sons, 1922.

Abun-Nasr, Jamil M. *A History of the Maghrib*. Cambridge: Cambridge University Press, 1971.

Adbury, H. J. *The Book of Acts in History*. London: Adam & Charles Black, 1955.

Africa, Thomas W. *The Ancient World*. Boston: Houghton Mifflin, 1969.

Akin, Daniel L. *A Theology for the Church*. Nashville: B & H, 2007.

Albright, William Foxwell. *From the Stone Age to Christianity: Monotheism and the Historical Process*. 2nd ed. New York: Doubleday Anchor, 1957.

———. *Samuel and the Beginnings of the Prophetic Movement (The Goldenson Lecture)*. Cincinnati: Hebrew Union College Press, 1961.

Alfoldi, A. *Conversion of Constantine and Pagan Rome*. Oxford: Oxford University Press, 1948.

Allen, Charlotte. *The Human Christ: The Search for the Historical Jesus*. New York: Free Press, 1998.

Allen, F., trans. *Four Discourses on Chrysostom: Chiefly on the Parable of the Rich Man and Lazarus*. Edinburgh: Ballantyne and Company, 1869.

Allert, Craig D. *Revelation, Truth, Canon, and Interpretation: Studies in Justin Martyr's Dialogue with Trypho*. Supplements to Vigiliae Christianae 64. Leiden: Brill, 2002.

Alslan, Reza. *No God but God: The Origins, Evolution, and Future of Islam*. Rev. ed. New York: Random House, 2011.

Alter, Robert. *The Five Books of Moses: A Translation with Commentary*. New York: W. W. Norton, 2008.

Anatolios, Khaled. *Athanasius*. The Early Church Fathers Series. London: Routledge, 2004.

Archer, Gleason L., Jr. *A Survey of Old Testament Introduction*. Rev. and expanded ed. Chicago: Moody, 1994.

Arius. "Arius Letter to Alexander of Alexandria—Greek Text with English Translation." https://earlychurchtexts.com/public/arius_letter_to_alexander_of_alexandria.htm.

Armitage, Angus. *The World of Copernicus*. New York: Signet Science Library, 1951.

Armstrong, Karen. *A History of God: The 4,000-Year Quest of Judaism, Christianity, and Islam*. New York: Ballantine, 1994.

———. *Holy War: The Crusades and Their Impact on Today's World*. 2nd ed. New York: Anchor, 2001.

———. *Islam: A Short History*. New York: Random House, 2002.
———. *Muhammad: A Biography of the Prophet*. New York: HarperCollins, 1992.
———. *Muhammad: A Prophet for Our Time*. New York: HarperOne, 2007.
Aslan, Reza. *No god but God: The Origins, Evolution, and Future of Islam*. Rev. ed. New York: Random House, 2011.
Athanasius. *Against the Heathen*. New York: Fig, 2013.
———. "de Synodis." In *Nicene and Post-Nicene Fathers*, vol. 4. 2nd ed., edited by Philip Schaff and Henry Wace. Peabody, MA: Hendrickson, 1996.
———. *The Festal Letters of Athanasius: Discovered in an Ancient Syriac Version (1848)*. Edited by William Cureton. Whitefish, MT: Kessinger, 2010.
———. *The Letters of Saint Athanasius Concerning the Holy Spirit*. Translated by C. R. B. Sharpland. New York: Philosophical Library, 1951.
———. *The Life of Antony and the Letter to Marcellinus*. Translated by Robert C. Gregg. Mahwah, NJ: Paulist Press, 1980.
———. *On the Incarnation*. New York: Fig, 2013.
Atiya, Aziz S. *The Coptic Encyclopedia*, vol. 4. New York: MacMillan, 1991.
———. *History of Eastern Christianity*. Notre Dame, IN: University of Notre Dame Press, 1968.
Aurelius, Marcus. *The Meditations*. Mineola, NY: Dover, 1997.
Ayer, Joseph Cullen. *A Source Book for Ancient Church History: From the Apostolic Age to the Close of the Conciliar Period*. New York: Scribner, 1941.
Ayerst, David, and A. T. Fisher. *Records of Christianity: Christendom*. New York: Barnes & Noble, 1977.
Bagnall, Roger S. *Egypt in Late Antiquity*. Princeton: Princeton University Press, 1995.
Bailey, Cyril. *Phases in the Religion of Ancient Rome*. Berkeley: University of California Press, 1932.
Baillie, John. *The Belief in Progress*. New York: Scribner, 1951.
Bainbridge, William Folwell. *Around the World Tour of Christian Missions*. Ann Arbor: University of Michigan Library, 1882.
Bainbridge, William Sims. *The Sociology of Religious Movements*. New York: Routledge, 1996.
Baldet, Jacques. *Jesus the Rabbi Prophet: A New Light on the Gospel Message*. Rochester, VT: Inner Traditions, 2005.
Balsdon, J. P. V. D. *Roman Women: Their History and Habits*. New York: Barnes & Noble, 1983.
Baly, Denis. *The Geography of the Bible*. New York: Harper & Row, 1974.
Bamberger, Bernard Jacob. *Proselytism in the Talmudic Period*. 2nd ed. Brooklyn: Ktav Publishing, 1968.
Barber, Malcolm. *The Cathars: Dualist Heretics in Languedoc in the High Middle Ages*. The Medieval World. New York: Routledge, 2013.
Barnard, Leslie W. *Justin Martyr: His Life and Thought*. Cambridge: Cambridge University Press, 1967.
———. *St. Justin Martyr: the First and Second Apologies*. New York: Paulist Press, 1997.
Barnes, Timothy D. *Constantine and Eusebius*. Cambridge, MA: Harvard University Press, 2006.
Barnett, Paul. *The Birth of Christianity: The First Twenty Years*. After Jesus Vol. 1. Grand Rapids: Eerdmans, 2005.
———. *Paul, Missionary of Jesus*. After Jesus Vol. 2. Grand Rapids: Eerdmans, 2008.

Baron, Salo Wittmayer. *A Social and Religious History of the Jews, Vol. 6: Laws, Homilies, and the Bible: High Middle Ages*. 2nd ed. New York: Columbia University Press, 1958.
Barrett, David B., George Thomas K., and Todd M. Johnson, eds. *World Christian Encyclopedia: A Comparative Survey of Churches and Religions in the Modern World*. 2nd ed. 2 vols. New York: Oxford University Press, 2001.
Batey, Richard A. *Jesus and the Forgotten City: New Light on Sepphoris and the Urban World of Jesus*. Grand Rapids: Baker, 1992.
Bauckham, Richard. *Gospel Women: Studies of the Named Women in the Gospels*. Grand Rapids: Eerdmans 2002.
———. *Jesus and the Eyewitnesses: The Gospels as Eyewitness Testimony*. Grand Rapids: Eerdmans, 2008.
———. *Jude and the Relatives of Jesus in the Early Church*. New York: Bloomsbury T. & T. Clark, 2004.
———. *The Testimony of the Beloved Disciple: Narrative, History, and Theology in the Gospel of John*. Grand Rapids: Baker, 2007.
Baumgarten, Albert I. *The Flourishing of Jewish Sects in the Maccabean Era. An Interpretation*. Atlanta: Society of Biblical Literature, 2005.
Beach, Harlan P. *A Geography and Atlas of Protestant Missions Vol. 2: Statistics and Atlas*. New York: Student Volunteer Movement for Foreign Missions, 1903.
Beard, Mary, John North, and Simon Price. *Religions of Rome*. Cambridge: Cambridge University Press, 1998.
Beckford, James A. *Cult Controversies: The Societal Response to New Religious Movements*. 2 vols. London: Routledge Kegan & Paul, 1985.
Benin, Stephen D. *The Footprints of God: Divine Accommodation in Jewish and Christian Thought*. Albany: State University of New York Press, 1993.
Benko, Stephen. *Pagan Rome and the Early Christians*. Bloomington, IN: Indiana University Press, 1986.
Berger, Peter L. *Heretical Imperative: Contemporary Possibilities of Religious Affirmation*. New York: Doubleday, 1980.
———. *The Sacred Canopy: Elements of a Sociological Theory of Religion*. New York: Anchor, 1990.
Beskow, Per. *Strange Tales about Jesus: A Survey of Unfamiliar Gospels*. Philadelphia: Fortress, 1983
Betz, Hans Dieter, Don S. Browning, Bernd Janowski, and Eberhard Jüngel, eds. *Religion Past and Present: Encyclopedia of Theology and Religion*, vol. 2. 4th ed. Leiden: Brill, 2007.
Beugnot, Arthur. *Histoire de La Destruction Du Paganisme En Occident*. Paris: Firmin Didot Press, 1835.
Bingham, D. Jeffrey "Justin and Isaiah 53." *Vigiliae Christianae* 53 (2000) 248–61.
Blomberg, Craig L. *The Historical Reliability of the Gospels*. 2nd ed. Downers Grove, IL: IVP, 2007.
Boak, Arthur E. R. *Manpower Shortage and the Fall of the Roman Empire in the West*. Ann Arbor: University of Michigan Press, 1955.
Bobichon, Philippe *Justin Martyr, Dialogue avec le Tryphon*. Fribourg, Switzerland: Departement de Patristique et d'Histoire de l'Eglise de l'Universite de Fribourg, 2003.
Bock, Darrell. *The Missing Gospels*. Nashville: Thomas Nelson, 2006.

Boff, Leonardo. *Ecclesiogenesis: The Base Communities Reinvent the Church*. Maryknoll, NY: Orbis Books, 1986.

Boorstin, Daniel J. *The Discoverers: A History of Man's Search to Know His World and Himself*. New York: Random House, 1983.

Bowden, Hugh. "Church Fathers." In *Christianity: The Complete Guide*, 243–44.

Bowersock, G. W. *Hellenism in Late Antiquity*. Ann Arbor: University of Michigan Press, 1990.

———. *Julian the Apostate*. Cambridge, MA: Harvard University Press, 1978.

Boyarin, Daniel. "Justin Martyr Invents Judaism." *Church History* 70 (2001) 427–61.

Brandon, S. G. F. *The Fall of Jerusalem and the Christian Church: A Study of the Effects of the Jewish Overthrow of AD 70 on Christianity*. 2nd ed. Eugene, OR: Wipf & Stock, 2010.

Braudel, Fernand. *Afterthoughts on Material Civilization and Capitalism*. The Johns Hopkins Symposia in Comparative History. Baltimore: The Johns Hopkins University Press, 1979.

Bridger, David, and Samuel Wolk, eds. *The New Jewish Encyclopedia*. Vol. 3. New York: Behrman House, 1976.

Brooten, Bernadette J. *Women Leaders in the Ancient Synagogue*. Atlanta: Brown Judaic Studies, 1982.

Brown, Peter. *Authority and the Sacred: Aspects of the Christianisation of the Roman World*. Canto Original Series. New York: Cambridge University Press, 1997.

———. *The Body and Society: Men, Women, and Sexual Renunciation in Early Christianity*. Columbia Classics in Religion. 2nd ed. New York: Columbia University Press, 2008.

———. *The Cult of the Saints: Its Rise and Function in Latin Christianity*. Chicago: University of Chicago Press, 1982.

———. *The Making of Late Antiquity*. Carl Newell Jackson Lectures. Cambridge, MA: Harvard University Press, 1993.

———. *Poverty and Leadership in the Later Roman Empire*. Hanover, MA: Brandeis University Press, 2002.

———. *Power and Persuasion in Late Antiquity: Towards a Christian Empire*. Madison, WI: University of Wisconsin Press, 1992.

Bruce, F. F. *The Epistle of Paul to the Romans: An Introduction and Commentary*. London: Martino Fine Books, 2011.

———. *The New Testament Documents: Are They Reliable?* Grassy Creek, NC: Eerdmans, 2003.

Bruce, Steve, ed. *Religion and Modernization: Sociologists and Historians Debate the Secularization Thesis*. New York: Oxford University Press, 1992.

Brunt, P. A. *Italian Manpower, 225 BC–AD 14*. Oxford: Oxford University Press, 1987.

Burckhardt, Jacob. *The Age of Constantine the Great*. Berkeley: University of California Press, 1983.

Burkert, Walter. *Ancient Mystery Cults*. Carl Newell Jackson Lectures. Cambridge, MA: Harvard University Press, 1989.

———. *Babylon, Memphis, Persepolis: Eastern Contexts of Greek Culture*. Cambridge, MA: Harvard University Press, 2007.

———. *Greek Religion*. Oxford: Harvard University Press, 1985.

Burridge, Richard A. *What Are the Gospels? A Comparison with Graeco-Roman Biography*. 2nd ed. Grand Rapids: Eerdmans, 2004.

Bush, L. Russ, ed. *Classical Readings in Christian Apologetics: AD 100–1800*. Grand Rapids: Academie Books, 1983.
Bush, R. Wheler. *St. Athanasius: His Life and Times*. London: Society for Promoting Christian Knowledge, 1888.
Bütz, Jeffrey J. *The Brother of Jesus and the Lost Teachings of Christianity*. Rochester, VT: Inner Traditions, 2005.
Calvin, John. *Institutes of the Christian Religion: 1536 Edition*. Philadelphia: Westminster, 1960.
Cameron, Averil. *Oi Buzantinoi*. Athens: Psychoigios, 2009.
Carcopino, Jérôme. *Daily Life in Ancient Rome: The People and the City at the Height of the Empire*. 2nd ed. New Haven, CT: Yale University Press, 2003.
Carlson, Stephen C. *The Gospel Hoax: Morton Smith's Invention of Secret Mark*. Waco, TX: Baylor University Press, 2005.
Carmignac, Jean. *The Birth of the Synoptic Gospels*. Chicago: Franciscan Press, 1937.
Carroll, James. *Constantine's Sword: The Church and the Jews, a History*. Boston: Mariner Books, 2002.
Carson, D. A. *Christ and Culture Revisited*. Grand Rapids: Eerdmans, 2008.
Case, Shirley Jackson. *The Historicity of Jesus: A Criticism of the Contention That Jesus Never Lived, a Statement of the Evidence for His Existence, an Estimate of His Relation to Christianity*. Chicago: University of Chicago Press, 1912.
———. *Jesus through the Centuries*. Chicago: University of Chicago Press, 1932.
Casey, Maurice. *From Jewish Prophet to Gentile God: The Origins and Development of New Testament Christology*. Louisville: Westminster John Knox, 1992.
Celsus. *On the True Doctrine: A Discourse against the Christians*. New York: Oxford University Press, 1987.
Chadwick, Henry. *Atlas of the Christian Church*. New York: Facts on File, 1987.
———. *Early Christian Thought and the Classical Tradition: Studies in Justin, Clement, and Origen*. Oxford: Oxford University Press, 1966.
———. *The Early Church*. The Penguin History of the Church. Rev. ed. London: Penguin, 1993.
Chandler, Tertius. *Four Thousand Years of Urban Growth: An Historical Census*. Rev. ed. Lewiston, NY: The Edwin Mellen Press, 1987.
Chandler, Diana. "Personal Soul-winning, Evangelism Task Force Named." June 15, 2017. https://www.baptistpress.com/resource-library/news/personal-soul-winning-evangelism-task-force-named/.
Chase, Frederic Henry. *Chrysostom: A Study in the History of Biblical Interpretation*. Cambridge: Deighton, Bell, and Co., 1887.
Chase, Frederic Henry, Jr., trans. *Saint John of Damascus: Writings*. New York: Fathers of the Church 1958.
Cheetham, Nicolas. *Keepers of the Keys: A History of the Popes from St. Peter to John Paul II*. New York: Scribner, 1983.
Chejne, Anwar G. *Islam and the West, The Moriscos: A Cultural and Social History*. Albany: State University of New York Press, 1983.
Chrysostom, Saint John. "An Address on Vainglory and the Right Way for Parents to Bring Up Their Children." In *Christianity and Pagan Culture in the Later Roman Empire*, translated by Max L. W. Laistner. Ithaca, NY: Cornell University Press, 1951. http://www.strobertbellarmine.net/books/Chrysostom--Vainglory_and_Children.pdf.

———. *Apologist: The Fathers of the Church*, vol. 73. Edited by Margaret A. Schatkin. Translated by Paul William Harkins. Washington, DC: The Catholic University of America Press, 1985.

———. "Chrysostom and Scripture." In *Homilies on Genesis 1–17: The Fathers of the Church*, vol. 74, translated by Robert C. Hill. Washington, DC: The Catholic University of America Press, 1986.

———. "Demonstration against the Pagans That Christ Is God." In *Apologist: The Fathers of the Church*, vol. 73, translated by Margaret A. Schatkin and Paul W. Harkins. Washington, DC: The Catholic University of America Press, 1985.

———."Discourse on Blessed Babylas and against the Greeks." In *Apologist: The Fathers of the Church*, vol. 73, translated by Margaret A. Schatkin and Paul W. Harkins. Washington, DC: The Catholic University of America Press, 1985.

———. "Discourses against Judaizing Christians." In *Apologist: The Fathers of the Church*, vol. 68, translated by Paul W. Harkins. Washington, DC: The Catholic University of America Press, 1999.

———. "Homily 1 on Matthew." In *Nicene and Post-Nicene Fathers, First Series*, vol. 10, translated by George Prevost, revised by M. B. Riddle, edited by Philip Schaff. Buffalo, NY: Christian Literature Publishing, 1888. Revised and edited for *New Advent* by Kevin Knight. http://www.newadvent.org/fathers/200101.htm.

———. "Homily 3 on the Gospel of John." In *Nicene and Post-Nicene Fathers, First Series*, vol. 10, translated by George Prevost, revised by M. B. Riddle, edited by Philip Schaff. Buffalo, NY: Christian Literature Publishing, 1888. Revised and edited for *New Advent* by Kevin Knight. http://www.newadvent.org/fathers/240103.htm.

———. "Homily 4 on Ephesians." In *Nicene and Post-Nicene Fathers, First Series*, vol. 10, translated by George Prevost, revised by M. B. Riddle, edited by Philip Schaff. Buffalo, NY: Christian Literature Publishing, 1888. Revised and edited for *New Advent* by Kevin Knight. http://www.newadvent.org/fathers/230104.htm.

———. "Homily 7 on the Gospel of John." In *Nicene and Post-Nicene Fathers, First Series*, vol. 10, translated by George Prevost, revised by M. B. Riddle, edited by Philip Schaff. Buffalo, NY: Christian Literature Publishing, 1888. Revised and edited for *New Advent* by Kevin Knight. http://www.newadvent.org/fathers/240107.htm.

———. "Homily 7 on Matthew." In *Nicene and Post-Nicene Fathers, First Series*, vol. 10, translated by George Prevost, revised by M. B. Riddle, edited by Philip Schaff. Buffalo, NY: Christian Literature Publishing, 1888. Revised and edited for *New Advent* by Kevin Knight. http://www.newadvent.org/ fathers/200107.htm.

———. "Homily 9." In *Homilies on Genesis 1–17: The Fathers of the Church*, vol. 74, translated by Robert C. Hill. Washington, DC: The Catholic University of America Press, 1986.

———. "Homily 9 on Colossians." In *Nicene and Post-Nicene Fathers, First Series*, vol. 10, translated by George Prevost, revised by M. B. Riddle, edited by Philip Schaff. Buffalo, NY: Christian Literature Publishing, 1888. Revised and edited for *New Advent* by Kevin Knight. http://www.newadvent.org/ fathers/230309.htm.

———. "Homily 21 on Ephesians." In *Nicene and Post-Nicene Fathers, First Series*, vol. 10, translated by George Prevost, revised by M. B. Riddle, edited by Philip Schaff. Buffalo, NY: Christian Literature Publishing, 1888. Revised and edited for *New Advent* by Kevin Knight. http://www.newadvent.org/ fathers/230121.htm.

———. "Homily 37 (John 5.7–13)." In *Commentary on Saint John the Apostle and Evangelist, Homilies 1–47: The Fathers of the Church*, translated by Sister Thomas

Aquinas Goggin. Washington, DC: The Catholic University of America Press, 2000.

———. "Homily 53 (John 8.20–30)." In *Commentary on Saint John the Apostle and Evangelist, Homilies 48–88: The Fathers of the Church*, translated by Sister Thomas Aquinas Goggin. Washington, DC: The Catholic University of America Press, 2000.

———. "Homily 55 on the Gospel of John." In *Nicene and Post-Nicene Fathers, First Series*, vol. 10, translated by George Prevost, revised by M. B. Riddle, edited by Philip Schaff. Buffalo, NY: Christian Literature Publishing, 1888. Revised and edited for *New Advent* by Kevin Knight. http://www.newadvent.org/fathers/200155.htm

———. "Homily 59 on the Gospel of John." In *Nicene and Post-Nicene Fathers, First Series*, vol. 10, translated by George Prevost, revised by M. B. Riddle, edited by Philip Schaff. Buffalo, NY: Christian Literature Publishing, 1888. Revised and edited for *New Advent* by Kevin Knight. http://www.newadvent.org/fathers/240159.htm.

———. "Homily 68 on Matthew." In *Nicene and Post-Nicene Fathers, First Series*, vol. 10, translated by George Prevost, revised by M. B. Riddle, edited by Philip Schaff. Buffalo, NY: Christian Literature Publishing, 1888. Revised and edited for *New Advent* by Kevin Knight. http://www.newadvent.org/ fathers/200168.htm.

———. *On Wealth and Poverty*. Translated by Catharine P. Roth. Crestwood, NY: St. Vladimir's Seminary Press, 1984.

Chuvin, Pierre. *A Chronicle of the Last Pagans*. Cambridge, MA: Harvard University Press, 1990.

Clark, Gordon H. *Thales to Dewey*. 2nd ed. Jefferson, MD: Trinity Foundation, 1989.

Clauss, Manfred. *The Roman Cult of Mithras: The God and His Mysteries*. New York: Routledge, 2001.

Cohen, Abraham. *Everyman's Talmud: The Major Teachings of the Rabbinic Sages*. New York: Schocken, 1995.

Cohen, Shaye J. D. *From the Maccabees to the Mishnah*. 2nd ed. Louisville: Westminster John Knox, 2006.

Collingwood, R. G. *Roman Britain and the English Settlements*. Oxford History of England. 2nd ed. Oxford: Oxford University Press, 1937.

Congar, Yves. *Lay People in the Church: A Study for a Theology of the Laity by a Master of Twentieth-Century Theology*. Louisville: Westminster John Knox, 1985.

Constantinou, Eugenia. "Select Quotes from St. John Chrysostom on the Benefits and Importance of Scripture Reading for Christians." http://www.saintjonah.org/chrysostom_scripture.htm.

Conway, Joe. "Pastors' Task Force to Address Declining SBC Baptism Trend." September 20, 2013. https://www.namb.net/news/pastors-task-force-to-address-declining-sbc-baptism-trend/.

Cooper, D. Jason. *Mithras: Mysteries and Initiation Rediscovered*. York Beach, ME: Red Wheel / Weiser, 1996.

Copleston, Frederick. *A History of Philosophy, Vol. 1: Greece and Rome from the Pre-Socratics to Plotinus*. New York: Doubleday, 1993.

Corrigan, John, Frederick M. Denny, Carlos M. N. Eire, and Martin S. Jaffee. *Readings in Judaism, Christianity, and Islam*. Upper Saddle River, NJ: Pearson, 1998.

Cosgrove, C. H. "Justin Martyr and the Emerging Christian Canon." *Vigiliae Christianae* 36 (1982) 209–32.

Cotton, Hannah M., Robert G. Hoyland, Jonathan J. Price, and David J. Wasserstein, eds. *From Hellenism to Islam: Cultural and Linguistic Change in the Roman Near East*. Cambridge: Cambridge University Press, 2012.

Countryman, L. William. *The Rich Christian in the Church of the Early Empire: Contradictions and Accommodations*. New York: Edwin Mellen, 1980.

Cox, Daniel, and Robert P. Jones. "America's Changing Religious Identity." September 6, 2017. https://www.prri.org/research/american-religious-landscape-christian-religiously-unaffiliated/.

Cross, F. L., and E. A. Livingstone, eds. *The Oxford Dictionary of the Christian Church*. 3rd ed. Oxford: Oxford University Press, 1997.

Crossan, John Dominic. *The Birth of Christianity: Discovering What Happened in the Years Immediately after the Execution of Jesus*. San Francisco: HarperOne, 1999.

———. *The Historical Jesus: The Life of a Mediterranean Jewish Peasant*. New York: HarperOne, 1993.

———. *Jesus: A Revolutionary Biography*. San Francisco: HarperOne, 2009.

Cumont, Franz. *Oriental Religions in Roman Paganism*. 2nd ed. New York: Dover, 1956.

———. *Recherches sur le Symbolisme Funéraire des Romains*. New York: Ayers Co., 1976.

Cureton, William. *The Festal Letters of Athanasius*. London: Society for the Publication of Oriental Texts, 1848.

Daniel, Norman. *Islam and the West: The Making of an Image*. Oxford: Oneworld, 1993.

Daniélou, Jean. *Origene*. Translated by Walter Mitchell. Paris: Table Ronde, 1948.

Daniel-Rops, H. *Daily Life in Palestine at the Time of Christ*. London: Phoenix Press, 2002.

DeConick, April D. *Recovering the Original Gospel of Thomas: A History of the Gospel and Its Growth*. New York: Bloomsbury T. & T. Clark, 2006.

———. *The Thirteenth Apostle: What the Gospel of Judas Really Says*. London: Bloomsbury Academic, 2009.

de Faye, Eugene. *Origene: Sa Vie, son Oeuvre, sa Pensée*. Paris: Ernest Leroux, 1923.

———. "L'Influence du Timee de Platon sur la Theology de Justin Martyr." *Bibliotheque de l'Ecole des hautes Etudes, Sciences Rel* 7 (1896) 172.

de Lubac, Henri. *History and Spirit: The Understanding of Scripture according to Origen*. Translated by Anne Englund Nash. San Francisco: Ignatius Press, 2007.

Dennett, Daniel C. *Breaking the Spell: Religion as a Natural Phenomenon*. New York: Penguin, 2007.

Denning-Bolle, Sara. "Christian Dialogue as Apologetic: The Case of Justin Martyr Seen in Historical Context." *Bulletin of the John Rylands University Library of Manchester* 69 (1987) 492–510.

di Berardino, Angelo, ed. *Encyclopedia of Ancient Christianity*. Downers Grove, IL: IVP, 2014.

Dibelius, Martin *From Tradition to Gospel*. Cambridge: James Clarke & Co, 1987.

Dodd, C. H. *The Founder of Christianity*. London: Collins, 1971.

Dodds, E. R. *Pagan and Christian in an Age of Anxiety: Some Aspects of Religious Experience from Marcus Aurelius to Constantine*. New York: Cambridge University Press, 1991.

Donalson, Malcolm Drew. *The Cult of Isis in the Roman Empire: Isis Invicta*. Lewiston, NY: Edwin Mellen, 2003.

Dowling, John. *The History of Romanism from the Earliest Corruptions of Christianity to the Present Time.* Lincolnshire, IL: Vance, 2002.

Drake, H. A. *Constantine and the Bishops: The Politics of Intolerance.* Baltimore: Johns Hopkins University Press, 2002.

Draper, James T., Jr. "Second Generation Syndrome." October 25, 2005. *The Christian Post.* http://www.christianpost.com/news/second-generation-syndrome-6481/.

Edgar, William, and K. Scott Oliphint. *Christian Apologetics Past and Present.* Wheaton, IL: Crossway, 2009.

Edwards, James R. *Is Jesus the Only Savior?* Grand Rapids: Eerdmans, 2005.

Ehrman, Bart D., ed. *After the New Testament: A Reader in Early Christianity.* New York: Oxford University Press, 1999.

———. *Lost Christianities: The Battles for Scripture and the Faiths We Never Knew.* Oxford: Oxford University Press, 2005.

———. *The Lost Gospel of Judas Iscariot: A New Look at Betrayer and Betrayed.* New York: Oxford University Press, 2006.

———. *Misquoting Jesus: The Story behind Who Changed the Bible and Why.* New York: HarperOne, 2007.

Elder, Ernie Dewey. "Contextual Impact on the Use of Scriptures in the Baptismal Homilies of John Chrysostom and Cyril of Jerusalem." ThM thesis, The Southern Baptist Theological Seminary, 1987.

Elders, Leo J. *The Philosophical Theology of St. Thomas Aquinas.* New York: E. J. Brill, 1990.

Eliade, Mircea, ed. *The Encyclopedia of Religion.* Vol. 3. New York: Collier Macmillan, 1987.

Ellerbe, Helen. *The Dark Side of Christian History.* San Rafael, CA: Morningstar & Lark, 1995.

Elliott, T. G. *The Christianity of Constantine the Great.* Scranton, PA: University of Scranton Press, 1996.

Elrod, Brandon. "Disciple-Making Task Force Report: Bible Engagement, Follow Up Key to Discipleship." June 21, 2018. https://www.namb.net/news/disciple-making-task-force-report-bible-engagement-follow-up-to-key-discussion/.

Encyclopedia Britannica. "Iconoclastic Controversy." *Britannica.com.* https://www.britannica.com/event/Iconoclastic-Controversy.

Erickson, Millard J. *Christian Theology.* 2nd ed. Grand Rapids: Baker, 1998.

Ernest, James D. *The Bible in Athanasius of Alexandria.* Atlanta: Society of Biblical Literature, 2004.

Eusebius. *Ecclesiastical History: Complete and Unabridged.* Translated by C. F. Cruse. Peabody, MA: Hendrickson, 1998.

———. *The Ecclesiastical History of Eusebius Pamphilus, Bishop of Cesarea, in Palestine.* Translated by C. F. Cruse. Grand Rapids: Baker, 1991.

Evans, Craig A. *Fabricating Jesus: How Modern Scholars Distort the Gospels.* Downers Grove, IL: IVP, 2008.

Fahlbusch, Erwin, ed. *The Encyclopedia of Christianity.* Grand Rapids: Eerdmans, 1999–2008.

Fairweather, William. *Origen and Greek Patristic Theology.* New York: Charles Scribner's Sons, 1901.

Farrar, Frederic. *Lives of the Fathers: Sketches of Church History in Biography.* Edinburgh: Adam and Charles Black, 1889.

Feldman, Louis H. *Jew and Gentile in the Ancient World*. Princeton, NJ: Princeton University Press, 1996.
Ferguson, Everett, ed. *Encyclopedia of Early Christianity*. Garland Reference Library of the Humanities. 2nd ed. New York: Garland Publishing, 1990.
Ferngren, Gary B. *Medicine and Health Care in Early Christianity*. Baltimore: Johns Hopkins University Press, 2009.
Ferrill, Arther. *The Fall of the Roman Empire: The Military Explanation*. New York: Thames & Hudson, 1986.
Filotas, Bernadette. *Pagan Survivals, Superstitions, and Popular Cultures in Early Medieval Pastoral Literature*. Toronto: Pontifical Institute of Mediaeval Studies, 2005.
Finley, M. I. *The Ancient Economy*. Updated ed. Berkeley: University of California Press, 1999.
———. *Atlas of Classical Archaeology*. New York: McGraw Hill, 1977.
———. *Economy and Society in Ancient Greece*. New York: Viking Adult, 1982.
Fletcher, Richard. *The Barbarian Conversion: From Paganism to Christianity*. New York: Henry Holt and Co., 1998.
Foltz, Richard. *Religions of the Silk Road: Premodern Patterns of Globalization*. 2nd ed. New York: Palgrave Macmillan, 2010.
Forster, E. M. *Alexandria: A History and a Guide*. New York: Oxford University Press, 1938.
Foster, Paul. "Justin and Paul." In *Paul and the Second Century*, edited by Michael F. Bird and Joseph R. Dodson, Library of New Testament Studies series, 108–25. London: T. & T. Clark, 2012.
Fox, Robin Lane. *Pagans and Christians*. New York: Knopf, 1987.
Frank, Harry Thomas. *Discovering the Biblical World*. Rev. ed. Maplewood, NJ: Hammond World Atlas Corp, 1988.
Freeman, Charles. *The Greek Achievement: The Foundation of the Western World*. New York: Penguin, 2000.
Fremantle, Anne. *The Age of Belief*. New York: Mentor Book, 1955.
———, ed. *A Treasury of Early Christianity*. Fort Collins: Roman Catholic Books, 1953.
Frend, W. H. C. *Martyrdom and Persecution in the Early Church: A Study of a Conflict from the Maccabees to Donatus*. Oxford: Blackwell, 1965.
———. *The Rise of Christianity*. Philadelphia: Fortress, 1984.
Froehlich, Karlfried, trans. and ed. *Biblical Interpretation in the Early Church: Sources of Early Christian Thought*. Philadelphia: Fortress, 1984.
Funk, Robert W. *Honest to Jesus: Jesus for a New Millennium*. San Francisco: HarperSanFrancisco, 1996.
Funk, Robert W., Roy W. Hoover, and the Jesus Seminar. *The Five Gospels: What Did Jesus Really Say? The Search for the Authentic Words of Jesus*. New York: HarperCollins, 1993.
Furseth, Inger, and Pål Repstad. *An Introduction to the Sociology of Religion: Classical and Contemporary Perspectives*. Aldershot, England: Ashgate, 2006.
Fustel de Coulanges, Numa Denis. *The Ancient City: A Study on the Religion, Laws, and Institutions of Greece and Rome*. Garden City, NY: Doubleday, 1956.
Gager, John G. *Kingdom and Community: The Social World of Early Christianity*. 2 vols. Englewood Cliffs, NJ: Prentice Hall, 1975.

———. *The Origins of Anti-Semitism: Attitudes toward Judaism in Pagan and Christian Antiquity*. Oxford: Oxford University Press, 1985.
Gallagher, Eugene V. "Divine Man or Magician? Celsus and Origen on Jesus." Chico, CA: Scholars Press, 1982.
Gambero, Luigi. *Mary and the Fathers of the Church: The Blessed Virgin Mary in Patristic Thought*. San Francisco: Ignatius Press, 2006.
Gamble, Harry Y. *Books and Readers in the Early Church: A History of Early Christian Texts*. New Haven, CT: Yale University Press, 1997.
Gardner, Jane F., and Thomas Wiedemann. *The Roman Household: A Sourcebook*. New York: Routledge, 1991.
Gasque, Ward. *A History of the Interpretation of the Acts of the Apostles*. Peabody, MA: Wipf & Stock, 2000.
Gaustad, Edwin S. *Faith of the Founders: Religion and the New Nation, 1776–1826*. Waco, TX: Baylor University Press, 2011.
Geisler, Norman L., and William E. Nix. *A General Introduction to the Bible*. Rev. ed. Chicago: Moody, 1986.
Gerhardsson, Birger. *The Reliability of the Gospel Tradition*. Ada, MI: Baker, 2001.
Gerlach, Luther. *People, Power, Change: Movements of Social Transformation*. Indianapolis: Bobbs-Merrill, 1970.
Gibbon, Edward. *The History of the Decline and Fall of the Roman Empire*. Edited by David Womersley. 3 vols. London: Penguin, 1994.
Gibbon, Edward, and D. M. Low. *Decline and Fall of the Roman Empire*. Abridged ed. London: Chatto & Windus, 1960.
Gierke, Otto. *Associations and Law: The Classical and Early Christian Stages*. Toronto: University of Toronto Press, 1977.
Glock, Charles Y., and Rodney Stark. *Religion and Society in Tension*. Chicago: Rand McNally, 1965.
Gonzalez, Justo L. *The Story of Christianity, Vol. 1: The Early Church to the Dawn of the Reformation*. San Francisco: HarperCollins, 2010.
Goodenough, Erwin R. *The Church in the Roman Empire*. New York: Henry Hold and Company, 1931.
———. *An Introduction to Philo Judaeus*. 2nd ed. Oxford: Basil Blackwell, 1962.
———. *The Theology of Justin Martyr: An Investigation into the Conceptions of the Earliest Christian Literature and its Hellenistic and Judaistic Influences*. Jena, Germany: Verlag Frommansche Buchhandlung, 1923.
Goodman, Martin. *Mission and Conversion: Proselytizing in the Religious History of the Roman Empire*. Oxford: Oxford University Press, 1996.
Goodspeed, Edgar Johnson. *Strange New Gospels*. Chicago: University of Chicago Press, 1931.
Gorman, Michael J. *Abortion and the Early Church: Christian, Jewish, and Pagan Attitudes in the Greco-Roman World*. Downers Grove, IL: InterVarsity, 1982.
Grant, Michael. *History of Rome*. New York: Faber and Faber, 1978.
Grant, Robert M. *Augustus to Constantine: The Thrust of the Christian Movement into the Roman World*. New York: Harper & Row, 1970.
———. *Early Christianity and Society*. London: Collins, 1978.
Green, Henry A. *The Economic and Social Origins of Gnosticism*. Atlanta: Scholars Press, 1985.

Green, Michael. *Evangelism in the Early Church*. Rev. ed. Grand Rapids: Eerdmans, 2003.
Grudem, Wayne. *Systematic Theology*. Grand Rapids: Zondervan, 1994.
Guthrie, W. K. *The Greek Philosophers: From Thales to Aristotle*. New York: Harper & Row, 1960.
Hall, Christopher A. *Reading Scripture with the Church Fathers*. Downers Grove, IL: InterVarsity, 1998.
Hammond, Mason. *The City in the Ancient World*. Cambridge, MA: Harvard University Press, 1972.
Hanson, R. P. C. *Allegory and Event: A Study of the Source and Significance of Origen's Interpretation of Scripture*. London: SCM, 1959.
Hanson, Richard A., and John S. Horsley. *Bandits, Prophets, and Messiahs: Popular Movements in the Time of Jesus*. San Francisco: Winston, 1988.
Hare, Douglas R. A. *The Theme of Jewish Persecution of Christians in the Gospel According to St. Matthew*. Cambridge: Cambridge University Press, 2005.
Harris, Sam. "Sam Harris: On Interpreting Scripture." April 17, 2007. https://www.youtube.com/watch?v=8zV3vIXZ-1Y.
Harvey, Susan Ashbrook. "Martyr Passions and Hagiography." In *Oxford Handbook of Early Christian Studies*, edited by Susan Ashbrook Harvey and David G. Hunter, 584–628. Oxford: Oxford University Press, 2010.
Hautsch, Ernst. *Die Evangelienziate des Origenes*. Leipzig, Germany: J. C. Hinrichs, 1909.
Haykin, Michael A. G. *Rediscovering the Church Fathers: Who They Were and How They Shaped the Church*. Wheaton, IL: Crossway, 2011.
Hechter, Michael. *Principles of Group Solidarity*. 2 vols. Berkeley: University of California Press, 1987.
Hemer, Colin J. *The Book of Acts in the Setting of Hellenistic History*. Edited by Conrad H. Gempf. Winona Lake, IN: Eisenbrauns, 1990.
Hengel, Martin. *Judaism and Hellenism: Studies in Their Encounter in Palestine during the Early Hellenistic Period*. 3 vols. Philadelphia: Fortress, 1975.
Herbermann, Charles G. *The Catholic Encyclopedia: An International Work of Reference on the Constitution, Doctrine, Discipline, and History of the Catholic Church*. London: Catholic Way, 2014.
Hitchcock, Susan Tyler, John Esposito, Desmond Tutu, and Mpho Tutu. *Geography of Religion: Where God Lives, Where Pilgrims Walk*. Washington, DC: National Geographic, 2006.
Hitchens, Christopher. *God Is Not Great: How Religion Poisons Everything*. New York: Hachette, 2007.
Hock, Ronald F. *The Social Context of Paul's Ministry: Tentmaking and Apostleship*. Philadelphia: Augsburg Fortress, 1980.
Hodgson, Marshall G. S. *The Venture of Islam, Vol. 1: The Classical Age of Islam*. Chicago: University of Chicago Press, 1977.
Hofer, Andrew. "The Old Man as Christ in Justin's Dialogue with Trypho." *Vigiliae Christianae* 57 (2003) 1–21.
Hoffmann, R. Joseph. *Porphyry's Against the Christians: The Literary Remains*. Amherst, NY: Prometheus, 1994.
Holmberg, Bengt. *Paul and Power: The Structure of Authority in the Primitive Church as Reflected in the Pauline Epistles*. Eugene, OR: Wipf & Stock, 2004.

Holte, Ragnar. "Logos Spermaticos: Christianity and Ancient Philosophy according to St. Justin's Apologies." *Studia Theologica* 12 (1958) 109–68.
Horner, Timothy J. *Listening to Trypho: Justin Martyr's Dialogue Reconsidered*. Contributions to Biblical Exegesis and Theology 28. Leuvan, Belgium: Peeters, 2001.
Hough, Lynn Harold. *Athanasius: The Hero*. New York: Eaton and Mains, 1906.
House, H. Wayne, and Dennis W. Jowers. Reasons for our Hope: An Introduction to Christian Apologetics. Nashville: B&H Publishing, 2011.
Hovhanessian, Vahan S., ed. *The School of Antioch: Biblical Theology and the Church in Syria*. Bible in the Christian Orthodox Traditions Series. New York: Peter Lang, 2016.
Hubík, Karl. *Die Apologien des hl. Justinus: Des Philosophen und Märtyrers. Literarhistorische Untersuchungen*. Theologische Studien der Leo Gesellschaft 19. Vienna: Mayer & Co., 1912.
Hurtado, Larry W. *The Earliest Christian Artifacts: Manuscripts and Christian Origins*. Grand Rapids: Eerdmans 2006.
———. *Lord Jesus Christ: Devotion to Jesus in Earliest Christianity*. Grand Rapids: Eerdmans, 2005.
Hyldahl, Niels. *Philosophie und Christentum: Eine Interpretation der Einleitung zum Dialog Justins*. Acta theologica danica 9. Copenhagen: Munksgaard, 1966.
James, William. *The Varieties of Religious Experience*. New York: Mentor / New American Library, 1958.
Janosik, Daniel J. *John of Damascus: First Apologist to the Muslims*. Eugene, OR: Pickwick, 2016.
Jeffery, Peter. *The Secret Gospel of Mark Unveiled: Imagined Rituals of Sex, Death, and Madness in a Biblical Forgery*. New Haven, CT: Yale University Press, 2007.
Jenkins, Claude. "Origen on 1 Corinthians." Journal of Theological Studies 9 (1908) 231–47.
Jenkins, Philip. *Hidden Gospels: How the Search for Jesus Lost Its Way*. New York: Oxford University Press, 2002.
———. *The Lost History of Christianity: The Thousand-Year Golden Age of the Church in the Middle East, Africa, and Asia—and How It Died*. New York: HarperOne, 2009.
———. *The New Anti-Catholicism: The Last Acceptable Prejudice*. Chapel Hill, NC: Oxford University Press, 2004.
———. *The Next Christendom: The Coming of Global Christianity*. The Future of Christianity Trilogy. 3rd ed. Oxford: Oxford University Press, 2011.
John of Damascus. *Writings*. Washington, DC: The Catholic University of America Press, 1999.
Johnson, Luke Timothy. *The Real Jesus: The Misguided Quest for the Historical Jesus and the Truth of the Traditional Gospels*. San Francisco: HarperOne, 1997.
Johnson, Paul. *A History of Christianity*. New York: Scribner, 1976.
———. *A History of the Jews*. New York: Harper Perennial, 1988.
Jones, A. H. M. *Constantine and the Conversion of Europe*. The Medieval Academy Reprints for Teaching. Toronto: University of Toronto Press, 1978.
Josephus, Flavius. "The Antiquities of the Jews." In *The Works of Josephus: Complete and Unabridged* translated by William Whiston. New updated ed. Peabody, MA: Hendrickson, 1987.

———. *The Complete Works of Josephus*. Grand Rapids: Kregel, 1960.
Judge, Edwin Arthur. *The Social Pattern of the Christian Groups in the First Century. Some Prolegomena to the Study of New Testament Ideas of Social Obligation*. London: Tyndale, 1960.
Justin Martyr. *The Apologies of Justin Martyr*. Edited by A. W. F. Blunt. Cambridge: Cambridge University Press, 1911.
———. *Dialogus cum Tryphone*. Edited by Miroslav Marcovich. Berlin: Walter de Gruyter, 1997.
———. *Justin, Philosopher and Martyr: Apologies*. Edited by Denis Minns and Paul Parvis. Oxford: Oxford University Press, 2009.
———. *The Works Now Extant of St. Justin the Martyr*. Translated by J. H. and Jas. Parker. Oxford: Oxford University Press, 1861.
Justin Martyr and Athenagoras. *The Complete Works of Justin Martyr and Athenagoras*. Edited by Alexander Roberts and James Donaldson. Edinburgh: T. & T. Clark, 1909.
———. *The Writings of Justin Martyr and Athenagoras*. Translated by Marcus Dods, George Reith, and B. P. Pratten. Edinburgh: T. & T. Clark, 1867.
Kanter, Rosabeth Moss. *Commitment and Community: Communes and Utopias in Sociological Perspective*. Cambridge, MA: Harvard University Press, 1972.
Kautsky, Karl. *Foundations of Christianity*. Translated by Henry F. Mins. New York: Russell & Russell, 1953.
Kee, Howard Clark. *Jesus in History: An Approach to the Study of the Gospels*. New York: Harcourt, Brace & World, 1970.
———. *Knowing the Truth: A Sociological Approach to New Testament Interpretation*. Minneapolis: Fortress, 1989.
———. *Medicine, Miracle, and Magic in New Testament Times*. Cambridge: Cambridge University Press, 1986.
———. *Miracle in the Early Christian World: A Study in Sociohistorical Method*. New Haven, CT: Yale University Press, 1983.
———. *What Can We Know about Jesus?* Cambridge: Cambridge University Press, 1990.
Kelly, J. N. D. *Golden Mouth: The Story of John Chrysostom: Ascetic, Preacher, Bishop*. Ithaca, NY: Cornell University Press, 1998.
Kimball, Dan. *The Emerging Church: Vintage Christianity for New Generations*. Grand Rapids: Zondervan, 2003.
King, Karen L. *The Gospel of Mary of Magdala: Jesus and the First Woman Apostle*. Santa Rosa, CA: Polebridge Press, 2003.
———. *What Is Gnosticism?* New ed. Cambridge: Belknap Press, 2005.
Kirchhofer, Johannes. *Quellensammlung zur Geschichte des Neutestamentlichen Kanons bis auf Hieronymus*. Zürich: Meyer and Zeller, 1844.
Kitchen, K. A. *On the Reliability of the Old Testament*. Annotated ed. Grand Rapids: Eerdmans, 2006.
Klauck, Hans-Josef. *The Religious Context of Early Christianity: A Guide to Graeco-Roman Religions*. Minneapolis: Fortress, 2003.
Klinghoffer, David. *Why the Jews Rejected Jesus: The Turning Point in Western History*. New York: Doubleday, 2005.
Knight, Margaret. *Honest to Man: Christian Ethics Re-Examined*. 2 vols. Buffalo, NY: Prometheus, 1974.

Knohl, Isræl. *The Messiah before Jesus: The Suffering Servant of the Dead Sea Scrolls.* Berkeley: University of California Press, 2002.
Koester, Helmut. *Ancient Christian Gospels: Their History and Development.* Philadelphia: Bloomsbury T. & T. Clark, 1992.
———. *Introduction to the New Testament: History, Culture, and Religion of the Hellenistic Age.* Vol. 1. New York: Walter de Gruyter, 1987.
Kraft, Heinrich. *Early Christian Thinkers: An Introduction to Clement of Alexandria and Origen.* Norwich, England: Page Bros., 1964.
Kroeber, A. L., and Clyde Kluckhohn. *Culture: A Critical Review of Concepts and Definitions.* New York: Random House, 1952.
Krupp, R. A. *Saint John Chrysostom: A Scripture Index.* Lanham, MD: University Press of America, 1984.
———. *Shepherding the Flock of God: The Pastoral Theology of John Chrysostom.* New York: American University Studies, 1991.
Lactantius. *Divine Institutes Books 1-7.* Fathers of the Church Series 49. New York: Catholic University of America Press, 1964.
Lamoreaux, John C. "Early Eastern Christian Responses to Islam." In *Medieval Christian Perceptions of Islam: A Book of Essays,* edited by John Victor Tolan, 3-32. New York: Garland, 1996.
Latourette, Kenneth Scott. *The First Five Centuries: A History of the Expansion of Christianity.* New York: Harper & Brothers, 1937.
Layton, Bentley. *The Gnostic Scriptures: A New Translation with Annotations and Introductions.* Garden City, NY: Doubleday, 1987.
Levick, Barbara. *Roman Colonies in Southern Asia Minor.* Oxford: Clarendon, 1967.
Liebeschuetz, J. H. W. G. *Ambrose and John Chrysostom: Clerics between Desert and Empire.* Oxford: Oxford University Press, 2011.
Lightfoot, J. B. *The Apostolic Fathers.* Edited by J. R. Harmer. Grand Rapids: Baker, 1988.
Litfin, Bryan M. *Getting to Know the Church Fathers: An Evangelical Introduction.* Grand Rapids: Brazos, 2007.
Livingstone, E. A. *The Concise Oxford Dictionary of the Christian Church.* Oxford: Oxford University Press, 2013.
Livy, Titus. *The Early History of Rome: Books I-V of the History of Rome from Its Foundations.* Translated by Aubrey de Sélincourt. New York: Penguin Classics, 2002.
Louth, Andrew. *St. John Damascene: Tradition and Originality in Byzantine Theology.* Oxford: Oxford University Press, 2002.
Lupton, J. H. *St. John of Damascus.* London: Society for Promoting Christian Knowledge, 1882.
MacMullen, Ramsay. *Changes in the Roman Empire: Essays in the Ordinary.* Princeton, NJ: Princeton University Press, 1990.
———. *Christianizing the Roman Empire: AD 100-400.* New Haven, CT: Yale University Press, 1984.
———. *Corruption and the Decline of Rome.* New Haven, CT: Yale University Press, 1988.
———. *Paganism in the Roman Empire.* New Haven, CT: Yale University Press, 1981.
———. *Roman Social Relations, 50 BC to AD 284.* Westford, MA: Yale University Press, 1974.

Malherbe, Abraham J. *Social Aspects of Early Christianity*. Baton Rouge: Louisiana State University Press, 1977.

Martens, Peter. *Origen on the Reading of Scripture*. Notre Dame, IN: University of Notre Dame, 2004.

Martens, Peter W. *Origen and Scripture: The Contours of the Exegetical Life*. Oxford: Oxford University Press, 2012.

Marx, Karl, Friedrich Engels, and Reinhold Niebuhr. *Marx and Engels on Religion*. New York: Schocken Books, 1967.

McDonald, Lee M., and James A. Sanders, eds. *The Canon Debate*. Grand Rapids: Baker, 2002.

McGavran, Donald A. *The Bridges of God: A Study in the Strategy of Missions*. Eugene, OR: Wipf & Stock, 2005.

McLaren, Brian D. *The Church on the Other Side: Doing Ministry in the Post Modern Matrix*. Grand Rapids: Zondervan, 2006.

Meeks, Wayne A. *The First Urban Christians: The Social World of the Apostle Paul*. New Haven, CT: Yale University Press, 1983.

———. *The Origins of Christian Morality: The First Two Centuries*. New Haven, CT: Yale University Press, 1993.

Meeks, Wayne A., and Robert L. Wilken. *Jews and Christians in Antioch in the First Four Centuries of the Common Era*. Missoula, MT: Scholars Press, 1978.

Metzger, Bruce M. "Antioch-on-the-Orontes." *The Biblical Archaeologist* 11.4 (December 1948) 69–88.

———. *The Canon of the New Testament: Its Origin, Significance and Development*. Oxford: Clarendon, 1987.

———. *The New Testament: Its Background, Growth, and Content*. New York: Abingdon, 1965.

Metzger, Bruce M., and Bart D. Ehrman. *The Text of the New Testament: Its Transmission, Corruption, and Restoration*. 4th ed. New York: Oxford University Press, 2005.

Meyendorff, John. "Byzantine Views of Islam." *Dumbarton Oaks Papers* 18 (1964) 113–32.

Migne, Jacques Paul. "Patrologia Graeca." Centre for Patristic Publications. http://patrologiagraeca.org/patrologia/en/patrologia-graeca.html.

Mohamed, Besheer. "New Estimates Show US Muslim Population Continues to Grow." January 3, 2018. http://www.pewresearch.org/fact-tank/2018/01/03/new-estimates-show-u-s-muslim-population-continues-to-grow/.

Momigliano, Arnaldo. *The Conflict between Paganism and Christianity in the Fourth Century*. Oxford: Clarendon, 1963.

Muller, Richard A. *Dictionary of Latin and Greek Theological Terms: Drawn Principally from Protestant Scholastic Theology*. Grand Rapids: Baker, 1985.

Najeebabadi, Akbar Shah. *The History of Islam*. Vol. 1. Riyadh, Saudi Arabia: Dar-us-Salam International, 2000.

Nautin, Pierre. *Lettres et Ecrivains Chretiens des II et III Siecles*. Paris: Cerf, 1961.

Nazianzus, Gregory. "Oration 21." In *Nicene and Post-Nicene Fathers*, vol. 7, 2nd series, edited by Philip Schaff and Henry Wace. Peabody, MA: Hendrickson, 1996.

Nelson, G. K. *Spiritualism and Society*. Routledge Revivals. London: Routledge, 2013.

Neyrey, Jerome H., and Eric C. Stewart, eds. *The Social World of the New Testament: Insights and Models*. Peabody, MA: Baker, 2008.

Niebuhr, H. Richard. *Christ and Culture*. New York: HarperCollins, 1996.

———. *The Social Sources of Denominationalism*. New York: H. Holt and Company, 1929.
Niebur, Barthold George. *The History of Rome*. London: Walton and Maberly, 1855.
Nock, Arthur Darby. *Conversion: The Old and the New in Religion from Alexander the Great to Augustine of Hippo*. Baltimore: Johns Hopkins University Press, 1998.
———. *Early Gentile Christianity and Its Hellenistic Background*. New York: Harper Torchbooks, 1963.
Nilson, Jon. "To Whom Is Justin's Dialogue Addressed?" *Theological Studies* 38 (1977) 538–46.
Origen. *Commentariorum in Matthaeum*. Die Griechischen Christlichen Schriftsteller 40. Leipzig: J. C. Hinrichs, 1935.
———. *Contra Celsum*. Cambridge: Cambridge University Press, 1980.
———. *The Fathers of the Church: Origen, Commentary on the Epistle to the Romans, Books 6–10*. Translated by Thomas P. Scheck. Washington, DC: Catholic University of America Press, 2002.
———. *The Fathers of the Church: Origen, Commentary on the Gospel according to John, Books 1–10*. Translated by Ronald E. Heine. Washington, DC: The Catholic University of America Press, 2001.
———. *The Fathers of the Church: Origen, Homilies on Genesis and Exodus*. Translated by Ronald E. Heine. Washington, DC: Catholic University of America Press, 2002.
———. *The Fathers of the Church: Origen, Homilies on Jeremiah, Homily on 1 Kings 28*. Translated by John Clark Smith. Washington, DC: Catholic University of America Press, 1998.
———. *Homélies sur les psaumes 36 a 38*. Edited by Emanuela Prinzivalli et al. Paris: Cerf, 1995.
———. *Origen on First Principles: Being Koetschau's Text of the de Principiis*. Translated by G. W. Butterworth. Gloucester, NY: Peter Smith, 1973.
———. *Origenes Werke*. 12 vols. Die Griechischen christlichen Schriftsteller der ersten drei Jahrhunderte. Leipzig: J. C. Hinrichs, 1899–1955.
———. *Philocalia*. Translated by J. Armitage Robinson. Cambridge: Cambridge University Press, 1893.
Oschwald, Jeffrey. "The Self-Evident Truth: Scripture and Apology in the *Contra Celsum* of Origen." PhD diss. University of Notre Dame, 1993.
Parkin, Tim G. *Demography and Roman Society*. Baltimore: The Johns Hopkins University Press, 1992.
Parvis, Sara, and Paul Foster, eds. *Justin Martyr and His Worlds*. Minneapolis: Fortress, 2007.
Payne, Robert. *The History of Islam*. New York: Barnes & Noble, 1959.
———. *The Holy Fire: The Story of the Fathers of the Eastern Church*. New York: Dorset Press, 1989.
Pelikán, Jaroslav. *The Excellent Empire: The Fall of Rome and the Triumph of the Church*. San Francisco: Harper & Row, 1987.
———. *The Christian Tradition: A History of the Development of Doctrine*. Chicago: University of Chicago Press, 1974.
Peters, Frances E. *Greek Philosophical Terms: A Historical Lexicon*. New York: NYU Press, 1970.
Pew Research Center. "America's Changing Religious Landscape." May 12, 2015. http://www.pewforum.org/2015/05/12/americas-changing-religious-landscape/.

———. "Hindus." April 2, 2015. http://www.pewforum.org/2015/04/02/hindus/.
Pfeiffer, Robert H. *Introduction to the Old Testament*. New York: Harper & Brothers, 1948.
Philo. *The Complete Works of Philo*. Translated by C. D. Yonge. Peabody, MA: Hendrickson, 1993.
Piper, John. *Contending for Our All: Defending Truth and Treasuring Christ in the Lives of Athanasius, John Owen, and J. Gresham Machen*. Leicester: InterVarsity, 2006.
Plato. *Plato's The Republic*. The Modern Library of the World's Best Books. Translated by Benjamin Jowett. New York: The Modern Library, 1941.
Polymnia, Athanassiadi. *Julian: An Intellectual Biography*. London: Routledge, 1992.
Potter, David S. *The Roman Empire at Bay: AD 180–395*. New York: Routledge, 2004.
Purves, George T. *The Testimony of Justin Martyr to Early Christianity*. New York: A. D. F. Randolph and Co., 1889.
Quasten, Johannes. *Patrology: The Golden Age of Greek Patristic Literature*. Vol. 3. Allen, TX: Christian Classics, 1983.
Rainer, Thom. "The Rise of the Religious 'Nones.'" March 12, 2012. https://archive.thomrainer.com/2012/03/the_rise_of_the_religious_nones/.
Ramsay, William M. *The Church in the Roman Empire before AD 170*. New York: G. P. Putnam's Sons, 1893.
Rawson, Beryl, ed. *The Family in Ancient Rome: New Perspectives*. 2 vols. Ithaca, NY: Cornell University Press, 1986.
———. *Marriage, Divorce, and Children in Ancient Rome*. OUP/Humanities Research Centre of the Australian National University. New York: Oxford University Press, 1996.
Remus, Harold. "Justin Martyr's Argument with Judaism." In *Anti-Judaism in Early Christianity, Vol. 2: Separation and Polemic*, edited by Stephen G. Wilson, 59–80. Studies in Christianity and Judaism. Waterloo, Ontario: Wilfrid Laurier University Press, 1986.
Riddle, D. W. *The Martyrs: A Study in Social Control*. Chicago: University of Chicago Press, 1931.
Roach, David. "Evangelism Task Force Releases Report, Recommendations." June 11, 2018. http://www.bpnews.net/51049/evangelism-task-force-releases-report-recommendations.
Robbins, Thomas. *Cults, Converts, and Charisma: The Sociology of New Religious Movements*. London: Sage, 1988.
Roberts, Alexander, and James Donaldson, eds. "Martyrdom of the Holy Martyrs: Justin, Chariton, Charites, Paeon, and Liberianus, Who Suffered at Rome." In *Ante-Nicene Fathers*, 504–06. New York: Scribner's Sons, 1905.
Roberts, Colin H. *Manuscript, Society, and Belief in Early Christian Egypt*. London: British Academy, 1979.
Robertson, Archibald. "Athanasius: Select Works and Letters." In *Nicene and Post-Nicene Fathers*. Vol. 4, 2nd series, edited by Philip Schaff and Henry Wace. Peabody, MA: Hendrickson, 1994.
Robinson, John A. T. *Redating the New Testament*. London: SCM-Canterbury, 1976.
Rokéah, David. *Justin Martyr and the Jews*. Boston: Brill, 2002.
Rostovtzeff, Mikhail. *Rome*. Translated by J. D. Duff, edited by Elias J. Bickerman. New York: Oxford University Press, 1960.

Russell, Jeffrey Burton. *The Devil: Perceptions of Evil from Antiquity to Primitive Christianity*. Ithaca, NY: Cornell University Press, 1977.

Sanders, Jack T. *Schismatics, Sectarians Dissidents, Deviants: The First One Hundred Years of Jewish-Christian Relations*. Valley Forge, VA: Trinity Press, 1993.

Sandmel, Samuel. *Philo of Alexandria: An Introduction*. Oxford: Oxford University Press, 1979.

Sawhill, John Alexander. "The Use of Athletic Metaphors in the Biblical Homilies of Saint John Chrysostom." PhD thesis, Princeton University, 1928.

Schaff, Philip, ed. "Homily XVIII: Acts VII. 54." In *A Select Library of the Nicene and Post-Nicene Fathers of the Christian Church, Vol. 11: Saint Chrysostom: Homilies on the Acts of the Apostles and the Epistle to the Romans*. Grand Rapids: Eerdmans, 1989.

———. *The New Schaff-Herzog Encyclopedia of Religious Knowledge*. 13 vols. Grand Rapids: Baker, 1949–56.

Schoedel, William R. *Ignatius of Antioch: A Commentary on the Letters of Ignatius of Antioch*. Edited by Helmut Koester. Philadelphia: Fortress, 1985.

Scholer, David M. *Social Distinctives of the Christians in the First Century: Pivotal Essays by E. A. Judge*. Peabody, MA: Baker, 2007.

Semisch, Charles. *Justin Martyr: His Life, Writings, and Opinions*. Vol. 41. Translated by J. E. Ryland. Edinburgh: Thomas Clark, 1843.

Shotwell, Willis A. *The Biblical Exegesis of Justin Martyr*. London: S. P. C. K., 1965.

———. *The Exegesis of Justin Martyr*. Chicago: University of Chicago, 1954.

Sibinga, Joost Smit. *The Old Testament Text of Justin Martyr: The Pentateuch*. Leiden: E. J. Brill, 1963

Simon, Marcel. *Verus Israel: Etude Sur Les Relations Entre Chrétiens Et Juifs Dans L'empire Romain. (135–425)*. Paris: Editions E. De Boccard, 1964.

Skarsaune, Oskar. "The Conversion of Justin Martyr." *Studia Theologica* 30 (1976) 53–73.

———. "Justin and His Bible." In *Justin Martyr and His Worlds*, edited by Sarah Parvis and Paul Foster, 53–76. Minneapolis: Fortress, 2007.

Smith, Charles Merrill, and James W. Bennett. *How the Bible Was Built*. Grand Rapids: Eerdmans, 2005.

Snyder, Graydon F. *Ante Pacem: Archaeological Evidence of Church Life Before Constantine*. Macon, GA: Mercer University Press, 1985.

Sordi, Marti. *The Christians and the Roman Empire*. Translated by Annabel Bedini. Norman: University of Oklahoma Press, 1986.

Sowers, Sidney G. *The Hermeneutics of Philo and Hebrews: A Comparison of the Interpretation of the Old Testament in Philo Judaeus and the Epistle to the Hebrews*. Richmond, VA John Knox, 1965.

Sparks, Kenton L. *God's Word in Human Words: An Evangelical Appropriation of Critical Biblical Scholarship*. Grand Rapids: Baker, 2008.

Stambaugh, John E. *The Ancient Roman City*. Ancient Society and History. Baltimore: Johns Hopkins University Press, 1988.

Stambaugh, John E., and David L. Balch. *The New Testament in Its Social Environment*. Library of Early Christianity. Philadelphia: Westminster John Knox, 1986.

Stanton, Graham. "'God-Fearers': Neglected Evidence in Justin Martyr's Dialogue with Trypho." In *Ancient History in a Modern University*, vol. 2 of Early Christianity, Late Antiquity and Beyond, edited by T. W. Hillard, 43–52. Grand Rapids: Eerdmans, 1998.

———. "The Law of Moses and the Law of Christ." In *Paul and the Mosaic Law*, edited by James D. G. Dunn, 99–116. Wissenshaftliche Untersuchungen zum Neuen Testament 89. Tübingen: Mohr Siebeck, 1996.

Stark, Rodney. *Cities of God: The Real Story of How Christianity became an Urban Movement and Conquered Rome*. New York: HarperCollins, 2006.

———. *The Rise of Christianity: How the Obscure, Marginal Jesus Movement Became the Dominant Religious Force in the Western World in a Few Centuries*. Princeton, NJ: Princeton University Press, 1997.

———. *The Triumph of Christianity: How the Jesus Movement Became the World's Largest Religion*. New York: HarperCollins, 2011.

Stephens, W. R. W. *St. John Chrysostom, His Life and Times: A Sketch of the Church and the Empire in the Fourth Century*. London: John Murray, 1880.

Stetzer, Claudia J. *Jewish Responses to Early Christians: History and Polemics, 30–150 CE*. Minneapolis: Fortress, 1994.

Stonequist, Everett V. *The Marginal Man: A Study in Personality and Culture Conflict*. New York: Charles Scribner's Sons, 1937.

Stott, John R. W. *The Lausanne Covenant: An Exposition and Commentary*. Minneapolis: World Wide Publications, 1975.

Suetonius. *Lives of the Caesars*. Translated by Catharine Edwards. Oxford: Oxford Paperbacks, 2009.

Swanson, Guy E. *The Birth of the Gods: The Origin of Primitive Beliefs*. Ann Arbor: University of Michigan Press, 1960.

Tacitus, Cornelius. *The Annals of Imperial Rome*. New York: Penguin Classics, 1989.

———. *The Annals: The Reigns of Tiberius, Claudius, and Nero*. Translated by J. C. Yardley. Oxford: Oxford University Press, 2008.

———. *The Histories*. Oxford World's Classics. Translated by W. H. Fyfe. Oxford: Oxford University Press, 2008.

Tanner, Norman. *Decrees of the Ecumenical Councils*. Vol. 1. Washington, DC: Georgetown University Press, 1990.

Thiede, Carsten Peter. "100 Most Important Events in Church History." *Christian History* 28 (1990) 1–49.

Theissen, Gerd. *The Social Setting of Pauline Christianity: Essays on Corinth*. 2 vols. Philadelphia: Fortress, 1982.

———. *Sociology of Early Palestinian Christianity*. Philadelphia: Fortress, 1978.

Thomson, Robert W., ed. *Athanasius: Contra Gentes and de Incarnatione*. Oxford Early Christian Texts Series. Oxford: Clarendon, 1971.

Thurston, Bonnie Bowman. *The Widows: A Women's Ministry in the Early Church*. Philadelphia: Fortress, 1989.

Trakatellis, Demetrios. "Justin Martyr's Trypho." *Harvard Theological Review* 79 (1986) 289–97.

Trigg, Joseph W. *Biblical Interpretation: Message of the Fathers of the Church*. Vol. 9. Wilmington, DE: Michael Glazier, 1988.

Tripolitis, Antonía, *Religions of the Hellenistic-Roman Age*. Grand Rapids: Eerdmans, 2001.

Troeltsch, Ernst. *The Social Teaching of the Christian Churches*. Translated by Olive Wyon. New York: Macmillan, 1931.

Van der Meer, F., and Christine Mohrmann. *Atlas of the Early Christian World*. Translated and edited by Mary F. Hedlund and H. H. Rowley. London: Thomas Nelson, 1958.

von Harnack, Adolf. *History of Dogma*. Vol. 1. Christian Classic Ethereal Library. London: Williams and Norgate, 1894.

———. *Marcion: The Gospel of the Alien God*. Durham, NC: Labyrinth Press, 1990.

———. *The Mission and Expansion of Christianity in the First Three Centuries*. Christian Classic Ethereal Library. London: Williams and Norgate, 1908.

———. *The Origin of the New Testament: And the Most Important Consequences of the New Creation*. Translated by John R. Wilkinson. London: Williams & Northgate, 1925.

———. *Porphyrius, "Gegen die Christen," 15 Bucher: Zeugnisse, Fragmente und Referate*. Abhandlunger der Koniglich Preussischen Akademie der Wissenschaften, Philosophisch-Historische Klasse. Berlin: Verlag der Königlichen Akademie der Wissenschaften, 1916.

von Hertling, L. "Die Zahl der Christen zu Beginn des vierten Jahrhunderts." *Zeitschrift für Katholische Theologie* 58 (1934) 245–64.

Walker, Williston. *Great Men of the Christian Church*. Chicago: University of Chicago Press, 1908.

Wallis, Roy. *Sectarianism: Analyses of Religious and Non-Religious Sects*. New York: John Wiley & Sons, 1975.

Walsh, Michael. *The Triumph of the Meek: Why Early Christianity Succeeded*. San Francisco: HarperCollins, 1986.

Wand, J. W. C. *A History of the Early Church to AD 500*. London: Routledge, 1990.

Washburn, Henry Bradford. *Men of Conviction*. New York: Scribners, 1931.

Watt, W. Montgomery. *Muhammad: Prophet and Statesman*. Oxford: Oxford University Press, 1961.

Weinandy, Thomas G. *Athanasius: A Theological Introduction*. Burlington, VT: Ashgate, 2007.

Weiss, Johannes. *Earliest Christianity*. New York: Harper & Row, 1959.

West, Thomas G. *Plato's Apology of Socrates: An Interpretation, with a New Translation*. Ithaca, NY: Cornell University Press, 1979.

Westcott, Brooke Foss, *A General Survey of the History of the Canon of the New Testament*. 3rd ed. London: Macmillan and Co., 1870.

Werline, Rodney A. "The Transformation of Pauline Arguments in Justin Martyr's Dialogue with Trypho." *Harvard Theological Review* 92 (1999) 79–93.

Wetzel, Richard. "Das Vierundzwanzigste Kapitel des Evangelisten Matthäus in der Auslegung durch die Griechischen Väter Origenes und Chrysostomus." PhD diss. Universität zu Tübingen, 1972.

White, K. D. *Greek and Roman Technology*. Ithaca, NY: Cornell University Press, 1984.

White, L. Michael. *Building God's House in the Roman World: Architectural Adaptation among Pagans, Jews, and Christians*. Baltimore: Johns Hopkins University Press, 1990.

Wilken, Robert L. *The Christians as the Romans Saw Them*. 2nd ed. New Haven, CT: Yale University Press, 2003.

———. *The First Thousand Years: A Global History of Christianity*. New Haven, CT: Yale University Press, 2012.

———. *John Chrysostom and the Jews: Rhetoric and Reality in the Late 4th Century.* Berkeley: University of California Press, 1983.

———. *Judaism and the Early Christian Mind: A Study of Cyril of Alexandria's Exegesis and Theology.* New Haven, CT: Yale University Press, 1971.

Williams, A. Lukyn. *Justin Martyr: The Dialogue with Trypho.* London: SPCK, 1930.

Wilson, Bryan R. *Religious Sects: A Sociological Study.* New York: McGraw-Hill, 1970.

Wilson, Stephen. "Dialogue and Dispute." In *Related Strangers: Jews and Christians, 70–170 CE*, 258–84. Minneapolis: Fortress, 1995.

Wright, N. T. *Christian Origins and the Question of God.* Minneapolis: Fortress, 1992.

———. *The New Testament and the People of God.* Minneapolis: Fortress, 1992.

Wrigley, E. A. *Population and History.* London: Littlehampton Book Services, 1969.

Zein, Assem. "The List: The World's Fastest-Growing Religions." May 14, 2007. https://foreignpolicy.com/2007/05/14/the-list-the-worlds-fastest-growing-religions/.

Zöllig, August. *Die Inspirationslehre des Origenes: Ein Beitrag zur Dogmengeschichte.* Freiburg, Germany: Verlag Herder, 1902.

www.ingramcontent.com/pod-product-compliance
Lightning Source LLC
Chambersburg PA
CBHW070918180426
43192CB00038B/1752